Interpreting Anime

Interpreting Anime

Christopher Bolton

University of Minnesota Press
Minneapolis
London

An earlier version of chapter 1 was previously published as "From Ground Zero to Degree Zero: *Akira* from Origin to Oblivion," *Mechademia* 9 (Minneapolis: University of Minnesota Press, 2014), 295–315. An earlier version of chapter 2 was previously published as "The Mecha's Blind Spot: *Patlabor 2* and the Phenomenology of Anime," *Science Fiction Studies* 29, no. 3 (November 2002): 453–74, and in *Robot Ghosts and Wired Dreams: Japanese Science Fictions from Origins to Anime*, ed. Christopher Bolton, Istvan Csicsery-Ronay Jr., and Takayuki Tatsumi (Minneapolis: University of Minnesota Press, 2007), 123–47. An earlier version of chapter 3 was previously published as "From Wooden Cyborgs to Celluloid Souls: Mechanical Bodies in Anime and Japanese Puppet Theater," *positions: east asia cultures critique* 10, no. 3 (Winter 2002): 729–71. An earlier version of chapter 4 was previously published as "Anime Horror and Its Audience: *3x3 Eyes* and *Vampire Princess Miyu*," in *Japanese Horror Cinema*, ed. Jay McRoy (Edinburgh: Edinburgh University Press, 2005), 66–76. An earlier version of chapter 6 was previously published as "The Quick and the Undead: Visual and Political Dynamics in *Blood: The Last Vampire*," *Mechademia* 2 (Minneapolis: University of Minnesota Press, 2007), 125–42.

Published by the University of Minnesota Press
111 Third Avenue South, Suite 290
Minneapolis, MN 55401-2520
http://www.upress.umn.edu

ISBN 978-1-5179-0402-9 (hc)
ISBN 978-1-5179-0403-6 (pb)

A Cataloging-in-Publication record for this book is available from the Library of Congress.

Printed in the United States of America on acid-free paper

The University of Minnesota is an equal-opportunity educator and employer.

24 23 22 21 20 19 18   10 9 8 7 6 5 4 3 2 1

For Kija, Mariko, and Erika

Contents

A Note on the Text

With the exception of one or two titles mentioned in passing, all of the anime discussed in this book have been released in North America, in DVD or Blu-ray editions with English subtitles. These subtitles provide reliable translations, but for the quotations in this book I have made my own translations from the original Japanese dialogue. (Readers consulting English dubbed versions of the anime may notice some differences, since dubs often feature freer translations and incorporate changes to the original scripts.)

Japanese names in the body of the text are given in Japanese order, family name first.

Read or Die

Reading Anime

This is a book about interpreting Japanese animation, or anime, but what does it mean to "read" or interpret a visual text? To address this question, I would like to begin this book about reading anime with an anime about reading books. Masunari Kōji's three-part anime *R.O.D: Read or Die* (2001–2) follows the adventures of a group of secret-agent superheroes employed by the British Library who are sent on missions to recover stolen volumes. The protagonist is Yomiko Readman, a bibliomaniac who has to surround herself with books and who possesses the ability to manipulate paper to form objects that do her bidding (Figure 1). Her nemesis is the legendary fifteenth-century Zen priest and poet Ikkyū, resurrected with cloning technology and now intent on world destruction. Ikkyū leads a band of history's great artistic, scientific, and literary figures, who have been similarly cloned, augmented with fantastic powers, and harnessed for Ikkyū's evil cause. These include the seventh-century Chinese monk Xuanzang (the historical protagonist of the Ming novel *Journey to the West*), the eighteenth-century artist, author, and scholar Hiraga Gennai, the nineteenth-century French entomologist and nature writer Jean Henri Fabre, World War I spy Mata Hari, and, in a key role, composer Ludwig van Beethoven.

Read or Die is an engaging comic drama with an entertaining setting, lively pacing (driven by Iwasaki Taku's strong musical score), striking visual compositions, and colorful, even compelling characters. The premise and especially the title seem tailor made for a literary critic. But in fact, this work has an interestingly ambivalent relationship with prose literature and the act of reading books. Although Yomiko's obsession with books is linked to her

FIGURE 1. *R.O.D: Read or Die*'s protagonist Yomiko is obsessed with books and can manipulate paper to construct tools or even stop bullets. But the paper is blank, and there is not much actual reading portrayed in the action-oriented anime. All stills are from the Manga Entertainment DVD (2003).

powers, the anime treats it as a kind of unhealthy preoccupation that cuts her off from reality, and a key theme is her gradual realization that real people and real relationships are more important than literature.

In this context, it is no accident that this anime's villains emerge largely from the world of literature and art, which is seen as a threat. The villains are plotting to recreate a lost Beethoven symphony, which is to be reconstructed from stolen books originally in Beethoven's personal library, then performed by the resurrected Beethoven clone and broadcast to the world. The symphony is a weapon, a doomsday device: it is such an immersive or powerful aesthetic experience that it causes its listeners to turn away from real life and kill themselves. In this way, the theme of *Read or Die* turns out to be the peril of becoming too obsessed with art and literature.

But even though the plot of *Read or Die* turns on reading, reading itself is not portrayed very explicitly or convincingly in this anime. With a cast of characters that references arts and literature ranging from Muromachi Zen Buddhism through Chinese classics to German Romanticism, one could imagine the series developing a very complex set of nested narratives, where the fictional plots of all these books and the characters' lives could weave together and comment on one another. But *Read or Die* does not have this sense of intertextuality: it never delves into the fictional worlds of these different literary texts.[1] Rather, the books in the anime seem to exist more as physical objects than as literary or textual ones: the villains' literary backstories supply their costumes and powers but little else; there are scenes of Yomiko wading through piles of books in her house or in bookstores, but there is virtually no discussion of the books' content; there are not even many scenes that show her reading the books she has collected. She does use her powers to assemble physical objects from reams of paper that she carries around in a suitcase, but each sheet is tellingly blank.

Overall, *Read or Die* seems divided: for the most part it immerses its audience in action and emotion in a way that short-circuits any self-conscious consideration of what it means to be reading or viewing this work. And yet it does have this metatextual layer, one that encourages the viewer to see him- or herself in Yomiko and ask if he or she is becoming too immersed in the fiction of this film. The opening credits seem to embody this division between the physical and the immediate on the one hand, and the mediated and the textual on the other. The credits begin with several screens of digital text that are cleared away by human hands, and then we see a series of action scenes intercut with stylized images of nude female bodies, painted with the names of the anime's creators. The written text, expressing the circumstances of the anime's creation, is forced to compete with these naked bodies for the viewer's attention (Figure 2).

All this suggests some interesting questions. Why does *Read or Die* return obsessively to the theme of reading and yet encounter such difficulty depicting the familiar experience of reading a book? Are there meanings that anime can represent (or ways of representing meaning) that elude other media? Most broadly, how is an audience's experience of anime different from other media like printed prose? This volume addresses these general questions by asking more specific ones about how specific anime work, visually and narratively.

This brings me back to the question of what it means to read anime, the subject of this book. Reading in the sense that I use it here is not simply collecting titles (physically or in a checklist of things seen), nor does it mean becoming so absorbed in a written or visual work that one loses oneself. The "reading" I am advocating means coming to a greater understanding of the text and its particular features through interpretation and critical consideration. This kind of reading has several steps, but it begins by looking carefully at the formal qualities of specific works: what is shown and how is it shown? How do different anime handle light, depth, and movement? How is each scene composed and edited, and how is the narrative structured? How does a given anime look—meaning what does it look like, but also how does it see the world? Here anime plots can be distracting: often they are so complex and so colorful that they monopolize critics' attention. But formal (especially visual) elements generate their own meanings that may either reinforce or upend conclusions we draw from the story. Ultimately my goal in reading anime is to interpret these formal qualities in order to extract or generate new meanings from

FIGURE 2. In the opening credits the textual must compete with the physical: human hands clear away screens of digital text, and the names of the series' creators appear painted upon (but overshadowed by) a succession of nude female forms.

the texts, particularly meanings that speak to broader issues of politics, gender, technology, and media.

In her work on Japanese print comics (manga), Jaqueline Berndt argues forcefully for this kind of attention to manga's formal visual structures, but also for a broadly comparative perspective on the medium. For Berndt, that means reading different authors and genres; considering Japanese and transnational critical and publishing contexts; and replacing single modes of reading with a wider range of critical approaches.[2] While it is impossible for one book to do everything, I have tried to embrace this comparative spirit by covering a wide range of anime, criticism, and critical theory. This is described in more detail below, but most centrally this book proceeds from the idea that an effective way to focus our attention on the specific formal qualities of anime is to contrast it with other media, so each chapter of this book juxtaposes anime with a different comparison medium to draw out these differences. The comparison media range from prose fiction to print comics, classical theater, and fine art. Some chapters compare specific texts (an anime and a manga, for example, or an anime and a stage play). Other chapters discuss media differences more abstractly, using media theory associated with specific media, like Vivian Sobchack's phenomenology of live-action cinema. Each chapter uses these comparisons to ask: what are anime's particular powers and what are its blind spots? Ultimately, what can anime do that other media cannot?

Anime's Oscillation

As an example of this kind of reading, let's return to the opening credits of *Read or Die*. While *Read or Die* feels very much like a single ninety-minute film, it is actually a three-part series released directly to video one part at a time—a format or medium referred to as original video animation (OVA or OAV). Three installments are certainly not enough to feel episodic, like television, and the transitions between parts are largely seamless, so it is tempting to analyze it as a single film. But one characteristic of the OVA that film lacks is the repeated opening sequence, which appears before each of the three episodes. The scenes in the opening are not borrowed from the series: they have been created and animated specifically for the credits, and they contain some motifs that shed light on the anime as a whole. Here let's resist the temptation to watch them once and then fast-forward through the second and third iterations. Instead, let's look at them in more detail.

Interpolated between the images discussed above (that seem to clear away a printed text and refocus attention on a concretely physical body), there is a series of other visuals that generally alternate between images of the characters and images of cities around the world. Looking more closely, we find that most of these scenes contain some conspicuous effect related to lighting or reflection: complex images reflected in windows, a glint off a watch crystal, the flash of light on Yomiko's glasses (Figure 3). In the most complex example, we see a view from the perspective of Nancy Makuhari, Yomiko's partner, as she looks through a window and sights down her gun at a target in the room on the other side. The window shows little of the room's interior, instead reflecting back Nancy's image ("our" image, in this point-of-view shot). Then Nancy shoots out the glass. Her own image continues to be reflected in the fragments of the exploding windowpane, but now we can also see a figure inside the room, silhouetted but still vaguely familiar (Figure 4).

Such complex reflections are a specialty of anime, which can portray intricate optical and lighting effects that might be difficult to capture in a live-action film or even a manga. The motif of reflecting glass is also a ready metaphor for the critical idea that language or media that seem to be "transparent" (that is, they seem to faithfully transmit the image of whatever lies on the other side) also distort that view and reflect back the viewer's own image. So while *Read or Die* seems reluctant to portray any printed text, the opening credits put us on notice that this work will center on the larger issue of how language represents or mediates the world.

Continuing, let us focus on just one of these reflecting, transmitting objects: Yomiko's glasses. These are prominent in the credits and throughout the anime, signifying not only Yomiko's reading habit but a kind of nerdiness, an awkward inability to relate to other people. The way the glasses represent mediation and the way they represent isolation come together in the final

FIGURE 3. The scenes in the opening credits almost always include some element of optical reflection, like the windows of this building or Yomiko's flashing glasses.

FIGURE 4. In the most elaborate sequence from the opening credits, Yomiko's partner Nancy shoots through a window that displays her own reflection.

scenes between Yomiko and Nancy, whose developing relationship is central to the story. It is this relationship (which ambiguously combines elements of sisterly affection and erotic tension)
that Yomiko learns to embrace in the course of the anime, finally
setting aside her books to do so. In the first episode, Nancy is teas-
ing Yomiko by nuzzling and pinching her cheek. Yomiko endures
this with a grimace until Nancy's hand gets near her glasses, at
which point Yomiko instinctively strikes out to protect herself. The
glasses thus come to represent a kind of shield between Yomiko's
intimate self and the people around her, a shield associated with
reading and mediation.

This romantic tension between the two characters comes to a
climax when it is revealed that Yomiko's partner is a double agent:
Nancy Makuhari is actually a clone of the famous spy Mata Hari
and lover to the evil mastermind Ikkyū. As Ikkyū puts his plot
in motion, Nancy seems to side with him. Yomiko, now in love,
cannot believe that she has "misread" Nancy so thoroughly, and
this is reflected (literally) in her glasses: at two climactic points
when Nancy embraces Ikkyū and her betrayal seems to reach a
peak, Yomiko's glasses are portrayed prominently (at one point
we are looking through them from Yomiko's point of view), and in
both scenes the lenses are made opaque with distorted reflections
or the fog of Yomiko's own heavy breathing (Figure 5). The result is
to show how clouded or blinded Yomiko's judgment has become.
So while *Read or Die* initially seems to recommend the solidity and
reality of emotional and physical relationships over the virtual
world of books, and while it makes us, the audience, root for the
happy consummation of this love story between the two women,
at other points the anime does seem to be about reading, albeit a
different kind. It turns on the difficulty of reading people, who are
compared to texts for the ways that their meanings and motivations remain hard to parse.

We return, then, to the idea of *Read or Die* as divided, embracing
concrete experience at one moment and then in the next moment
revealing the slippery layers of perception and mediation that
compose experience (and anime itself). This division points to an
idea that runs through all my readings in this book: anime's ability to move the viewer very rapidly back and forth between these

FIGURE 5. In two climactic scenes, Yomiko's apparent inability to "read" Nancy is expressed in the way her glasses are clouded by fog or reflections.

two poles of immersion and distance. Above all it is this quality of oscillation that for me defines the particular character and the unique power of anime.

For example, in many anime, including *Read or Die* and virtually all of the films treated in the chapters that follow, the visual physical action, the suspense of the plot, and the emotional depiction of the characters all encourage a kind of immersion on the part of the viewer, who can suspend disbelief and experience the events and characters as immediate—as somehow real, or at least realistic—in order to feel the excitement, suspense, joy, sadness, etcetera that make the work engaging and entertaining. I use "immersion" broadly here, as an experience of resonance (emotional, visual, or other) between the world of the text and the viewer's own world, with a sense that the language of the text functions transparently, representing things clearly, effectively, and invisibly in a way that allows the viewer to enter seamlessly into that world. Elements that provoke an immediate bodily reaction (like the sex, violence, or horror common to so many anime) can create a sense of physical immersion. But a film with clear historical resonances and a transparent political argument could also be termed immersive if it allows the viewer to focus comfortably on the message without considering the complexities of how that message is represented.[3]

However, in many anime this immersive or immediate experience is regularly interrupted by self-conscious textual devices that call attention to the form of the text itself, turning its language opaque and making the viewer remember self-consciously that he or she is encountering a created world. Examples might include visual effects that somehow call attention to their own artificiality (for example constantly altering the visual style of the anime) or metafictional elements that break the frame of the story (for example discussions by characters of what it means to be a character, or obvious visual quotations from other very different films). By and large *Read or Die* seems intent on limiting these effects, which may be why there are so few scenes of Yomiko reading: too many of these might break the spell of the story as effectively as scenes of Yomiko watching anime, or Yomiko watching *Read or Die*. But the motif of reflection and the clouded glasses disrupt this transparency, encouraging us to think about mediation and distortion.

It reminds us viewers that we too are wearing a pair of glasses that influences the way we see things, and that pair of glasses is the anime itself. Of course, for many of us there is tremendous pleasure in these kinds of postmodern and metafictional gestures, though it seems to be a qualitatively different, even a diametrically opposite sort of appeal from the immersive one.

Jay David Bolter and Richard Grusin argue that new media in particular are characterized by a combination of both impulses: these media strive to present an experience that appears unmediated, but they also tend to multiply layers of mediation in a way that makes us hyperaware of language itself.[4] But historically, literary theory had many ways of naming this dichotomy before the advent of new media. The term used above, "suspension of disbelief," was coined by Samuel Taylor Coleridge in 1817 to suggest that the experience of literature is a delicate balance between skepticism and credulity, a "poetic faith" prompted by "a human interest and a semblance of truth." Modernist avant-garde playwright Bertolt Brecht formulated one of the best-known versions of this duality, phrased in terms of "identification" versus "alienation." In the mid-twentieth century, structuralism focused attention on the gap between a represented meaning (the signified) and the linguistic form that does the representing (the signifier). And more recently, postmodern literature and theory have suggested that if politics and ideology often function invisibly through the illusion of transparent language, then art and criticism can respond by focusing attention on the functioning of language itself, with devices like self-referentiality, irony, and pastiche. For our reading of Read or Die, the most evocative characterization comes from Roland Barthes, who describes this alternation by comparing a literary text to a partially reflective window: you can look through the glass and see outside, or you can focus your eyes on the surface of the glass itself, so literary language (in any medium) alternates between being transparent and calling attention to itself.[5]

Some critics see literature as essentially immersive and assign to criticism the role of breaking that spell, by helping us step back and consider how the effect is achieved. But here I am interested in anime as a text that can perform this critical operation on itself, through its own oscillation between immersive and distancing effects. Of course, almost any literary text combines these effects to some degree: a narrator's voice (or voiceover) may intrude to break the spell of involvement in the most realistic-feeling novel or film, and some of the most structurally complex and experimental postmodern narratives are anchored by a sympathy or empathy we feel for their recognizably human protagonists. But I think anime is unusual, perhaps unique, in its ability to move so rapidly between the extremes of immersion or identification on the one hand, and alienation or distance on the other.

As an artifact of mass or popular culture, anime has evolved the same strategies as other popular genre fictions for involving the audience and making them come back for more. But something about anime's particular context (perhaps the relatively cheap cost of producing anime in comparison to Hollywood film, the sheer number of titles in competition with one another in Japan, and/or the increasing number of distribution routes and niche audiences) has simultaneously encouraged formal experimentation and nurtured an audience for that kind of experimentation. Anime can be moving and involving but also highly ironic and metatextual. Some of the medium's most gifted directors have produced amazing work by harnessing anime's ability to traverse the full range of these different possibilities.

In *Read or Die*, we experience this oscillation particularly through the relationship between Yomiko and Nancy. At some moments we are immersed and invested in this emotional story, which is portrayed as more concrete than the world of books; but then Nancy is revealed to be dissembling, and she herself becomes a text to be read and interpreted. And beyond this, everything about the way Nancy is depicted makes her both realistic and unrealistic, a solid body and an insubstantial text. Nancy's voluptuous figure, for example, has the exaggerated proportions common to many anime heroines, and her skintight costume is both "transparent" and "realistic" in the sense of leaving nothing to the imagination. (Reportedly designed to resemble dominatrix gear, it counterpoints Yomiko's masculine trench coat, necktie and vest.)[6] But Nancy's secret power is the ability to make her body insubstantial so that solid objects pass right through it. She is alternately a palpably arousing presence and an ephemeral special effect. This is certainly a specialty of many anime, where even the most realistic bodies are an uncanny combination of real and unreal—their proportions, movements, and voices real enough to be desirable but also pervasively artificial or doll-like.

In fact, *Read or Die* takes this a step further by doubling Nancy's body both narratively and visually. We eventually discover that Ikkyū has made two Mata Hari clones, Nancy #1 and Nancy #2, and when the first begins to fall in love with Yomiko, the two mirror images face off against one another. This explains the image from the opening credits, where Nancy shoots her own reflection and sees a second version of herself on the other side of the glass. Nancy is thus a literal double agent, and her alternate dominance and submissiveness toward Yomiko throughout the anime are retroactively explained by the fact that we have been watching two different Nancy characters. (Perceptive fans have pointed out that they are distinguishable or readable in that one is left-handed and one right-handed. This encourages viewers to rewatch the series and locate each point where Nancy #1 and #2 switch places.)[7] In the climax, good Nancy sides with Yomiko and fatally wounds Ikkyū, but then chooses to die with him. Evil Nancy survives, but conveniently loses her memory of everything so that she can regain her innocence and once again form a bond with Yomiko in the coda (and the sequels).

So on the one hand *Read or Die* provides a satisfying ending for those of us who have become immersed in the story and involved with these characters: Nancy stays true to Yomiko, dying heroically and simultaneously surviving so their relationship can continue. But at the same time the anime presses this idea of the virtual by making Nancy into something less than solid, a virtual creation that is not only readable but writable and rewritable, a clone who can be copied and edited seemingly at will. If in one sense *Read or Die* is about choosing "real" life over fiction, the conclusion also upends that by suggesting that real lives and even real bodies may themselves be sorts of fiction. Fiction is not what we choose, but what we are. This suggests the ultimate stakes of the title, and why the alternative to reading is an end to life.

This interpretation is brief, not much more than a sketch, but it illustrates the kind of readings undertaken in the chapters that follow. These readings use media comparison to focus on specific details, with the goal of unfolding new or unexpected ideas about the film texts; they are linked by this larger idea of oscillation between immediacy and distance; and finally they share some common thematic concerns that link anime to pressing issues outside the text. These include issues of media, technology, and representation; issues of body and gender; and finally issues of memory, history, and politics. (History and memory are not treated in the abbreviated reading above, but *Read or Die* could certainly accommodate such a reading, with an international cast and canvas that creatively recapitulate elements of Japan's colonial past.)[8]

Texts and Contexts

This is certainly not the only possible approach to reading *Read or Die*. Anime scholarship has flourished in the last decade, and there are excellent books in English that take up anime from many different angles, from Susan Napier's landmark survey by theme and genre, *Anime: From "Akira" to "Howl's Moving Castle,"* through Thomas Lamarre's brilliantly abstract media theory of animation, *The Anime Machine.* Other important studies specialize in anime's history as a medium, its international fan communities, or its production techniques.[9]

My own approach is informed by my background. I have been teaching Japanese literature and visual culture to college students for twenty years, meaning that I received my graduate training at a time when studying Japanese literature meant studying Japanese poetry, stage drama, or prose. My own interest was the postwar Japanese novel, but my years in graduate school corresponded to the anime boom in the 1990s, and I was excited by the ways that anime seemed to challenge conventional ways of reading literature and film. My first articles on anime, published in 2002, were among the earliest literary critical readings of anime films in English. They were also informed by my earlier work on prose and live-action film, and my position teaching in a comparative literature program—two factors that have influenced the comparative approach I have taken ever since. In the decade and a half that followed, I coedited several anthologies of anime criticism during a time when scholars in Japanese studies were engaged in some exciting debates and decisions about the most productive and interesting ways to read this new medium.

One purpose of this book is to trace that critical history by reading a range of anime from the past three decades and by surveying a range of writing on anime, from early interventions to the current state of the art. But for me, looking at a range of films and critical work is not just an end in itself but a way to help readers of this book develop their own original ways of reading and interpreting anime, in order to make these works even more interesting, compelling, and relevant for individual viewers. To permit very close readings grounded in each anime's specific visual, structural, and narrative characteristics, each chapter in this book focuses on just one or two works, mostly feature-length anime films but also a few short series like *Read or Die* that feel like single films.

This book begins in the 1980s, with Ōtomo Katsuhiro's breakthrough film *Akira* (1988). Of course one could go back further. The history of Japanese animation begins at the turn of the century, though some critics reserve the term "anime" for more recent Japanese animation that shares certain qualities beyond its medium: for example, stylistic features, genre conventions, or specific reception contexts. I am not particularly interested in drawing narrow boundaries around the word *anime*. I will use this term to refer broadly to Japanese animation based on a drawn image (leaving out things like stop-motion animation made with movable dolls, or 100 percent computer-rendered 3D animation in the style of a video-game cut scene or a Pixar film).[10] Certainly anime existed before *Akira*, and I will mention some earlier works in passing, but I have chosen to discuss *Akira* in the first chapter because it marks the beginning of a Japanese renaissance in long-form theatrical anime for more adult audiences—or perhaps more accurately, crossover audiences that included adults as well as teens. It is also the first anime film to receive wide theatrical distribution in the United States and arguably marks the beginning of the latest and largest anime boom in North America.

The chapters that follow span the next twenty-five years of anime's history, continuing to focus on feature-length anime films. (The arrangement of chapters is roughly but not strictly chronological.

See the chronology at the back of the book for a year-by-year list of the principal anime discussed.) This includes work by some of the most interesting and internationally successful Japanese directors of the past three decades, in any medium: Ōtomo, Oshii Mamoru, Kon Satoshi, and Miyazaki Hayao. Born in a span of about twenty years, these four directors also dwell on some common themes we might trace to their generational experiences, particularly economic and social changes in the decades following World War II. (We will see this in the first two chapters with *Akira* and *Patlabor 2*: these two films from around 1990, by two different directors born in the early 1950s, both view contemporary Japan through the lens of 1960s social and political protests, but with very different results.)

This focus on feature-length theatrical films and short OVAs sets aside a great deal of anime broadcast as television series, which typically have twenty-five half-hour episodes per season and often multiple seasons. The length of these series allows them to develop complex plots, but feature-length films provide better support for the kinds of close visual readings I am arguing for: they focus our attention on a smaller number of scenes, and their higher production standards often make them visually more rewarding to read. Beyond this, it might be argued that even when television anime incorporates some of the same formal devices as feature-length films, it often fails to generate the kind of oscillation between immersion and distance discussed above. (We will investigate this in more detail in chapter 6, where the comparison is between feature-length and television anime.)

Finally, besides ranging through different decades, directors, and comparison media, the different chapters represent a range of critical approaches. They not only cover a wide spectrum of anime criticism from the past twenty years but also progress deliberately through several distinct bodies of critical theory: structuralist analysis, phenomenological film theory, psychoanalysis, theories of postmodernism and posthumanism, queer theory, and some recent media theory focused specifically on Japanese animation. So besides comparing different media to ask what anime does best, the book also encourages readers to compare a wide range of critics and critical theories to ask which provide the most compelling readings and interpretations. In that spirit of exploration, the presentation of the theory does not assume any specific critical background on the part of the reader—just an open-minded willingness to consider how these ideas might enhance our understanding of anime.

Applying these theories to anime also increases our understanding of the theories themselves. Critical theory is after all an exercise in abstraction, positing general ideas that apply to different kinds of texts. Often these theories have been developed to explain other media, and in some cases the application of these theories to certain media and texts has become so familiar that it becomes hard to separate the theory from the examples. Can phenomenological film criticism, developed to consider the body in live-action film, also be applied to anime? Can cyborg feminism shed light on a text that does not look conventionally feminist? Such questions challenge the ways we understand and evaluate these theories at a productively fundamental level.

Here it may be useful to provide a brief overview of the specific titles, media comparisons, and theoretical frameworks treated in the chapters that follow. The first and penultimate chapters discuss the interplay of the two-dimensional and the three-dimensional in two films separated in time: 1988's *Akira,* an apogee of hand-drawn and hand-painted cell-based animation, and 2000's *Blood: The Last Vampire,* which combines conventional 2D animation with digital composition and computer modeling. Both of these anime have strong political subtexts, and my readings suggest that they are both trying to choose between a realistic, grounded three-dimensional world and a fantastic two-dimensional one—though the question of which world enables more productive political engagement remains complex.

These films also differ in other ways: *Akira* is a single film based on an epic manga series by the same creator, and the media comparison is the obvious comparison between the manga and the film. But *Blood: The Last Vampire* is the beginning of a long franchise that spans more than a decade and includes multiple TV and manga series, additional films, and several novels, so the chapter discusses what happens when the same plot, character, and visual tropes jump through multiple media and genres. The book thus begins with a focus on landmark titles and directors, but eventually considers theories of anime that focus on larger franchises or "media mixes."

The book's middle chapters look at a series of canonical anime films by Oshii Mamoru and Kon Satoshi, and suggest some less expected media comparisons—with Japanese puppet theater, contemporary stage drama, or early cinema. In *Patlabor 2* (*Kidō keisatsu patoreibaa 2 The Movie*, 1991), *Ghost in the Shell* (*Kōkaku kidōtai*, 1995), and *Millennium Actress* (*Sennen joyū*, 2001), the oscillation between immediacy and distance relates more directly and more personally to the body, and to the divide between human bodies and mechanical ones. We may be tempted to regard the human body as something immediate or intimate, and the robot or puppet body as something more alien, but this is not inevitably the case: the poststructural and phenomenological work of critics like Roland Barthes, Donna Haraway, Vivian Sobchack, and Judith Butler collapses this distinction in productive ways, making us see that our own putatively natural human bodies are also artificial or constructed. At the same time, the idea of the machine body can be developed to include the animated body, prompting the question of whether we can regard an anime film as having a natural (or unnatural) body of its own.

Part of this discussion recasts the idea of media comparison by asking how we might compare the medium or mediation of anime with the idea of *unmediated* human experience—if such a thing exists. This is a key question in many theories of anime fandom, particularly psychoanalytic theories of single-minded fans known as otaku. In one definition, otaku are fans for whom anime has become a dangerous substitute for actual experience (in particular sexual experience). But some theories of the otaku suggest that their unwillingness to distinguish between real and virtual relationships represents a savvy awareness of the extent to which all relationships are mediated by multiple layers of language. The anime horror series discussed in chapter 4 resemble *Read or Die* in that these questions and anxieties are taken up self-reflexively by anime itself: Takenouchi Kazuhisa and Nishio Daisuke's *3x3 Eyes* (*Sazan aizu*, 1991–92, 1995–96) and Hirano Toshiki's *Vampire Princess Miyu* (*Vanpaia Miyu*, 1988–89) alternately encourage us to become absorbed in the fiction and then pull us back, forcing us to self-consciously observe ourselves.

Finally the book's last chapter considers Miyazaki Hayao, a major director whose work does not encourage the kind of oscillation we see in other anime films. We will look at *Howl's Moving Castle* (*Hauru no ugoku shiro*, 2004), based on a young-adult novel by the British writer Diana Wynne Jones. Like most of Miyazaki's films, this one strives for a completely immersive experience, largely rejecting the kind of alienation effects that I identify in other Japanese animation. This becomes particularly clear when we compare it with Jones's novel, which has metafictional interludes that constantly interrogate the boundaries of its own medium and genre. In the final chapter, then, this book considers the limits of its own generalizations about anime, and asks why some anime seem to aim deliberately at different effects.

As this summary suggests, there will always be tradeoffs between focus and coverage. For example I have not undertaken a broad survey of new media theory, to leave time for other kinds of theory; the comic end of the anime spectrum is underrepresented, in order to focus on films that treat similar themes and talk to one another; and finally some landmark series like *Gundam* and *Evangelion* are left out simply because the sprawling complexity of each franchise seems to deserve a book of its own. But ultimately the goal of the book is to outline new ways of reading anime that will serve as a model for the reader's own creative engagement with any and all anime: the chapters that follow suggest a range of approaches to some important directors and films, but these are also approaches that the reader can apply to a wide range of other anime by these directors and others. To this end, while most chapters focus on a single anime, several conclude with a brief discussion of some alternate film—a sequel, for example, or a similar work by a different director—to suggest how the reader might begin to apply or adapt the arguments to other texts. In the same vein, I hope that my interpretations are convincing, but they are not intended to be exhaustive or definitive; it is my hope that readers will ultimately devise their own interpretations, particularly where they find my readings incomplete.

This book's most ambitious hope is that thinking about how

to read anime, particularly in comparison with other media and in conjunction with a wide range of critical theory, will suggest new ways of reading those other media as well. In the latter part of the twentieth century, film criticism made its way into literature departments and challenged our thinking about what it means to read a text. Different ways of thinking about fiction and representation, discovered or rediscovered by film theory, subsequently spilled over into our ways of reading prose. In the twenty-first century, academic attention to animation now challenges us to ask new questions about literature in its broadest sense. By asking how anime sees the world, and what anime can do that other media cannot, we also address much broader questions about film, fiction, and language itself.

Let me close by returning one more time to the idea of reading, and one last time to *Read or Die*. Like many anime, this one is known by a shortened version of its title, *R.O.D.* One of its sequels is a manga series that plays on this abbreviation by titling itself *R.O.D: Read or Dream*. In the context of the franchise, the latter title might be said to (once again) equate reading with daydreaming, as something pleasant but unproductive. However, I prefer to interpret this title as an expression of the two poles I have described: the pleasure and immediacy of an immersive engagement in a dreamt-of world, and the pleasure and distance of the critical engagement I associate with reading and interpretation. I hope readers and dreamers alike will find both sorts of pleasure in the pages that follow.

1
From Origin to Oblivion

Akira as Anime and Manga

In surveying a medium as broad and diverse as anime, the first question is "where to start?" This book begins with the 1988 anime *Akira*, which marks a turning point for the sophistication of anime film in Japan and also for the popularity of anime in North America. But as these dual credentials suggest, behind this question of anime's history or chronology is another about geography: in a book about Japanese animation for English speaking readers, should we make our starting point Japan or the West?

In some ways, any discussion of the history of anime has to start with our own individual anime histories—the texts and ways of reading that resonate for us. My own history with anime begins with childhood memories of Japanese television animation from the 1960s and 1970s, rebroadcast a decade later on American TV. During my first trip to Japan in 1984 (before I understood any Japanese), I saw Kawajiri Yoshiaki's *Lensman* in a Japanese theater and glimpsed the possibilities of anime on a larger scale. But it was in the spring of 1990, shortly after I had graduated from college, that I watched *Akira* at the Music Box Theater in Chicago, and that was the point when everything seemed to change. It was one of a series of encounters with Japanese film and fiction that year that eventually led me to quit my job as a software engineer and go to graduate school in Japanese literature—as if the light coming off the theater screen had set off a reaction in me parallel to the film's story of psychic radiation, mutation, and transformation. Many readers will have stories of their own first encounters with anime. One goal of this book is to preserve and extend the sense of wonder and surprise that originally drew us to these texts, by helping readers develop new meanings and interpretations for themselves.

Another, less individual goal is to unfold some of the broader cultural context for anime—whether we think of that in terms of Japan's specific history and politics, its media landscape, or broader, vaguer things like Japanese "culture." My own academic background teaches me to think that these contexts are crucial but that they are also complex. In describing anime's cultural background, for example, one should be wary of explanations that neglect a careful reading of the work and instead rush to explain it with broad generalizations about what Japanese audiences think, feel, or believe. In a very real sense Japanese culture is not a stable, definable, or locatable thing that can explain why anime is the way it is. Rather, what we call Japanese culture is formed through and by a wide range of discourses from inside and outside of Japan, discourses that include anime within them. In other words anime is Japanese animation, but in another sense it is not Japan that makes anime; rather, it is our readings of anime that constitute our idea of Japan.

One of the central themes of this chapter and this book is how to maintain a balance between these two ways of reading: on the one hand cultural, historical, political, or contextual readings that seem to explain a given anime in definitive ways, grounding one interpretation at the risk of closing off others; and on the other hand original, individual interpretations that multiply potential readings but also potential uncertainty. *Akira* is a perfect place to begin this discussion. First, it occupies a key place in several different contexts: we can discuss its status in 1988, at the beginning of a new era for anime film in Japan and a broader anime boom abroad; we can investigate the Japanese historical context of the 1960s–1980s that informs its politics; and we can talk about its continued relevance and interest for international audiences today. But even more fascinating, the critical debates over *Akira* inside and outside Japan have centered squarely on this balance or tension between stable and unstable meanings.

This chapter looks concretely at the visual language of *Akira* by comparing the anime with the epic *Akira* manga, the print comic that was created in parallel. The comparison shows more specifically how the visual language of the anime and manga support or undermine the search for the kind of historical and political narratives we might associate with decisive meanings and origins.

Introducing *Akira*

Akira was directed by Ōtomo Katsuhiro, based on a landmark manga of the same name that Ōtomo drew from 1982 to 1990. When the *Akira* manga began serialization, Ōtomo was already a ten-year manga veteran with dozens of celebrated titles to his credit. But *Akira* was a bona fide cultural phenomenon, proving so popular that it spurred interest in a film well before it was complete. Ōtomo actually interrupted serialization of the manga in the middle to make the anime—the first feature film he would direct. It was released in theaters in July 1988 in Japan and late the following year in the United States.

In Japan, it was one of the most lavishly produced anime films to date, setting a new technical bar for the medium. Its making occupied a production committee of eight different companies and a hundred animators for more than two years, with a budget of a billion yen—more than any other Japanese animated film to that time.[1] *Akira* was in many ways the apogee of traditional cel animation, a process whereby each frame of the action is hand-drawn and hand-painted on a transparent piece of celluloid (a cel), which is then layered over a background painting (sometimes with other cels) and photographed to make a single frame of film. In this system, character designers set the look of each character, lead animators draw the "key-frames" that represent key points in the movement of characters and objects, and "in-betweeners" then draw the intermediate frames that move the characters from one key pose or position to another. In the decade after *Akira*, computers would begin to automate some of these steps, like coloring the cells, rendering intricate lighting or reflections, and animating the movements of complex three-dimensional shapes or backgrounds. But in 1988 *Akira* was famous for the massive scale of this hand-made product: 2,212 separate shots or sequences created with 160,000 hand-drawn and hand-painted cels.[2] Finally, the film's eclectically experimental musical soundtrack, by Yamashiro Shōji, combined traditional gamelan percussion with synthesizers and a range of choral and vocal gestures to brilliant effect.

In the United States, the film's technical achievements and sophisticated themes awakened audiences to the potential of

Japanese animation. Japanese television anime had been broadcast on American TV as early as the 1960s, and a grassroots network of North American anime fans was already active in the 1980s, but *Akira* was an event on a different scale. It was the first Japanese anime to receive wide North American theatrical distribution, bringing anime to the big screen—a large format that suited the epic physical scale of Ōtomo's story. It reached a wide audience, with extended reviews appearing in many major newspapers. Jerry Beck, who supervised *Akira*'s North American distribution at Streamline Pictures, told me that they had only about ten prints of the film, but that "with those ten prints we played every art-theater (and college) in the country . . . roughly 150 playdates." For this reason *Akira* is often characterized as the origin or ground zero of anime's spread to North America.[3]

This characterization of *Akira* as a kind of bombshell that set off the anime boom is all the more tempting given the film's memorable opening sequence, which is a literal explosion. The film fades in on an aerial view of a city, with the superimposed title "1988.7.16. Tokyo" (the date of the film's Japanese release). As the camera pans up to take in more and more of the distant city, there is the sound of wind on the otherwise silent soundtrack, and then a dome of alternating light and darkness appears at a distant point in the city's center. It illuminates the entire city in a harsh glare and then expands toward the viewer, obliterating the buildings in the foreground until the light fills the frame (Figure 6). Slowly, an aerial view of a new transformed city resolves itself out of this whiteness. An echoing drumbeat marks a transition to a more musical soundtrack, and a second title appears: "31 years after WW III. AD 2019 Neo Tokyo."

This ninety-second opening image—of a detonation that heralds violent change and renewal—became a metaphor for the influence of *Akira* on North American popular culture and anime's fortunes in the United States. "Just as the bubble of Japan's economy of the 1980s was about to burst," writes one popular anime guide, "a bomb of a more positive nature detonated, with the premiere of *Akira*."[4] But of course the more disturbing parallel is between this opening detonation and the atomic bombings of Japan. To see *Akira* in the United States around 1990 was to be transported

FIGURE 6. The opening sequence of the 1988 *Akira* anime, with an explosion that seemed to signify both a past war and a future media revolution. All *Akira* stills are from the twenty-fifth anniversary edition Blu-ray disc (Funimation, 2013).

back in history to the moment of Hiroshima, at the very same instant one seemed to be lifted out of the story and out of the theater to see the flash of a new future for Japanese film (Figure 7).

In fact, these two senses of the explosion—a celebratory, artistic, metatextual one that seems to productively explode the rules or boundaries of a whole genre or medium, and the dark immersive or illusionistic historical reminder—these sum up the oscillation that is at the heart of *Akira*, a version of the oscillation between distance and immersion that is at the heart of all the anime treated in this book. Critical appraisals of *Akira*, both at the time of its release and since, have tended to focus explicitly or implicitly on this oscillation by offering two very different interpretations of the film. Let us consider each of these interpretations in turn.

Ground Zero: *Akira*'s Nuclear Origins

For some critics, *Akira* represents a fixation on destruction that supposedly lies at the heart of Japanese popular culture, a legacy of the atomic bombings. This reading suggests Hiroshima and Nagasaki as original traumas that are then worked out and mastered through their repetition in popular culture. "It is easy

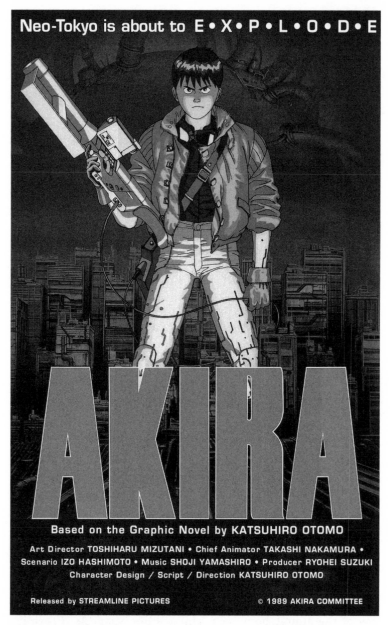

FIGURE 7. A movie poster used to advertise *Akira* for its 1989 U.S. theatrical release. Note the focus on explosion.

to recognize the outlines of the Japanese A-bomb anxiety that has been embedded in their popular culture from Godzilla onward," Dave Kehr writes in an early review of the film.[5] And academic readings have often taken a similar tack, foregrounding the way *Akira* and related films deal with fears of nuclear technology and memories of Japan's defeat in World War II. This idea is supported not only by the film's apocalyptic opening but by political references that run throughout: the groups and factions that drive the film include an army clique led by "the colonel" *(taisa)*, who is connected with experiments designed to create psychic weapons, and a group of antigovernment guerrilla fighters plotting to expose or disrupt the colonel's work. The colonel is easily associated with the militarization in the 1930s that led Japan into World War II, as well as the looming threat of remilitarization that many feared in the postwar. (True to form, he stages a military coup midway through the film and overthrows the government.) Meanwhile the guerrilla revolutionaries and the film's graphic images of street protests recall the mass demonstrations and political violence of Japan's postwar period.[6]

To understand *Akira's* politics, it is important to understand this history of postwar political protest in Japan, a history that could also be said to have its origins in the atomic bombing and Japan's defeat. The massive public demonstrations of the 1950s and 1960s brought together a range of left-leaning and left-wing groups (including unions, student organizations, and progressive political parties) around a cluster of related progressive causes like labor law, university conditions, and Japanese foreign policy. But the catalyst in each period was the adoption and renewal of the security treaty that defined the defense relationship between Japan and the United States, a relationship that began to take shape immediately after the end of World War II.

Following the atomic bombing of Hiroshima and Nagasaki, Japan surrendered and the United States began a seven-year occupation of the country that imposed a range of reforms designed to make Japan more democratic in the American mold, including a new constitution written by lawyers on the occupation staff. Prominent in the new constitution was a radical clause, Article 9, that renounced Japan's right to wage war and maintain armed forces. But when the occupation ended in 1952, the two countries signed a mutual security treaty that gave the United States the continuing right to base troops in Japan, with Japan eventually bearing much of the cost. The forces were justified as necessary for Japan's own defense, but a result was that Japan continued to act as a staging area for American military operations in Asia, including the Korean War in the early 1950s and the Vietnam War in the 1960s and 1970s. Throughout the Cold War, this treaty and its successors afforded the United States an operating base just a few miles from the Soviet Union's eastern seaboard. Japan also developed an advanced army, navy, and air force of its own, though it ostensibly adhered to Article 9 by characterizing these as "Self Defense Forces" and refusing (up until the 1990s) to deploy them outside the country. Even Japan's nuclear policy was divided: while it never constructed nuclear weapons, it tacitly permitted U.S. nuclear weapons to be based there, and a postwar nuclear power program created with the help of the United States generated a stockpile of weapons-grade nuclear material.

Japan's compromising (or compromised) position prompted opposition from several different political directions. Pacifists and strict constitutionalists opposed Japanese complicity in U.S. wars and feared Japanese remilitarization, while nationalists and anti-American factions (on the left and the right) argued for a more independent Japanese foreign and military policy. This prompted demonstrations in 1952, when the treaty was promulgated, and again in 1959–60, when it was revised, then a third time in 1968–70, at the time of its renewal.

In 1969 huge crowds demonstrated in Tokyo, and student occupations forced the closure of Tokyo University and other schools. After the conservative government forced through the treaty renewal, these public demonstrations came to an end, but they were succeeded in the 1970s by a series of dramatic airline hijackings and anti-Western, antigovernment terrorist actions by "urban guerrilla" groups like the Red Army Faction (*Sekigunha*) and the Japanese Red Army (*Nihon Sekigun*)—the Japanese counterparts to violent left-wing groups like the Red Army Faction in Germany and the Weathermen in the United States. In name and appearance, *Akira*'s urban guerrillas are clearly modeled on these groups

(Figure 8). Born in 1954, Ōtomo is part of a generation of Japanese artists and writers shaped by this history and by 1960s counterculture. Manga critic Yonezawa Yoshihiro writes, "The drug culture, flower power, the underground, the rock revolution, protests over the 1970 security treaty—these movements that dominated Japan in Ōtomo's middle-school and high-school years surely left a strong impression on him."[7]

Recently, popular visual artist Murakami Takashi has suggested that the history of the 1950s and 1960s has shaped not only Ōtomo's work but generations of Japanese popular culture. As an artist and curator, Murakami has advanced his idea that Japan's contemporary pop culture reflects not just the trauma of the atomic bombing and defeat but Japan's subservience to the United States throughout the postwar period. In 2005 Murakami curated a high-profile exhibition titled "Little Boy: The Arts of Japan's Exploding Subculture" at the Japan Society in New York City, where he exhibited anime, manga, monster films, and toys alongside his own paintings and sculptures and the work of his artistic circle. The exhibit drew a direct line from the Hiroshima bomb (codenamed "Little Boy" by its inventors) to the "otaku" or geek fans (the "little

FIGURE 8. The urban guerrilla character Kei emerges from a cloud of tear gas during a demonstration that visually recalls the public demonstrations of the 1950s and 1960s. Kei's hat seems calculated to evoke the helmets worn by demonstrators at the time, and she bears a passing resemblance to Shigenobu Fusako, a telegenic founder and leader of the Japanese Red Army.

boys") who produce and consume the narratives of disaster, mutation, and invasion that figure so prominently in Japan's popular media. "These images bespeak a profound psychological repression," wrote Sawaragi Noi in the exhibition catalog, suggesting that memories of defeat and later fears of Cold War nuclear annihilation "have never been channeled into a legitimate political consciousness. Instead, they have been transformed into the monstrous catastrophes and apocalyptic delusions depicted in the bizarre world of manga and anime." Ōtomo's *Akira* manga occupied a central place in the exhibition catalog: Murakami's programmatic essay in the catalog referred to the anime as "the epic film that would define an era," and devoted more text to the *Akira* manga than to any other single work in the exhibit.[8]

The popularity of the "Little Boy" show clearly owes much to the rhetorical power of Murakami's thesis, which is hard to refute and temptingly easy to understand and repeat.[9] The idea that the nuclear explosions over Hiroshima and Nagasaki are the origins of Japanese popular culture (a big bang from which all else springs) satisfies our desire for origins or explanations. Faced with the bewildering variety of Japanese pop culture products and the disturbing mix of the familiar and alien that we find there, it is not surprising that we feel the desire for some kind of historical key that will unlock the meaning of these images. This is what Murakami provided to his non-Japanese audience. And this interpretation is anchored by the fact that it is largely immune to interrogation, at least from outside Japan, since it is founded on Japan's particular status as the victim of atomic weapons, a position (the argument goes) that no other nation can occupy, question, or fully comprehend.

These ideas received renewed attention in the wake of the March 2011 earthquake, tsunami, and nuclear disasters in northeastern Japan. For some foreign journalists, these events provided yet another opportunity to explain Japan's apocalyptic popular culture (or even its broader culture) as stemming from a history of real disasters. Three weeks after the earthquake the *LA Times* wrote, "The apocalyptic streak in post–World War II Japanese pop culture has two primary sources: the country's precarious geography, perched at the intersection of shifting tectonic plates; and the Allied bombing raids that devastated Japanese cities, culminating in the horrors of the atomic attacks of August 1945."[10]

This is a powerful and in many ways a plausible idea, but it has some genuine pitfalls. By focusing on Japanese wartime suffering and postwar victimization, for example, it seems to encourage a passivity that elides Japan's past responsibilities as a wartime aggressor and refuses to think through its international responsibilities today. But when it comes to reading (whether it is interpreting anime or the world around us), the pitfall for Murakami's thesis is its reductionism, the way its sense of a decisive historical origin seems to close off more complex, more original, and more imaginative interpretations.

Returning for a moment to the disasters of 2011, at that time I was living in western Japan, which felt simultaneously very near and very far from the devastation. The events I watched unfold on the nightly news were so difficult to grasp, intellectually or emotionally, that they felt straight out of science fiction. I know I was not the only one who felt that in a situation where our individual lived experience provides no useful points of reference, it is only fictional narratives that give us any purchase on these events or any hope of coming to terms with them. In other words, rather than see the earthquake as a concrete reality that explains the texts of popular culture, a more productive possibility may be to use the texts of popular culture to help make sense of an otherwise baffling reality.[11]

Literary theory has long been suspicious of unitary meanings and has frequently argued that destabilizing firm meanings can be a more productive and progressive way of viewing literary texts and the wider world. Indeed, the recent history of critical theory could be characterized as a gradual erosion of the origins that would ground those meanings. In the first half of the twentieth century, New Criticism set aside authorial intent as a ground for interpretation and shifted the responsibility for producing meaning to the reader and critic. Later structuralism and deconstruction carried this project further and questioned the received faith in literary language as a transparent vessel that could convey a clear, stable, or reliable meaning. Jacques Derrida writes of "the moment when language invaded the universal problematic, the moment when, in the absence of a center or origin, everything became discourse."[12] This in turn fed the idea discussed at the outset of this chapter, that history and culture are not stable backgrounds against which texts can be written and interpreted, but that they are constructed from those very texts.

There is a range of shorthand for the core or irreducible meaning these theories call into question, including "presence," "transcendence," "depth," and the "origin" Derrida refers to above. In this chapter, the range of things I associate with this idea of "origin" thus starts from historical or cultural origins that are called on to explain why anime is the way it is, but ultimately it extends to anything that might fix or ground a single "correct" interpretation of a text: a reliance on the author or director to explain the work's meaning, a sense that only certain readers or critics are qualified interpreters, or even just a faith that the language and images of the work convey a single clear message. The counterpart to such an origin is the sense that literary meaning is always in play, that it can never be pinned down. In Derrida's words, "The absence of the transcendental signified extends the domain and the play of signification infinitely."[13]

In fact, at the same time they talk about its atomic origins, many academic readings of *Akira* have also been inclined to see it as just such a loss or effacement of origins, a work that undermines the search for unitary meaning and instead portrays a world in which there is no stable ground that could anchor interpretation. Literary criticism's suspicion of origins arguably reached a peak with poststructuralism in the late 1980s and early 1990s, just when *Akira* appeared, so it is not surprising that these approaches suggested themselves at the time; but even today many of these readings remain convincing in their core contention that *Akira* is a text about the unreliable function of language itself.

Degree Zero: *Akira*'s Postmodernism

These readings of the *Akira* anime as an effacement of origins often associate it with the postmodern, a theoretical paradigm that builds on the critical legacy outlined above to link the bewildering pace and unstructured quality of language and imagery in contemporary art and literature with the erosion of meaningful political language and activity. In other words, this approach sees *Akira*'s imagery and narrative neither as a traumatic repetition of the atomic bombing nor as a rereading of postwar Japanese history and politics; instead, *Akira* represents a kind of narrative oblivion that erases that history or finds itself unable to represent it.

The term "postmodern" has been applied repeatedly to *Akira*, notably in Susan Napier's influential 1993 article "Panic Sites," the first English academic article on anime in the field of Japanese studies, and arguably itself the origin of academic anime criticism in North America.[14] These readings focus on the film's frantic visual pacing, which looked to some like a ceaseless rotation of vivid images unconnected by any coherent plot. The American Marxist critic Fredric Jameson identifies the postmodern closely with this kind of rapid but unstructured flow of language and imagery, which he links with modern media technologies and, more fundamentally, with the way that capital and the market accelerate the spread of commercial language while alienating us from lived, historical reality in a way that erodes our sense of grounded meaning.

Jameson compares the resulting state with a Lacanian notion of schizophrenia, whereby the individual is unable to link and structure successive instants of time or language to form a linear personal or historical narrative. "With the breakdown of the signifying chain," Jameson writes, "the schizophrenic is reduced to an experience of pure material signifiers, or, in other words, a series of pure and unrelated presents in time." The result is that the "present suddenly engulfs the subject with undescribable vividness, a materiality of perception properly overwhelming, which effectively dramatizes the power of the material—or better still, the literal—signifier in isolation." We can relate Jameson's erasure of deep meaning to what Jean Baudrillard calls the "triumph of superficial form, of the smallest common denominator of all signification, degree zero of meaning."[15]

Jameson views the fragmentation of linear narrative negatively, as a loss of history. But other critics of the postmodern, like Jean-François Lyotard, have seen this overturning of time as potentially revolutionary, as a way to escape some of the more oppressive "modern" narratives of history and the subject and start anew. Below we turn to Lyotard and the question of whether *Akira* can be viewed with this kind of optimism. But for now let's remain with

Jameson's Marxist critique, which is that today in an age of multinational capital, we no longer have access to the kind of language that would permit us to understand and change our place in history and our lived political reality. The loss of time and self referenced above not only erases our sense of historical narrative (historical cause and effect), it also undermines the kind of firm subjectivity that allows one to see oneself as an individual actor who can intervene to affect the course of future events. For Jameson, the resulting sense of freedom or lightness (exhilarating but disturbingly empty) is what it feels like to live in the postmodern world.

Writing after Napier, Freda Freiberg and Isolde Standish separately described *Akira* as postmodern precisely in Jameson's terms: "In the absence of narrative coherence, the film grabs and grips the viewer by its visceral excitement, a constant bombardment and battering of the senses, a barrage of high intensity experiences."[16] This reading of *Akira* is supported not only by the pace and impact of the film's visuals but also by the confusion of its plot. Many initial reviews of *Akira* found the story incomprehensible, and even later critics with the luxury of a DVD player have asserted that it somehow defies summary.[17] In fact, the events of the story are fairly straightforward; however, the editing is complex, as the film skips back and forth between several different characters and locations, and the politics and motivations that link these different factions are often confounding.

The first characters to be introduced, Kaneda and Tetsuo, are teenage friends and rivals in a motorcycle gang. One night while out riding, Tetsuo crashes his bike into a young boy with strangely aged features, who turns out to be a test subject escaped from a psychic weapons lab overseen by the colonel. The collision sets off a series of transformations in Tetsuo that give him psychic powers like those of the test subjects. As these powers grow, Tetsuo becomes increasingly unbalanced and destructive, first killing his fellow gang members and eventually battling the colonel's troops through the streets of Tokyo. Tetsuo follows a series of clues toward the font of psychic power at the heart of the colonel's project, a force known to us only as "Akira." This force, we learn, is the source of the original explosion that touched off World War III at the start of the project, thirty-one years ago. Throughout the film Tetsuo is pursued by his rival Kaneda, the colonel, the three aged "children" who are original test subjects, and the guerrilla fighters, among other factions. All form shifting alliances with one another to try to possess, control, kill, or rescue Tetsuo before he locates Akira and risks reawakening its power. The chase scenes become increasingly frenetic and the combat increasingly kinetic until the film's climactic reveal, when Tetsuo locates Akira and exposes its true form, and all the forces converge for a final apocalyptic showdown.

Some of these factions resemble the historical Japanese political actors discussed above: compromised politicians, a grasping military, left-wing revolutionaries, and a doomsday weapon. But if the anime's cast of characters is familiar, the web of politics that connects them is confused. Viewers experience the film from constantly shifting perspectives as various characters take center stage, one after another, in a confusing rotation that continually complicates their motivations and their relations to each other. Isolde Standish calls the film's politics a "pastiche," Fredric Jameson's keyword for the postmodern accumulation of historical styles (like the hodgepodge of architectural elements in postmodern buildings) that robs those elements of any historical context or meaning and reduces them to free-floating signifiers. Standish suggests that Ōtomo's film quotes indiscriminately from the preceding fifty years of Japanese political struggle: the militarization of the 1930s, World War II, and cold-war politics are all intermixed in a way that collapses past, present, and future. For Standish, *Akira*'s images of strikes and street demonstrations become generic representations of "unrest" that suggest our inability to understand or come to terms with real Japanese politics or history. Critiques like these suggest that *Akira* and other texts of mass-market culture are the symptoms of our postmodern condition, in which market forces have undermined individual agency and meaningful language, to the point where we can no longer affect or even grasp the economic and political forces that shape our lives.

When we combine the political confusion of the plot with the hallucinogenic quality of Ōtomo's luminous cityscapes, the kinetic excitement of the motorcycle chase scenes, and the detailed scenes of the city's destruction that begin and end the film, it all contributes to this sense of an aggressive, even uncontrolled propagation of images that cannot be reined in by meaning. A culminating image comes in the climax of the film, when Tetsuo's psychic powers increase to the point where his body can no longer contain them, and he metamorphoses into a pulsating, pustulating mass of flesh and machinery that explodes outward, absorbing or consuming everything in its path. As Napier points out, the dissolution of bounded individual subjectivity (what Jameson traces at the level of schizophrenic language) is here enacted literally as the disintegration of the body's physical boundaries.[18]

The Beginning of the End: *Akira* as Both Origin and Oblivion

The interpretation of *Akira* as a postmodern rejection of origins and decisive explanations seems to be at odds with the nuclear origin theory, the notion of a single traumatic historical event that forms the source of *Akira's* imagery and anxiety. But in fact the two readings have been combined by interpreters like Murakami Takashi into the single idea that the atomic bombing represents the end of conventional history and representation, and the inauguration of a Japanese postmodern.

Jameson already argues that the dawn of the electronic and atomic age is a singularity, a moment when the developing power of multinational capital becomes manifest in new technologies that influence the ways we communicate and that pose new threats to progressive politics. Murakami's narrative is more specifically Japanese: it is precisely the atomic bombing and its aftermath (from Japan's defeat and occupation through the politics of the Cold War) that have rendered impossible any hope of constructive political engagement, and with it any hope of understanding and representing that history constructively or realistically in literature and art. Arguments like Murakami's see the postwar as a long series of defeats and setbacks for progressive political reform in Japan: even as the protests of the 1950s and 1960s escalated in scale and violence, the mutual defense treaties were consistently supported by the conservative forces of the ruling Liberal Democratic Party, which held power almost continuously from its formation in 1955 until the end of the century, and after 1970 these mass protests ended. Violent left-wing groups of the 1970s (like the Red Army Faction and United Red Army) alienated the broader public and were eventually hunted down by police or consumed by violent infighting.

At the same time, the impetus and appetite for widespread popular political activism were undoubtedly undermined by the nation's focus on industrial and economic growth in the 1960s and 1970s (displayed triumphantly to the world at the 1964 Tokyo Olympics) and then later by the prosperity of the superheated "bubble" economy in the 1980s. For some on the left it seemed as if productive political activism had been sabotaged by the ascendance of corporate and consumer culture. Oshii Mamoru, an anime director of the same generation as Ōtomo, lamented in 1989, "I mean, it used to be that young people's desires were in conflict with society's demands on them. Now, however, young people are the ideal consumers."[19]

Meanwhile, outside of Japan the global expansion of Japanese manufacturing and media industries during this final phase of the Japanese economic miracle fed foreign interest in Japanese culture, setting the stage for the anime boom a decade later. So when Jameson's Marxist critique of postmodern society appeared in the mid-1980s, the contemporary image of Japan as a land of hyperconsumption, hypermediation, and conservative politics seemed to match perfectly his description of a society where the market-driven expansion of the image had replaced and disabled political engagement.[20]

In this narrative, then, the events of the postwar (historically and symbolically concentrated into the single initiating event of the atomic bomb) somehow evacuate political and historical meaning from the present, in a way that is reflected by the frantic propagation of imagery in texts like *Akira*. This is how *Akira* comes to represent an origin and a lack of origins at the same time: the film's opening explosion blows away meaning along with everything else.[21]

Ultimately neither the origin nor the oblivion thesis by itself is exceedingly interesting or productive: each tends to foreclose interpretation, by seeing *Akira*'s meaning as either overdefined by the atomic (not up for discussion) or completely indefinable (and undiscussable). And interpretations like Murakami Takashi's seem to accomplish both gestures at once. I would agree that *Akira* reflects both the impulse to locate origins and the impulse to efface them, but not in the way Murakami suggests. For me, *Akira* oscillates productively between these two positions: it has a realism that provokes a shock of historical recognition and a search for real political solutions, but it also has a presentation that makes spectators question how that politics, history, or reality can be represented to begin with. This is *Akira*'s version of the oscillation traced in this book: this power to alternate rapidly between an illusionistic realism that expresses a concrete truth and a productively skeptical deconstruction of expression itself.

This oscillation manifests itself concretely in *Akira* in different ways: in terms of its tone, scenes of farce and slapstick violence (often accompanied by less realistic, more visually cartoony animation) intrude in a way that breaks the spell of the film's realistic politics and realistic violence. This can make the film seem to drift uncomfortably back and forth between juvenile and adult literature.[22] But the jarring juxtaposition of different registers that is so common in anime (and other postmodern art) can also be seen as the medium's way of injecting some irony or skepticism into the film's portrayal of history: at regular intervals *Akira* is compelled to remind us that in some sense this is simply a cartoon version of real life.

It is also easy to see the film's plot as politically divided. There is a desire for a law-and-justice conclusion that would resolve the plot conflicts and uphold moral or political values (represented by Kaneda or even the colonel, who gradually morphs from sinister dictator to protective father figure). But there is also a conflicting delight in destruction for its own sake, represented by Tetsuo. Of course, the film's desire for destruction also has a political dimension, linked to the dream of a violent revolution in which youth will dismantle the city and the political system built by earlier generations, and start again from zero. This is a dream we might associate with the radical politics of the 1960s and 1970s and the radical art movements of the same period, which embraced the modernist hope that artistic expression could intervene to disrupt or redirect the political status quo. To that extent, the film still seems grounded in politics, and the choice between a conservative and a revolutionary alternative. But many theories of postmodernism are skeptical that we can still make that kind of revolutionary choice, and frequently the destruction in *Akira* seems to pass beyond the realm of meaning in just the way that Jameson predicts. Violence becomes a purely sensory experience cut off from any political significance or efficacy. As Tetsuo's body metamorphoses fantastically and spreads uncontrollably across the screen, we seem to see a celebration of destruction that has largely left the plot behind: having lost all political meaning and connection to reality, the anime simply revels in the visual and representational possibilities of the medium itself.

Some theorists of the postmodern, like Jean-François Lyotard, suggest that this renewed focus on representation—with its attendant skepticism of realism and historical narrative—is a healthy impulse. Lyotard sounds a bit like Jameson when he writes, in *The Postmodern Condition,* that the "grand narratives" of historical progress that guided the eighteenth, nineteenth, and early twentieth centuries no longer seem believable or compelling to us today, and also when he warns of the market's baleful influence on our pursuit of knowledge. But Lyotard sees an alternative in a range of "little narratives," multiple ways of understanding the world that can productively shape our understanding precisely because they are unpredictable, local, and contingent. Lyotard's advocates suggest that these are healthier than the grand narratives of advancement that underwrote the horrors of our modern history, culminating in two world wars. (Theorizing Japan's postmodernity is complicated by the question of whether Japan's modernity was the same as the West's, but clearly it is possible to see Japan's early twentieth-century history of colonialism, militarism, and imperialism as driven by quintessentially modern narratives of progress, civilization, and rationalization. And the death of the grand narrative and the rise of little ones have been the focus of Japanese theorists like Ōtsuka Eiji and Azuma Hiroki, whose theories of narrative are discussed in chapter 6.)[23]

Discarding these grand narratives, writes Lyotard, "is what the postmodern world is all about. Most people have lost the nostalgia for the lost [grand] narrative. It in no way follows that they are reduced to barbarity. What saves them from it is their knowledge that legitimation can only spring from their own linguistic practice and communicational interaction"—their own little narratives. This chaotic arrangement of competing stories certainly seems to describe the narrative structure of *Akira*. Writing more specifically on literary and artistic style, Lyotard sees the postmodern as continuing modernism's radical project in a different way: if the modernist avant-garde used conventional forms (like the novel) but did away with conventional meaning, postmodernism accomplishes something similar by undermining conventional forms.[24] Jameson is more pessimistic than Lyotard, but even he allows that postmodern art and literature (including popular culture and science fiction) have the potential to expose the crisis of postmodernity and perhaps even hint at a way out of it. Might *Akira* be productive in the ways Lyotard and Jameson hope?

To analyze the dynamic between *Akira*'s politics and its postmodernism, we need to move beyond general observations (about the rapid pace of imagery, for example) and examine the film's visuals in more detail. As discussed in the Introduction, one of the most powerful critical tools we have for focusing attention on anime's formal properties is to compare it with another medium, and in this chapter I would like to make the comparison with Ōtomo's *Akira* manga. Here it is not my intent to treat the manga as a backstory or a better story that will answer all our questions about the anime. That would simply substitute one origin for another, replacing *genbaku* (the nuclear bomb) with *gensaku* (the nucleus of the franchise, the original text). Instead, I want to use the comparison to focus our attention on the distinctive visual styles and devices these two texts employ, and reveal how the same author working in different media can accomplish very different effects and even reach very different destinations. This in turn tells us something about the specific powers of anime as a medium, the things it can and cannot depict, and the problems and solutions it can and cannot prompt us to think through.

Akira as Manga

In the same way that the *Akira* anime had an influence on anime that followed, the *Akira* manga became a major publishing event in Japan when it was serialized in the 1980s. Archie Goodwin writes that *Akira* helped establish *Young Magazine*, driving its circulation over a million and paving the way for an entire genre of Japanese manga magazines aimed at young men. *Young Magazine* originally appeared biweekly, with one installment of *Akira* (usually twenty pages) in every issue. This was a slower pace than other manga serials, which allowed Ōtomo to invest his drawings with the almost excruciating level of visual detail that helped make his style so popular. At intervals these biweekly installments were collected, sometimes revised again by Ōtomo, and published in thick, large-format paperback volumes (an innovation at the time, when collected volumes were typically published in formats smaller than the original magazine publication). Eventually the series ran to 120 installments, published from 1982 to 1990 and collected in six volumes totaling 2,200 pages. But the story became popular enough in its first few years to spur interest in making an anime film, which was started and finished before the manga narrative was complete. (In early 1987, about three-quarters of the way through the story, Ōtomo stopped serialization for a year and a half to work on the anime full time.)[25] The plot of the anime follows the content of the first thirty installments or so, but also carries the story forward to a final resolution. Then after the anime was released, serialization of the manga resumed, and over the next year and a half it worked its way toward a conclusion that borrowed some elements from the film but changed others.

These circumstances suggest that many of the Japanese fans who saw the film when it opened in theaters would already have known the first part of the story, just as many readers of the serialization probably had the film in mind as they read the final installments. The anime and manga were thus interlocking parts of a single franchise (a dynamic addressed in detail in chapter 6), and this undoubtedly explains some of the difficulty that non-Japanese viewers and reviewers had following the plot.

But that difficulty stems from more than just a lack of background; it also traces to the ways that manga influences the film's form and narrative structure—particularly the rapid, fragmentary editing that critics associated with the film's postmodernism. Standish suggests that the manga's serial form resists narrative

closure, giving both it and the anime a fragmented quality associated with the postmodern, and I would also emphasize the way
the manga can shift rapidly among different subplots between
and within its many short installments.[26] For readers accustomed
to manga, the transitions from frame to frame, page to page, and
episode to episode have a rhythm that is dynamic but not chaotic;
however, when this structure is translated into the medium of
anime film, it becomes more difficult to parse.

Consider the first few minutes of the anime, which jumps rapidly from place to place and from one set of characters to another.
Part of the action focuses on a gang war Kaneda's crew is fighting
with a rival biker group, and there are several scenes of different
gang members riding violently through the night city. These alternate with scenes of a guerrilla fighter who has kidnapped or
liberated one of the three child test subjects (Takashi) from the
colonel's lab, and who is fleeing from security forces when he runs
into a street demonstration. We also cut back and forth to the interior of the colonel's helicopter as he searches for the guerrillas
and the escaped test subject. Finally the guerrilla is gunned down
by security forces, and a terrified Takashi teleports away to the outskirts of the city. He materializes in front of Tetsuo's bike, causing a
crash. Moments later the colonel's helicopters land, and his troops
seize Takashi and Tetsuo. Kaneda and the guerrilla Kei are both
detained in the aftermath, and meet in police custody the next day.

This opening sequence serves to introduce most of the story's
different factions (or reintroduce them, for viewers who had already read the manga) and bring them into contact with one another. But while this action unfolds over the first 100 pages of the
manga (five episodes, or about two months, in the original serialization), it happens in the first fifteen minutes of the anime, and
the frequent transitions can make it confusing. This confusion is
magnified by the fact that links between scenes are often provided
by visual associations and by cues in the soundtrack, rather than
clear narrative connections. In one shot, for example, the bikers
speed through flames, smoke, and firefighting foam inside a burning highway tunnel, then we cut to a scene of demonstrators turning over a burning car while riot police aim water hoses at them.

If the opening suggests that the manga is more clearly organized than the anime—better able to orient the reader—that difference becomes even clearer as both texts progress, and it is particularly evident in their conclusions. The remainder of this chapter examines these differences by comparing the endings of the two works.

The Anime's Inconclusive Conclusion

Let's begin with the ending of the film. In the anime's climactic reveal, Tetsuo locates the force that has until now been identified by the cryptic term "Akira" and learns it was the name of a child, the most powerful of the military's original test subjects, whose psychic awakening generated the explosion that opens the film. Akira now exists only as a series of tissue samples in glass jars, housed in a supercooled vault in the old city, in a secret base located beneath the explosion crater. (The base is concealed by a symbol of reconstruction that mirrors a central symbol of Japan's postwar reconstruction: a new Olympic stadium being built over the old ground zero.) As Tetsuo breaks open the vault, his rival Kaneda and the colonel bring increasingly powerful weapons to bear on him, but to no avail. Growing stronger by the minute, Tetsuo begins to lose control of his growing power and transforms dramatically into a monstrous fleshy growth that begins to consume everything and everyone around him. To stop him, Takashi and the other two test subjects use their own powers to reawaken Akira, who is reassembled and reappears momentarily as an embodied child and who almost immediately generates an expanding globe of light like the one in the opening scene, a widening sphere that destroys the surrounding city and engulfs Tetsuo, Kaneda, and the test subjects.

This finale is full of light imagery. The glowing ball of light that emanates from Akira seems to absorb and eventually reconcile everything and everyone. Swirling clouds and surging seas topple the surrounding buildings to the accompaniment of a dramatic organ fugue, but this ends relatively quickly, and the clouds are shown clearing as rays of sunshine pierce them and shine down on the city. Inside the sphere of light, Kaneda and/or Tetsuo recall their friendship in a series of flashbacks that seem to restore their relationship, then Kaneda is transported back to the city. We

see him crouched in the rubble, cupping a tiny light that is the remains of the now contracting explosion, a personal illumination
(memory, realization, enlightenment) that he takes into himself
(Figure 9). He is then reunited with Kei, and they ride off into the
city on his motorcycle. The screen fades to white, and there is a series of light/dark images (abstract flashing shapes, then stars and
galaxies) accompanied by a voiceover saying "I am Tetsuo."

This imagery is distinctly spiritual, from the accompanying
organ and choral music and beams of light descending from the
heavens, to Kaneda's entering the light and taking it inside himself, and finally to the suggestion that Tetsuo presides over the
birth of a new universe. But neither this suggestion of religious
transcendence nor the suggestion that friendship conquers all
can really tie up the anime's many threads or provide a satisfying
sense of closure. They certainly do not resolve the political issues
that are in the background of the film. For example, consider the
conflicted symbolism of Akira: is he like the colonel, the symbol of
a regrettable military past buried beneath a reconstructed Japan?
Or is he the victim of war like Takashi and his fellow test subjects—
the blameless child, the fallen soldier, the buried casualty now dis-
interred? Or is he some combination of Tetsuo, Kaneda, and Kei:

FIGURE 9. Kaneda emerges from the giant sphere of light generated by Akira
and then cups the shrinking ball of light in his hands, in a gesture that seems
intended to signify growth and resolution. Note, too, the relatively flat background, which contrasts with the volumetric portrayal of rubble in the manga.

youthful revolution personified, the hope of a future that is cut off from the sins of the past, an idealistic, violent cleansing that will undermine every existing political signification and wipe every slate clean? This conflicting symbolism can be resolved only by making Akira and these other ambiguous signifiers disappear in a ball of light. The future seems to belong to Kaneda and Kei, a new Adam and Eve who survive and embrace in the wreckage, but it is not easy to determine what this domestic couple of biker and guerrilla stands for politically.

One could speculate that Ōtomo resorted to the cheat of this final divine light because he could not think of a way to tie up the different threads of the anime's plot and politics. But here I would like to point out that light and darkness form the visual grammar that Ōtomo uses throughout the whole film, starting with the opening explosion and the nighttime motorcycle chase. As we will see below in our comparison with the manga, the anime's visual language or grammar is effective for expressing confusion but not as good for portraying solutions or resolutions. In other words, I will argue that the anime is inconclusive not because Ōtomo could not think of a solution but because he could not animate it. His anime does not possess the visual language to describe how the characters might resolve these political contradictions.

And yet, seen through the lens of postmodern theory, the film's ability to evoke political realities without being able to tie them together in a single narrative might represent either failure or success: either the failure of narrative and political imagination that Jameson decries or success in replacing Lyotard's dangerous or discredited grand narrative with many little ones. Here again we will be helped by a comparison with the manga, which provides the narrative closure that the anime lacks, but in a way that may make us prefer the anime's uncertain resolution.

How The Manga Ends, and How It Ends Again

About a third of the way through the manga Tetsuo awakens Akira from his thirty-seven-year sleep in the cryogenic vault, which causes a second explosion that wrecks a part of the city—just as in the anime. But in the manga this explosion does not carry away

Tetsuo or the psychic child test subjects. Instead, Tetsuo survives to form a gang and rule the ruins, holding United Nations aid workers at bay and keeping Tokyo effectively cut off from the world. All the main characters live on in the isolated city, scattered and forced to survive in the rubble, but many of them are transformed as factions shift and old villains like the colonel become new heroes. The manga also introduces some new factions, including an interventionist U.S. military and a religious leader with psychic powers, Miyako, who opposes Tetsuo and his army in order to create a pacifist utopia in the ruins. These struggles and transformations make up the entire second half of the manga narrative.

Ōtomo is famous for his meticulous draftsmanship, and these ruins are unquestionably the manga's visual signature.[27] The manga lavishes much more attention on the city's destruction and transformation than the anime does, devoting page after page to depictions of toppled buildings. These images resonate realistically and powerfully with scenes of devastation and reconstruction in the immediate postwar period, and they represent both destruction and survival. Many of the subnarratives revolve around characters' efforts to navigate this wreckage—to find a path or a person, to fight through a barrier, and so on. In the second half of the manga, then, characters struggle to restart from zero (or ground zero) and redefine their position geographically, socially, and morally. This is figured not only in terms of the plot, which involves a lot of travel through the city on various quests, but also in terms of the visuals, which depict the characters in long-distance views that display these symbolic and actual journeys through the ruins (Figures 10 and 11). There are also numerous sequences where we start with a view of a building in the distance and then zoom in one panel at a time to a close-up of a previously invisible character in a window or doorway, locating the character in a geographical context.

Some of these spatial contexts are highly symbolic: the curving profile of Miyako's temple rises out of the rubble looking like a huge revival tent, big enough to shelter the city's refugees but always with her in the tower at its apex. Tetsuo occupies a stone throne that sits in imperial isolation on a concrete island floating

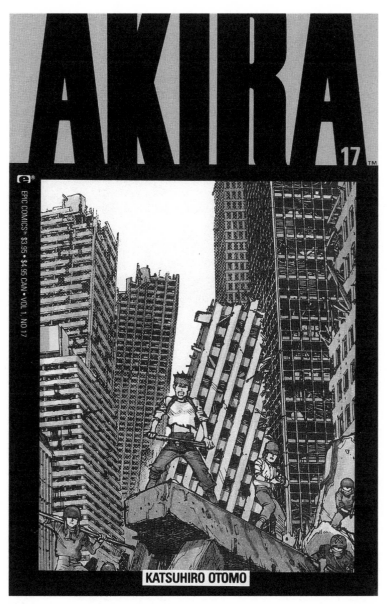

FIGURE 10. Much of the *Akira* manga is dominated by scenes of rubble, which characters navigate in a visual and narrative attempt to locate their place in the city. Cover image from the English color version of the manga, issued serially by Marvel's imprint Epic Comics (issue 23, 1990).

FIGURE 11. Tetsuo with the city spread out beneath him. The scene conveys his power and points to the reassuring but also sinister quality of the bird's-eye view, which locates the characters in a stable context but also establishes a hierarchy of surveillance and control. Cover image from the Marvel serialized English version (issue 17, 1990).

in the middle of the half-flooded Olympic stadium—a visual riff on Tokyo's imperial palace and its moats, as well as the idea of Japan as an independent, self-sufficient island empire. In other words, the manga's three-dimensional landscapes become metaphors for the political worlds that the characters are trying to build or locate themselves within.

For technical reasons, the anime cannot give the city the kind of volume or depth that the manga can: in the latter, Ōtomo is able to draw still images of collapsing architecture in exquisite detail, but these kinds of images were impossible to animate even with *Akira's* budget, and except for a brief sequence of crumbling buildings at the end, the film defaults to a typical animation pattern of moving the characters across relatively flat, stationary backgrounds. Even in the opening scenes where it is introduced, the city remains a backdrop of two-dimensional sliding layers. No matter how far or in what direction the characters ride in that opening scene, the buildings do not seem to get any nearer or farther away, but exist as a kind of looming backdrop, impossibly large and impossibly distant, like mountains (Figure 12).

The light/dark dynamic that characterizes the anime also flattens the film's third dimension and makes everyone seem lost in the darkness. The characters and their machines hurtle through the night, struggling to light their own way, but these lights rarely

FIGURE 12. Distant, unmoving, and impossibly large, the skyline in the background of the anime's opening sequence obeys no laws of linear perspective.

seem to penetrate more than a few feet into the gloom. The result is that the characters seem trapped in a foreshortened space they cannot escape. By the time obstacles appear in their headlights (literally or figuratively), it is already too late to avoid a collision. This is a central motif of the opening sequence: the black screen that follows the title credit is revealed to be the inside of the bomb crater, but only after the camera manages to pull back and show the crater edges, and this is the last time for a while that the spectator or anyone in the anime will achieve that kind of perspective. After a shot of the flickering light outside the Harukiya bar where the characters hang out, the motorcycles take off in a flash of sparking wheels, light trails, and glaring headlights, but as the characters shoot out of the brightly lit new city and into the darkness of the old city's ruins, their headlights illuminate only small patches of road ahead (Figure 13).

At the climax of the opening, the rival biker that Tetsuo is pursuing crashes when an obstacle looms up out of the darkness directly in front of him, and then Takashi appears suddenly in Tetsuo's headlights, too close to avoid. Moments later, the colonel's helicopters materialize in the darkness at point-blank range: magically the huge machines have remained undetected (un-

FIGURE 13. The bikers hurtling through the darkness near the beginning of the film can see only a few feet ahead, a visual figure for the postmodern world the film portrays.

heard, unseen, unfelt) until their probing searchlights reveal them directly overhead.

Several critics have commented on the play of light and darkness in the film.[28] In my reading, it is this device that makes the characters seem unable to gain a sense of distance or perspective, or to place themselves in the wider world. The faster they drive, the less warning they have of what is ahead, so that the quicker they try to get somewhere, the more compressed or foreshortened their world becomes. The only way for the film to escape this regime is to light up everything, with the ball of illumination that magically shows all—from Kaneda's past with Tetsuo to the future of a new universe. But after the effective claustrophobia that has preceded it, that solution seems both too sudden and too trite. Unlike the manga, the visual dynamics of the anime are optimized for portraying the characters' confusion or oblivion, the flattened world from which they cannot escape.[29]

Jameson associates the postmodern strongly with this kind of flatness or depthlessness, his central figure that connects the flat picture plane of artists like Andy Warhol with all the symptoms of metaphorical depthlessness discussed above: the loss of deep meaning, historical perspective, and psychological interiority. This plays out dramatically in the work of Murakami Takashi, whose "Superflat" art borrows ideas like Jameson's. Above we discussed Murakami's thesis that Japanese fine art and political discourse have both been unable to capture the political meaning of the atomic bomb and occupation; only popular media like anime, manga, and character design have come close to portraying these issues, but always in a flattened (distorted, indirect, "repressed") way that corresponds to their two-dimensional visual aesthetic. Superflat art emulates that aesthetic deliberately, with very two-dimensional compositions that defeat any sense of perspective and even sculptures that seem intended to mimic the flat images of anime. Like Jameson, Murakami suggests that there is something simultaneously empty and liberating about this art. Critiquing Murakami, and wondering whether anime can offer something more, Thomas Lamarre writes, "The important question is whether the . . . flattening and dehierarchizing of the image allows us to think technology differently or whether, like Murakami's superflat, it leaves us suspended in ambivalence, with projections of precocious impotence into the future."[30]

Jameson finally extends this issue of aesthetic flattening to a reading of urban geography and the way in which the corporatized architecture of Los Angeles produces buildings and neighborhoods that are increasingly difficult for the individual to navigate. Unable to chart a course through this flattened space, we become physically lost in a way that mirrors our political disorientation. But in the case of *Akira*, the manga seems to cling to something that the anime and Jameson's Los Angeles have lost or given up. The city portrayed in the manga is both mappable and navigable. The kind of three-dimensional representation we see in the manga represents the persistence of an origin that could orient the characters: it is now literally the origin coordinate or vanishing point of a linear geometric perspective.[31]

Consider the conclusion. In plot terms, the manga's finale is similar to the anime's, but with more factions (including, significantly, an invading contingent of U.S. military forces) battling Tetsuo and each other. But on the final pages of the manga, Akira again envelops Tetsuo, Kaneda, and the test subjects in a sphere of light, and the emphasis on friendship as a resolution is repeated. Kei calls Kaneda back from inside the light, and when the smoke clears, the two find themselves at the top of a ruined building looking out on a sunrise. This was the final image of the serialized version of *Akira* as it appeared in *Young Magazine*. The sunrise is a symbol of optimism about the future, but significantly this kind of light imagery is hard to see and understand on the page: here as elsewhere the manga eschews chiaroscuro in favor of an evenly lit deep focus that reveals every detail of the cityscape, so it cannot harness contrast the way the anime does.[32] But for readers attuned to the use of perspective and the path-finding motif in the manga, the way Kaneda and Kei survey the city's wreckage from on high creates a kind of visual closure that subtly suggests they will be able to locate themselves in the world (geographically, and perhaps ethically and politically) and move forward.

This final image of Kaneda and Kei is carefully balanced between vulnerability and power: their aerial view of the ruined but paradoxically beautiful city suggests a degree of agency but also unpredictability. It suggests a future where youth can exert control over their own home and their own destiny, without exercising the totalitarian control of adult authorities like the colonel or the religious leader Miyako, but without surrendering to Tetsuo's terrorist anarchy either. Read carefully, this final image of the serialized version becomes a promisingly utopian evocation of revolution.

In its way, this ending is also much clearer than the ending of the anime. But even this ending was apparently still too inconclusive for Ōtomo or the manga's fans, because the author added a thirty-five-page epilogue when the serialized episodes were collected into the final paperback volume, a new ending that renders the conclusion more blunt and more decisive, both in terms of its plot and its perspectival visuals. Significantly, it also becomes more conservative and nationalistic. In that epilogue, Tetsuo's gang collapses with his disappearance, and U.N. aid workers are finally able to enter Tokyo. But at this point the remaining bikers and guerrillas join forces to repel these foreign intruders and form a new state based on the one Tetsuo attempted to build, the Great Tokyo Empire Akira (*Dai Tōkyō Teikoku Akira*). In the final image, Kaneda rides off into the city in an exaggerated perspectival shot that outdoes even the earlier panorama from the top of the building.

In this new final image, the road extends to a clean vanishing point, while buildings tower dramatically and geometrically on either side, making the city's structures seem to rise again from their own ruins. This second ending has an architectural solution that is even more clearly expressed and more optimistically inflected: we can locate ourselves geometrically and geographically in the city, we can restore the city's sleek lines from the rubble, and we can chart our own future direction.[33] But along with this increased optimism or confidence comes a renewed nationalism: the rebuilding of a state, even an empire, with a military to defend it. As it gestures toward the future, the manga also moves us into the past: it rewrites the end of World War II, so that the bomb explodes but the subsequent foreign occupation is repulsed. And it seems to invoke the prewar era of Japanese colonialism and imperialism that led to the war. In the first part of the story, "Akira" is the mysterious name for the unknown fount of all power; on the last pages of the manga it becomes the name of the empire.[34]

At the level of its plot and its visuals, then, the manga has a stronger sense of direction and perspective than the anime, and this translates into a kind of historical or political certainty as well. But with that confidence and certainty comes a kind of chauvinism, and the text eventually gravitates to a nationalist politics that threatens to recreate the political mistakes of the past. Returning to the anime, then, we can see how its combination of recognizable political history and postmodern uncertainty about Japan's political present may actually be more realistic, more optimistic, and more constructive.

Writing about the bewildering but potentially liberating possibilities of postmodern space, Jameson says we cannot and should not hope to return to "some older and more transparent national space, or some more traditional and reassuring perspectival or mimetic enclave." What we require are new kinds of art to serve as "cognitive maps" for understanding the fraught political and geographic spaces of modernity and postmodernity and for navigating our contemporary world. These cognitive maps might "enable a situational representation on the part of the individual subject to that vaster and properly unrepresentable totality which is the ensemble of society's structures as a whole."[35] In other words, though Jameson sees the bewildering state of art and language as a symptom of our postmodern dilemma, he also hopes (with Lyotard) that certain kinds of postmodern art might help us grasp our position in postmodernity, might help us begin to place ourselves in society and in history as well as in space.

As we have seen, the *Akira* anime oscillates between real political and historical referents, on the one hand, and a deconstruction of political, historical, and literary narrative, on the other. But as Lyotard hoped, it also manages to avoid the pitfalls of the modern political narratives seen in the manga, where clarity and perspective become linked to certainty and control, surveillance, and empire. In this sense, perhaps the anime could constitute one of Jameson's cognitive maps—one that helps us begin to fix our position, but one that also supplies a healthy skepticism about language, a productive confusion that keeps us from being too sure of where we stand.

Onward and Inward

So far we have defined the positive value of the *Akira* anime mostly in terms of negatives: it represents a way of escaping from a dominant narrative, a productive source of uncertainty or creativity, a consciousness of the difficulty of representation itself, and perhaps the kernel of a new (as yet undefined) mode of representation that would convey in a roundabout way what straightforward representations (transparent language or realism) cannot.

All this remains rather general. More recent anime criticism, specifically the work of Thomas Lamarre, has delved more deeply into these issues of depth and flattening to conduct a much more elaborate reading of anime's layered sense of space. We will investigate Lamarre's work in chapter 6, and have a chance to revisit these issues of political and visual perspective in a more rigorous way. In the meantime, we will see how some of the anime that followed *Akira* became more politically sophisticated and concrete, extending *Akira's* general skepticism about politics and representation into more focused critiques of specific political situations and their media representation. We can see this development in the work of Oshii Mamoru, whose anime films are the subject of chapters 2 and 3.

Oshii is a member of Ōtomo's generation, and his early anime are arguably informed by the general concerns of the student movement; but Oshii's political critiques are much more specific and clearly articulated than we see in *Akira*. At the same time, Oshii narrows the focus in other ways, moving from *Akira's* broad interest in the place of individuals in society toward a more concrete interest in the fate of physical bodies and embodied subjects in postmodern space. To examine this, the next two chapters move from Jameson, Lyotard, and Murakami's broad theories of art and society to phenomenological film theory and theories of the post-human body, both of which focus on the ways that film and media define individual embodied subjects. For example, Oshii's *Patlabor 2* is a film about giant anthropomorphic robots and the human pilots that control them from within. Its universe shrinks in comparison with *Akira*'s: if the latter's action spans a city, a planet, a new universe, much of the drama of *Patlabor 2* takes place inside a single cockpit.

2
The Mecha's Blind Spot
Cinematic and Electronic in *Patlabor 2*

In the opening sequence of Oshii Mamoru's animated film *Patlabor*, a small army of men and machines hunts down an elusive quarry, but what they finally capture is an absence that lies at the heart of the film's fears. The hunters are a mixed group of soldiers, tanks, and the "labors" of the film's title—giant, often human-shaped robots with living pilots. Their target is a rogue labor, but when they finally capture it and open its hatch to apprehend the pilot, they find only an empty cockpit. The machine is unmanned.

The scene encapsulates the central threat in the film, that these robotic tools might go berserk, rising up without pilots and rampaging en masse. But the even more frightening threat implied in *Patlabor* and its sequel *Patlabor 2* (*Kidō keisatsu patoreibaa The Movie*, 1989 and *Kidō keisatsu patoreibaa 2 The Movie*, 1993) is that the labors are images of us, human–machine hybrids that have lost all humanity, increasingly technologized bodies that turn out to be empty shells.

These giant mechanical puppets carrying tiny human souls are an evocative metaphor for the ways that technology magnifies the body's reach and power, but also changes what the body is. Susan Napier writes that they are "simultaneously appealing and threatening, offering power and excitement at the expense of humanity."[1] Her discussion focuses on the mecha's outward body, but one of the most prominent figures for this trade-off in *Patlabor 2* is the trope of vision and mediated vision. The labor pilots and virtually everyone else view the world magnified and filtered by sensors, displayed on screens, enhanced and distorted by electronics. The motif of an enhanced vision that has its own blind spots is made to reflect the trade-offs between technological amplification of bodily experience and an alienation from our original bodies, threatening dehumanization.

Oshii's film connects this motif of technologized vision with another kind of mediation closer to our own everyday lives—the idea that the mass media we consume daily is the most thorough and pervasive electronic filter of all. This chapter reads *Patlabor 2* as an examination of a contemporary society in which media has replaced firsthand experience, and as a critique of the resulting political situation, in which the disconnect between reality and representation undermines any sense of political agency or responsibility. This immediately raises the question of whether Oshii's anime, itself an example of popular media, can effectively critique its own milieu. I will argue that Oshii stages this critique by moving the film back and forth between two different visual modes: a digital or electronic world (associated with the look of animation and computer animation) in which representation usurps reality, and an analog or "cinematic" world (associated with the look of live-action film) that holds out the hope of a less mediated engagement with the world. To distinguish between these two modes, we turn from the broad theories of postmodernism in the last chapter to Vivian Sobchack's more detailed and more concrete phenomenology of electronic and cinematic experience, to see how it applies to the trope of vision in Oshii's film.

Oshii Mamoru and the *Patlabor* Franchise

Oshii's *Patlabor* films are examples of the "mecha" or "mobile suit" genre of anime. These towering humanoid robots piloted by human operators have occupied a place in anime for decades, from *Mazinger Z (Majingaa Z)* in the 1970s and later staples like *Gundam (Gandamu,* 1979–) and *Macross (Makurosu,* 1982–) to *Neon Genesis Evangelion (Shinseiki evangerion,* 1995–).[2] Oshii's two *Patlabor* films are part of a larger *Patlabor* franchise that includes a television series, direct-to-video (OVA) releases, manga, and novels. *Patlabor* was conceived as a franchise that would originate and develop simultaneously in different media. The group called Headgear that came together in the late 1980s to create *Patlabor* included creators with a range of different backgrounds: manga artist Masami

Yūki, mecha designer Izubuchi Yutaka, character designer Takada Akemi, and scriptwriter Itō Kazunori. Oshii was the final addition, though he was in some ways an unlikely choice at the time, with his reputation as an experimental filmmaker who liked to upend the conventions of genres and franchises he worked on. Born in 1951, Oshii graduated from university in 1976 and almost immediately began work in television animation. In the 1980s he directed several seasons of the *Urusei Yatsura* TV series, based on a colossally popular manga by Takahashi Rumiko, and two *Urusei Yatsura* films, including a brilliantly creative metafictional entry, *Beautiful Dreamer (Urusei yatsura 2: Byūtifuru doriimaa*, 1984), in which all the characters discover they are being dreamed by another. Following these successes, Oshii quit his studio job in 1984 and began to produce more experimental work as an independent director—including the anime *Angel's Egg (Tenshi no tamago,* 1985) and the live-action film *The Red Spectacles (Akai megane,* 1987), both of which featured arresting visuals and surreal plots that aggressively undermined viewers' expectations.[3]

Oshii reports a sense of resignation, even despair, at having to return to serial popular anime after facing a backlash for this experimental work, and Headgear's existing members are said to have worried that Oshii's style might be too adventurous. But his work on *Patlabor* proved to be a turning point for Oshii and the medium: in this period he directed a six-episode *Patlabor* series for direct-to-video release in 1988 *(Patlabor: Early Days)* and expanded on the themes of the series in his two *Patlabor* films, the first in 1989 and the second in 1993. In between these projects, Oshii wrote scripts for some of the later television and OVA episodes. As Oshii tells it, he used the success of each installment in the franchise to gain more control over the next piece and push it into more daring territory. Without ever losing his audience, he shifted attention from cute young characters, comic stories, and action sequences to slower, more mature, and more political plots, culminating in *Patlabor 2*.[4]

In fact, the *Patlabor* films arguably set the tone for all of Oshii's subsequent anime. *Patlabor* represented the beginning of his long-running association with Production I.G, the anime studio that would become closely associated with the look, feel, and visual polish of Oshii's work.[5] With Production I.G and several members of the *Patlabor* production team (including scriptwriter Itō and composer Kawai Kenji), Oshii would borrow and extend the look and themes of *Patlabor 2* in his next film, *Ghost in the Shell* (1995)—a popular and critical phenomenon that brought Oshii to the attention of international fans and critics. So while *Patlabor 2* does build on the characters and situations that had come before, it also breaks new ground in terms of its look, content, and tone. One need not have seen the earlier work to understand this film, and despite the "2" in its title, it is an excellent place to start looking at Oshii's work.

In the near-future world of the series, the labors have been developed as heavy military and construction equipment, and the police force, too, has formed a "special vehicles division"—the "patrol labors" of the title. In the simplest version of the mecha formula, these human-shaped robots with human operators inside them represent a transparent fantasy of bodily augmentation, in which the machines' youthful pilots magnify the power of their own small bodies in order to save the world (Figure 14). The politics are similarly straightforward: the pilots' youth represents a purity and clarity of purpose as they battle the evil villains. But the *Patlabor* anime directed by Oshii transform this formula into one that is more ambivalent about the machines and their politics.

FIGURE 14. The bodies of the labors mirror and magnify the human body, in a fantasy of transparent empowerment. All *Patlabor 2* stills are from the Maiden Japan Blu-ray disc (2015).

Oshii is a political director. He participated in the student wing of the protest movement described in chapter 1, starting in high school. He was seventeen in early 1969, when street demonstrators were clashing with riot police and protesting students closed Tokyo University, and Oshii has suggested that the politics of his films are influenced by the political culture of his youth. It would be oversimplifying to identify the politics of *Patlabor 2* entirely with the causes of the student movement, three decades earlier, but the two definitely share a consciousness of Japan's complex place in global politics, a desire to confront authority (including U.S. authority), and an urge to challenge the political status quo. At the same time, Oshii and his films have an overwhelming fascination with military technology and culture that can seem to clash with this antiauthoritarianism—though it may help to remember that radical left-wing groups in 1960s Japan certainly had their nationalistic and militaristic sides.[6]

We can see these ambivalences in both of Oshii's *Patlabor* films: the heroes are police, but they are members of the labor division's "Section 2," stationed on the outskirts of Tokyo and marginalized within the larger police force. Much of the film consists of political jockeying rather than action sequences, and when the characters finally do suit up, it is not always clear which faction they stand with or whom they are fighting (as suggested by the rogue labor with its empty cockpit). Furthermore, donning these powerful mobile suits is not the euphoric experience of empowerment we see in some other robot anime. There is a clear fascination with the details of how the labors function, but in *Patlabor 2* there is also a feeling of claustrophobia or confinement inside their dark, isolated cockpits: even with the labors' advanced sensors, the pilots and the anime's viewers never quite connect with what is going on outside.

Screening Reality: Mediation and Politics in *Patlabor 2*

Consider the first scene of *Patlabor 2*, which opens with a United Nations military mission somewhere in Southeast Asia. A group of experimental Japanese military labors is on U.N. maneuvers under the command of Japan's top labor engineer and tactician,

Tsuge Yukihito. When Tsuge's group is cut off and threatened by advancing enemy troops, headquarters denies him permission to fire, telling him to wait for reinforcements. But the enemy attacks first, and Tsuge must watch helplessly as his force is wiped out. It is this disaster that twists Tsuge into the noble villain of the story, but his horrified frustration has two different sources, one related to politics and the other related to representation. First there is the command from headquarters that paralyzes Tsuge's forces, denying them the opportunity to fight back and defend themselves—a reference to contemporary debates about whether Japanese troops should be deployed abroad and in what capacity, if any, they should be permitted to fight. But there is also the problem of the gap Tsuge experiences between the violence on the battlefield and the sensory deprivation inside his labor as he watches the fight unfold on his monitors. Like *Akira*, *Patlabor 2* deals with these two parallel ideas: the confusing politics of postwar Japan and also the more abstract difficulties of representation in our technologized and mediated postmodern world.

First let's examine how the opening scene unfolds as a critique of mediated experience. Tsuge watches the enemy troops advance toward his position on a screen whose image fills the movie screen; we never see the enemy troops directly, but the animation shows an intricate computer display that zooms in on their heat signatures (Figure 15). Just as we cannot see the enemy in the flesh, Tsuge's face is concealed from us by his helmet visor, two small mechanical lenses taking the place of his eyes. But when a wave of incoming enemy rockets appears on his monitor, Tsuge's fear is signaled by the dilation of these lenses, a mechanical analog of wide-eyed shock.

As the rockets strike Tsuge's group, the bipedal labors double over and fall like human figures, more human in fact than the immobile pilots inside their cockpits. Throughout the scene, the film cuts back and forth between the carnage outside and the dark interior of the labor, with its cool green displays that are all that Tsuge can see. Over the radio he hears the anguished cries of his men screaming "Commander!" but the sounds are distant and distorted, filtered through layers of static. When one panicked pilot realizes his labor is about to be destroyed and screams "I can't eject!" he

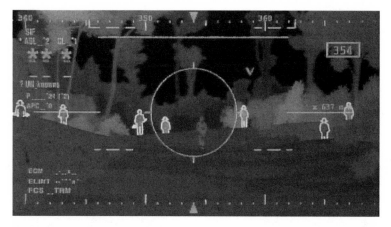

FIGURE 15. Inside his labor, Tsuge can see the enemy only as an abstracted image on his display. At the same time, note the detailed realism with which the screen itself is portrayed.

voices the fears of the whole scene and eventually the whole film: that the humans will be trapped permanently inside their mechanical shells. (The opening scene of the first *Patlabor* film might indicate the next step, when the human pilot has become totally absorbed, leaving only an empty chair. At that point the human–machine hybrid we have become retains no inward or outward human traces at all.) This opening scene of *Patlabor 2* is followed by a credits sequence that shows a labor pilot in a virtual reality training exercise, and the same elements are featured: the goggled pilot, the labor's cameras, and the cockpit displays that show a flickering virtual world (Figure 16). From this opening, the film goes on to become entirely dominated by these kinds of images.

Media and film theorist Vivian Sobchack describes the fear of insulation and absorption as a defining quality of electronic media. The theories of the postmodern discussed in chapter 1 took up the increasing pace of images in art and media (an acceleration driven by technology) and linked those to the increasing difficulty of expression and self-expression. The result was a destabilization of the individual subject—be it a historical subject, a political subject, or a psychological one. Sobchack's media theory builds on this general foundation but focuses much more specifically and concretely on the body and vision—the twin preoccupations of *Patlabor 2*.

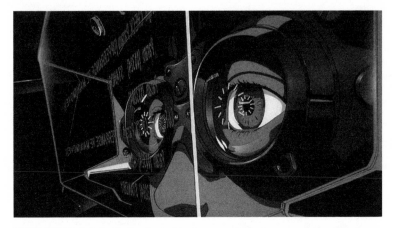

FIGURE 16. *Patlabor 2* is dominated by images of windows, goggles, glasses, and other screens that interpose themselves between us and our world.

Sobchack's theory is phenomenological: it dwells on the perception and experience of embodied subjects and on how language works to mediate or communicate between them. In Sobchack's phenomenological scheme, film is both a kind of language that communicates between subjects and a simulation that allows one subject to share the experiences of another—a kind of virtual reality. Drawing on Don Ihde's phenomenology of technology, Sobchack writes that wide-eyed fantasies about virtual reality frequently center on the desire for technological augmentations that are simultaneously powerful and transparent, whether these are science fiction's dreams of perfect computer-generated experiences indistinguishable from reality or just utopian ideas about an Internet that will allow us to read, see, and hear everything. In other words, we want to increase the power of our perceptions by getting free from the constraints of the physical body, but we don't want the technology to intrude in a way that changes the nature or quality of those perceptions: we want it to feel like we're really there, like we're really everywhere. Sobchack focuses on the naiveness of this dual dream: film, electronic media, and all forms of mediation change the nature of experience, and the more we extend our sensoria, the more radical and destabilizing these changes are likely to become.[7]

Implausibly shaped just like human beings, *Patlabor's* robots are a figure for this impossible desire to extend the body yet keep it as it is. But in the disconnection of the pilots, we see exactly the problems that Sobchack predicts: she could easily be talking about *Patlabor 2* when she writes that the prevalence of computer readouts and computer graphics in late twentieth-century American science-fiction films expresses the threat of dehumanization. Citing Fredric Jameson's idea of a flattened postmodern space linked to a flattened affect or a loss of psychological depth, which we discussed in chapter 1, Sobchack writes: "In these films . . . the 'deep' and indexical space of cinematographic representation is deflated—punctured and punctuated by the superficial and iconic space of electronic simulation. . . . Indeed, only superficial beings without 'psyche,' without depth, can successfully maneuver in a space that exists solely to display."[8]

Asked why Tsuge does not ignore his orders and fire on the enemy, Oshii describes the same waning of the subject, suggesting that it is partly because the commander cannot feel any sense of danger from what transpires on his screens.[9] Here we have returned to the dynamic of depth and flatness that structured our reading of *Akira*. But while chapter 1 identified manga as the medium that can portray geometric depth and political or geographic perspective, Sobchack identifies these powers with a "cinematographic representation" that she associates with earlier styles of live-action film, in contrast to the flatter "electronic" regime of post-1970s science-fiction films that rely increasingly on computer graphics.

We will return to the comparison between the electronic and the cinematic later in the chapter, and try to place *Patlabor 2* more carefully on this scale. For now, let's observe that there is another, diametric way of reading this opening scene: at the same time that it portrays the difficulty of connecting with the world outside the labor, it also contains some very specific connections to the broader world of geopolitics outside the film. Many of these are references to the 1991 Gulf War, which brought to a head some of the tensions in Japan's postwar foreign policy.

As introduced in chapter 1, for decades after World War II, the Japanese constitution was interpreted as limiting the role of the

Japanese armed forces to self-defense, and specifically as prohibiting any deployment of Japanese troops outside the country. At the same time, Japan supported U.S. military policy diplomatically, logistically, and financially, by helping the United States to maintain its own bases in Japan. In the 1991 Gulf War, a coalition of powers headed by the United States invaded Iraq in response to Iraq's occupation of Kuwait and its oil fields the year before. This was the largest U.S. combat operation since the Vietnam War and the protest era of the 1960s. In the interim Japan had become the second-largest economy in the world—an economy heavily dependent on foreign oil. When Japan supplied money for the war but no troops, this compromise renewed domestic and international debates about Japanese foreign policy, with some arguing that Japan should reinterpret or revise its constitution to allow it to send Self Defense Force troops abroad, and others staunchly opposed.

In the wake of the Gulf War, restrictions were relaxed to allow the Japanese forces to participate in certain noncombat operations abroad, including support operations like mine clearing in the Persian Gulf and United Nations peacekeeping operations, starting with a 1992 operation in Cambodia. But Japanese soldiers still faced restrictions on their ability to engage in combat—a situation that arguably just extended the divisions or contradictions of past policies. This is the situation referenced in the opening scene of *Patlabor 2.*

Although I have described the focus on politics and the focus on representation as two distinct ways of reading the opening scene, Oshii loses no time in connecting them. In this, *Patlabor 2* is different from *Akira*, which moves restlessly back and forth between these two worlds without really synthesizing them, like its biker rebel heroes who seem torn between style and substance. Oshii describes being inspired by *Akira*'s rebellious impulses when he was working on the first *Patlabor* film, but also wanting to take a more disciplined approach:

> I saw *Akira* before I started on the storyboards for this movie, and it got me thinking in a lot of ways. It's saying, in a hysterical way, "Tokyo be damned! Burn it all, men and mechas alike!" . . . *Akira*

represents a type of death wish, a primal scream. . . . But I was thinking, there must be some other way of depicting that.[10]

In contrast with *Akira, Patlabor 2* has a plot and a wealth of didactic dialogue that articulate clear arguments about the relationship between politics and representation. One of those arguments is that the labor pilots watching the battles on their monitors resemble the Japanese nation, insulated from the realities of the wars it wages by proxy. Tsuge's accomplice Arakawa describes this national insulation using the metaphor of the display screen: "We reap the fruits of these conflicts, prosecuting the wars that rage on the other side of our monitors, forgetting that we are standing just behind the front lines. Or pretending to forget. Someday we'll be punished for our lies."

By relating the sensory deprivation inside the labors to the idea of a war that does not register on the screens of everyday life, Oshii takes aim at the way electronic sensation and communication distance us from reality, whether it is the labor's sensors or the mass media. When asked what god will dole out the punishment he refers to, Arakawa answers: "In this city everyone is like a god. Omniscient, all seeing, but unable to touch any of it from where they sit—gods who never lift a finger."

Tsuge upsets this complacency by staging a series of attacks that heighten political tensions—first a missile attack on the Yokohama Bay Bridge, then an invasion of Japanese airspace by a phantom plane. By playing the police, the military, and the United States against one another, Tsuge's plan provokes a declaration of martial law that leads to the presence of troops in the streets of Tokyo and sets the stage for a new war on Tsuge's own terms.

Tsuge's Strategy: A Shooting War or a Shooting Script?

What are the terms of Tsuge's war? Tsuge himself remains a phantom throughout most of the film, rarely appearing or speaking. In his place we have Arakawa, who initially contacts the heroes claiming he is hunting Tsuge but who eventually turns out to be Tsuge's accomplice. Arakawa describes Tsuge's plan as an effort to strip away Japan's insulation and bring the Japanese closer to the conflicts that they are accustomed to seeing only on television, if at all. Tsuge, Arakawa says, will start "a genuine war that will make up for this passive, empty peace."

A number of critics have taken Arakawa's words as the heart of the film, and argued implicitly or explicitly that the reality of physical conflict ultimately trumps the ambiguities of representation. In these readings Tsuge's plot is a decisive, if violent, act that pierces the veil of illusion and mediation, in Ihiroi Takashi's words an act that finally "closes the distance" between the formerly insulated self and the world. Michael Fisch's early, impressive analysis similarly treats Tsuge's operation as a real war (and more specifically a replay of World War II) that shatters Japan's political illusions, awakening the country to the real possibility of its own destruction and pushing the film's characters and viewers toward a more aggressive and interventionist foreign policy, justified as self-protection.[11]

Noda Makoto gives more attention to the radically mediated and virtual quality of experience and perception in *Patlabor 2*, seeing those features in all of Oshii's early films. He acknowledges "Tokyo's condition of isolation, as a city unable to escape the chains of media and technology." But Noda, too, sides with the Arakawa character in seeing Tsuge as a figure whose commitment is able to punch through this fiction in the end. In fact, Noda views *Patlabor 2* as a turning point in Oshii's work because, he says, its characters are actually able to emerge from the shells of their individual virtual realities and join with others in a real world.[12]

Oshii's own statements suggest that representation and politics are not easily separated. Oshii tells Brian Ruh that "Tsuge is the other self of Mamoru Oshii. Tsuge's political thoughts and opinions, if there are any, are all mine."[13] But this formulation also points out the layers of mediation at work: Oshii's thoughts are mediated through his other self, Tsuge, and as for Tsuge's thoughts, we cannot even say for certain "if there are any," presumably because we hear about his motives only through Arakawa. Regarding his own politics, Oshii emphasizes his involvement with the radical student movement, but describes it as equal parts political engagement and escapist fantasy. Comparing his student political activities with his interest in science fiction, he writes: "At the time, I didn't see any contradiction between this embrace of radical politics and this extreme escapism. They were just two sides of the same coin, two different ways of leaving behind the insufferable reality and suffocating conventions around me."[14]

In another discussion of the connection between the politics of his films and the politics of his youth, Oshii says he was attracted to *Patlabor* for the chance to make a movie about the police. Then he continues:

> Ultimately the most natural thing for me was for it to develop into something like a story about how to take revenge in that era. For a long time I've wanted to see what it would be like to destroy the Section 2 station house. I wanted to portray the hangar and the labors inside it being demolished, or rather dismantled, to destroy them as carefully and meticulously as possible. . . . In other words, I wanted to take a machine gun to every memorable place in that building. I think all directors have that in them—that kind of mean streak.[15]

Oshii's vengeance here seems to have one foot in the world of politics and one in the world of media—part 1960s-inspired revenge fantasy against the police and partly a revenge against the franchise itself. The final comment brings us full circle by again suggesting a parallel between Oshii and Tsuge, this time as the directors or producers of a violence staged through media and against media.

If we look closely at Tsuge's plot, it is arguably not the shooting war that Arakawa posits, but a kind of scripted action, an illusory war conducted in and on the media that make discourses of war and peace possible. Tsuge's plot proceeds as follows: after a few carefully staged violent incidents have raised tensions and provoked a domestic and then an international power struggle, martial law is declared, Japanese Self Defense Force troops take up stations around Tokyo, and the city waits tensely for an all-out conflict. At this point Tsuge's forces conduct a series of surgical strikes on the city's bridges and communication facilities. While the hardwired communication grid goes down, powerful jamming disrupts radio communication, figured in the film by an evocative soundtrack that features static interspersed with garbled bits of speech. At the same time, Tsuge launches a series of doomsday weapons, giant unmanned blimps that function by remote control. When the authorities try to disable one of these airships, it crashes and releases a cloud of yellow gas that envelops several blocks of downtown. After an initial panic, the gas is revealed to be harmless, but the authorities learn that the blimps are capable of releasing real toxins as well, and they realize Tsuge now holds the city hostage.

Each of these strategies—the feints, the jamming, the gas scare—is designed not to wreak physical destruction but to create the appearance and the perception of war. Tsuge's operations are rhetorical, both in the sense of being symbolic acts of destruction and in the sense of acting mainly through language and image. So even before the blimps rise into the air above Tokyo, the image of war has been created. In fact, the declaration of martial law midway through the film is Tsuge's real victory, for he has achieved a state of war without an actual war. The long, elegiac montage of troops taking up their positions is the visual and emotional center of the film, and the role of media representation is highlighted by the way the troops are shown reflected in various other media. We witness the maneuvers on televisions in a store window; we hear reports on a series of radios; we see soldiers and military vehicles in a bystander's snapshot or elaborately reflected in the glass windows of skyscrapers. The viewer knows that whatever comes later, Tsuge has already won the war of words and images (Figure 17).

Gotō, the labor-squad police captain who is trying to foil Tsuge, says that Tsuge's plot is about "constructing a state of war. Or rather, producing a 'wartime' on the stage of Tokyo." Answering Arakawa's theory about a real war to expose the fake peace, Gotō counters: "Arakawa-san, what you said about fraudulent peace and real war was interesting. But if you're right that this city's peace is a lie, the war Tsuge has created is a lie as well."

Watching *Patlabor 2* today, we may be struck by the way that narratives created in the media can take on the force of reality, even as they remain too insubstantial to analyze in a concrete way. Two years after *Patlabor 2* was released, Japanese domestic

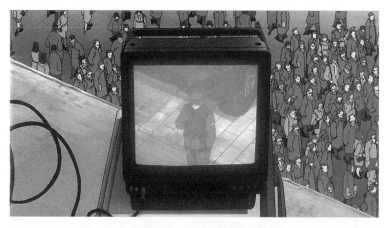

FIGURE 17. The Self Defense Force troops who occupy Tokyo are shown reflected in various media, here in a television crew's monitor and a wall of windows. The image on the monitor flickers in a way that recreates the effect of a camera filming a video screen.

terrorists associated with the Aum Shinrikyō cult released nerve gas in the Tokyo subway system, and then a few years later the 9/11 terrorist attacks irrevocably changed the political and media landscape in the United States and beyond.[16] In one sense the fictions of Oshii's film seemed to have come true; but in another sense the line between truth and fiction blurred further, as subsequent terrorist threats portrayed in the mass media gained importance and power precisely in proportion to their uncertainty. Today in the age of the "Global War on Terror," the threat predicted by *Patlabor 2* may be the way that media and the state can portray a perpetual state of danger that justifies violence abroad and curtailed freedoms at home, even as the threat and the response remain too ambiguous or too secret to be examined openly—what Mark Anderson calls the "blurring line between terror and warfare and thus between war and peace." Anderson's more recent reading of the film attempts to describe a more complex relationship between warfare and media, at some points questioning the division between the two and at others suggesting the first steps toward a synthetic treatment of both.[17]

Besides its interest in Japanese politics, one thing that Anderson's approach shares with most of the readings discussed above is a focus on the anime's plot and dialogue, which have a complexity and clarity that have attracted the bulk of attention in English-language criticism of the film. Here I would like to undertake a more visual reading of *Patlabor 2*, with the goal of asking what kind of political critique an anime might be able to make—using its own unique visual qualities—that other media cannot.

This presents an interesting problem. If Tsuge's attack on the virtual reality of the mass media is itself a virtual attack, then it immediately raises the question of how effectively representation can critique representation, or media critique itself. This is slippery, but it is among the most interesting and important questions that the film raises, because it leads directly to the question of whether and how anime (or any product of the mass media) can ever stage a media or political critique. At its heart, this is a question of how we experience this medium—the phenomenology of watching anime—as well as the question of how to read it.

Here Ueno Toshiya's interpretation of the film is helpful, not only because it focuses on the anime's visuals but because it connects the broad issues of representation and mass media back to the individual's body and vision. Ueno's canonical book on mecha anime, *Kurenai no metaru sūtsu* (Metalsuits the red, 1998), contains a memorable formulation comparing the mecha (also frequently referred to as "mobile suits") with the larger situation of society: both the city and its residents, he says, are suited up. As labor-assisted construction projects refit Tokyo, weaving it a new, networked skin, "this invisible (mienai) city is becoming a suit or a machine itself. The city is a suit that its residents get into; a 'media suit' that makes communication (im)possible. This is the expansion of the invisible domain."[18]

"Invisibility" is Ueno's term for the indeterminability of postmodern media society and its multiple images, a confusion that Tsuge exacerbates and exploits. One kind of invisibility results from the profusion of images in electronics and the media, to the point where the distinction between reality and simulation becomes meaningless. (And here Ueno lists many of the same examples of screens and images discussed above and below.) For Ueno, the political situation in the film is analogous, with the reversible discourses of vision and power (as well as the shifting circumstances of politics) producing a battlefield on which the enemy is always invisible or unknown, and the good guys are indistinguishable from the villains. Hence the film's confusing plot, in which the identities of Tsuge's plotters are never really certain, even at the end.[19]

Ueno describes Oshii's world as a radical version of the postmodernism introduced in chapter 1. Rather than juxtapose the media with a reality it distorts, Ueno largely abandons the distinction between the two. Reality in Oshii's work emerges "from within the folds of multi-dimensional fiction . . . and each repetition is the next successive materiality or reality."[20] In this situation the 1960s dream of popular political intervention is radically curtailed: the anime can urge us to reflect on the ways that technology changes our perceptions and our society, but we can no longer escape those changes. For Ueno, Tsuge or Gotō can battle to bring these changes to our attention, but both are fighting a losing "rear-guard action," because they themselves are caught up in the networks of data and power that are bringing these changes about.[21]

Ueno's reading suggests that anime as a medium can struggle to bring those changes to the viewer's attention, but only with some difficulty, because anime like Oshii's are a part of the mass media they want to critique. This returns us to postmodernism's idea that we can no longer escape the discourses of mass media and politics long enough to stage a critique of them from the outside. Those discourses supply the only language we have (that is the sense in which they remain "invisible"), so that any critique must be bootstrapped precariously from inside the discourses themselves—Ueno's "rear-guard action."

Ueno's idea that a material reality can emerge only "from within the folds" of a repeated fiction is a powerful one for later anime we'll examine, where successive layers of fiction seem to be nested even more deeply than in *Patlabor 2*. But I would argue that *Patlabor 2* itself is not as trapped within media as Ueno's interpretation suggests—that it actually oscillates between portraying a "real" world and a mediated one in a way that tries to give us some purchase and perspective on the differences between the two. The film maintains a strong dichotomy between insides and outsides, for example, the claustrophobia of the labor clearly juxtaposed with less mediated kinds of views. In these ways I think *Patlabor 2* holds out hope for a more authentic or less mediated kind of experience, even if the virtual is never entirely escaped.

One of the most interesting things about *Patlabor 2* is the range of visual strategies it evolves for contrasting the mediated and the real, and the way it moves back and forth between these two regimes in order to ground its critique of mediated experience. The second half of this chapter tries to characterize and theorize that visual oscillation. But before we dive into this, let's quickly examine the remainder of the plot and see how it holds out a hope (perhaps a tentative hope) that we can penetrate Ueno's invisibility and witness or achieve something genuine.

Finally, an Unmediated View?

The anime's conclusion is the part that seems to suggest most decisively that we can break through the curtain of mediation; yet, even this final shift contains some ambiguity. As the film moves toward its climax, Tsuge attacks mediated communication itself, with radio jamming and a series of helicopter attacks that destroy the city's bridges, communication lines, antennae arrays, and command centers, but leave everything else untouched. Amid all the explosions, the only casualty we are shown is communication: we see few or no humans injured, but there are pointed scenes of TVs and radios helplessly bleeding static into the air. As Gotō sur-

mises when the jamming begins, "Cutting off information, causing confusion—that's not the means, but the end." Tsuge puts all
of Tokyo in the situation he experienced inside his labor, blind and
cut off, and so urges citizens to shed their electronic shells, just
as he must emerge from his ruined labor after the battle in the
opening scene.

Tsuge is opposed by Gotō and other members of Section 2, including Gotō's beautiful and conflicted co-captain, Nagumo, who
is also Tsuge's ex-lover. Gotō and Nagumo eventually foil Tsuge's
plans, but in order to triumph, the good guys must heed Tsuge's
warning, opening their eyes and reclaiming their own senses from
the machines; in the end, they too must emerge from their suits in
order to defeat him.

In the climactic battle, Gotō and Nagumo have tracked Tsuge to
a spot of reclaimed land in Tokyo harbor, where he is controlling
the blimps and the jamming. The only path of attack is through a
narrow underwater tunnel guarded by Tsuge's own labors, a pair
of advanced "Ixtl" models. The Ixtls represent the apex of technological dehumanization: crab-like, clickingly mechanical, and
unmanned, they are controlled by remote operators via radio and
cable. The heroes eventually defeat the Ixtls by cutting their control cables and then jamming the radio signals from their human
operators, in effect turning Tsuge's jamming strategy against his
own machines. But in order for the police forces to see through
their own electronic countermeasures, they must abandon their
labors' special sensors and use their naked eyes. When Nagumo
activates the jamming, her labor's electronic displays dissolve into
static, while her face, hidden until now, is revealed. She turns off
her now useless data-visor, and her pilot's chair rises on elevators
out of the labor's stomach cockpit so that she can see outside. As
her labor joins the battle, her face is framed in the window of the
machine's giant head, stressing the human heart or soul at the
core of the good labors, in contrast to Tsuge's soulless Ixtls and
unmanned airships.

The Ixtls are only narrowly defeated, and when Nagumo's victo-
rious labor rises to the surface of the reclaimed island on a freight
elevator, it is a ruined hulk, hunched and still. Nagumo ejects, the
labor's abdomen blowing off explosively as she jumps out from

between its legs—as if the labor were giving birth to the human, or the human were being reborn. Her arrival startles a massive flock of seagulls into flight, one scene among several in which animals (particularly dogs and birds) are shown to possess the acute, unmediated senses that humans lack. Having shed her steel skin, Nagumo now enters that unmediated world. She dramatically doffs her visor and helmet and goes to meet Tsuge face to face.

For most of the film, Tsuge has remained unseen. Like the incidents he stages, he is a ghost onto which other characters map their fears and expectations. Now Nagumo finds him staring at the city across the bay through binoculars. For the first time, he speaks at length: "From here the city looks just like a mirage, doesn't it? . . . Three years ago when I returned to Tokyo, I lived in the midst of that illusion. And I tried to tell people it was an illusion. In the end, no one noticed until the first shot rang out. Even now, maybe they haven't." Then we see the city, shimmering in the distance. To this point the film has taken every opportunity to look through instruments like the binoculars, forcing mediated views on the spectator. But now for the first time it refuses us this augmented vision: we see the city as Nagumo sees it, with her naked eyes. She presses her physical reality upon Tsuge, saying, "Even if it is an illusion, there are people there living it as real life. Or are those people ghosts to you too? . . . The woman standing in front of you now is no phantom."

As Nagumo places the cuffs on her former lover, a lingering close-up shows them clasping hands in a briefly intimate gesture. And in the final shot, when a policeman asks Tsuge why he allowed himself to be captured alive, Tsuge takes off his glasses (a last layer of mediation) and admits that he wants to stay and "see a little more" of the city's future. All of this suggests to some critics that in the end, the real, physical world of humanity has triumphed over mechanical, mediated existence.[22]

But there are a few things qualifying this optimistic ending. With Tsuge's arrest, the police are able to shut down the jamming and restore regular electronic communication, with all the problems that entails. So while Tsuge's defeat might seem to highlight the importance of unmediated experience, it actually restores the mediation that he had interrupted. Furthermore, parallels between the final scene and the opening scene suggest that the victors may be indistinguishable from the defeated: when Nagumo exits her labor and pulls off her helmet, the motion exactly mirrors Tsuge's movements at the end of the opening scene.[23] And when the junior pilots emerge battle-torn from the tunnel where they fought the Ixtls and see Gotō in the distance, in their excitement they call out to him by screaming "Commander!"—echoing the dying pilot who screams the same word to Tsuge over the radio in the film's opening. All this suggests that there is little difference between the winners and the losers, perhaps even that Gotō and Nagumo might have enough sympathy for Tsuge to take up where he left off. Structurally, the way the end returns us to the beginning suggests that simulation never ends but simply loops in the way Ueno points out, that "simulacra are generated as in a kaleidoscope: the same incident is repeated endlessly."[24]

The Machine's Blind Spot

The love story between Nagumo and Tsuge is one of the narrative devices the anime uses to create an immersive story that will pull us into the fiction and make us momentarily forget the mediation. Like Tsuge, we are asked to feel that the woman standing before us now is no phantom. Some of the concrete political images—like the images of the Southeast Asian peacekeeping operation that recall the real Cambodian PKO operation undertaken just a few months before the film's release—accomplish the same kind of grounding by making a firm connection with the real world outside the film. Both of these realities contrast with the anime's visual foregrounding of media, which constantly reminds us we are watching a piece of media ourselves. This tension between a realistic plot and a patently mediated view is part of what creates the movement between immersion and distance that is at the heart of all the anime and all the readings in this book.

But the tension that is most interesting is not the contrast between *narrative* immersion and *visual* mediation, but rather the anime's purely visual oscillation between realistic visual images and more obviously mediated ones, an oscillation that also moves the viewer rapidly back and forth between immersion and distance. Ultimately it is this visual alternation that enables the anime to portray both a mediated and an unmediated view: the contrast between them grounds the anime's critique of media representation, while at the same time their rapid and radical mixing expresses the important idea that this critique is not an easy one. As Ueno suggests, we can never completely discard the suit and its mediated view, any more than we can escape language itself.

To characterize the way the anime works visually, I would like to replace Ueno's "invisibility" (and its suggestion of the epistemologically undecidable or unknowable), with a different metaphor—an obstacle to vision that can be sensed but never seen directly. It is not a blindfold that Tsuge can rip off us, but more like a blind spot: a hidden point in a view that is otherwise unimpaired. It may be large or small. It may be consciously sensed (like the area outside the range of a vehicle's rear-view mirror) or unconsciously missed (the rodless, coneless region on our retina that invisibly swallows up details). It moves. Sometimes it can be overcome by looking in a different direction, and sometimes not. Like the space "on the other side of our monitors," it is a shifting area that is always in our view, but that we do not notice or cannot see.

To understand how Tsuge and Oshii direct our attention to our own blind spots, consider a series of scenes in which Japanese defense radar picks up an unidentified warplane moving on an attack course toward Tokyo—a plane that is actually a computer ghost the plotters have created by hacking the defense net and exploiting its own blind spots. The action alternates between the air over Tokyo, where the pilots of the interceptor fighters search fruitlessly for the intruder, and various defense control centers, where operators in darkened rooms plot the course of the phantom plane on a series of computerized displays. Screens dominate the command centers: technicians stand in front of monitors or are silhouetted against them, their faces lit from below by readouts, their eyeglasses flashing in the screens' reflected light. The audio in the scene also portrays the humans as buried under layers of technology, emphasized by the static-laden radio dialogue between the pilots and their controllers. As in the Southeast Asian scene, the communications become more frantic as the situation escalates, yet the static renders it remote.

In one of the interceptor planes, we watch the outside world from the pilot's point of view, through the heads-up display (HUD) in the plane's cockpit. The HUD is a device in use on real planes, a clear pane of glass in front of the pilot on which luminous instrumental readings are projected. It lets the pilot see the sky in front of the plane through the glass, but with an overlay of digital information about the plane's course, speed, and weapons. This technology is duplicated in the labors by the graphic overlays that appear in their pilots' helmet visors. It is the literal incarnation of what Sobchack identifies as the sought-after "transparent" technology, one that allows us to see in the same way, only more.

But the idea that the technology does change its users is indicated symbolically by shots of a pilot from a viewpoint outside his plane; we look back through the HUD so that the digital readouts now appear superimposed (in mirror image) on the pilot's face. The same shot is used in the control room sequence, where we gaze down at the operators from a position behind the wall-mounted display screens. The screens appear partly transparent to us, allowing us to see the operators behind the reversed readouts, though now it is they who are overlaid with information. *Patlabor 2* is full of these shots: images of the characters through semi-transparent windows, display screens, and visors that flash with digital information (Figures 16 and 18). These shots force the spectator to look through this technology just as the characters do, and they also symbolize the idea that, however transparent the technology, it nevertheless alters the people who use it.

In Oshii's film, even ordinary car and building windows display complex combinations of transmitted and reflected light that layer images of people and scenery one over the other. This is almost exactly the visual metaphor we explored in the Introduction, in the context of *Read or Die*. There, we encountered Roland Barthes's image of a window that is alternately or simultaneously opaque and transparent, depending on whether we focus on the window or beyond it; we read this as a metaphor for anime and other kinds of literature that combine an immersive experience we can identify with transparently, and a distancing or alienating effect that calls attention to the medium and the act of interpretation. As with *Read or Die*, the oscillation between these two different views might allow *Patlabor 2* to stage a critique of mediation,

FIGURE 18. Frequently in *Patlabor 2* we are positioned behind television and display screens, looking back at the humans watching those screens. Here, the way the display data is overlaid on the human bodies suggests that information technology is not a transparent tool, that it always changes the user in some way. (See also Figure 16.)

a critique of the mass media from a position that is neither wholly inside nor wholly outside it.

Here some might ask skeptically whether a medium like anime can really produce a sense of visual contrast between the real and the mediated, given that everything in the frame is a stylized, two-dimensional representation. There is the paradox that the anime appears most immediate and realistic when it is depicting the mediation of computer screens (since it can mimic these digital displays with a high degree of visual fidelity), while the ostensibly unmediated views of human faces must remain cartoonish or stylized. Is it meaningless or even naive to pose a contrast between arbitrary versus illusionistic simulation in anime?

What is implied in these questions is a comparison of anime with live-action film, which is typically judged more visually realistic than anime, but live-action film is filled with stylizations and abstractions of its own. More broadly, visual realism is not necessarily synonymous with visual immersion or identification. What we need is a more rigorous theorization of the link between identification and vision, and this is precisely what Sobchack provides. Her work offers a framework for exploring mediated experience in contexts (like film) that are already more or less mediated themselves. Earlier we used her observations about technologically augmented experience; we now turn to her more detailed phenomenology of film experience.

Sobchack's is a theory of live-action film, and her examples come from that medium, so by applying her ideas to anime, we can compare the two media. Sobchack divides live-action film into two different historical and phenomenological categories, the cinematic and the electronic. Asking how anime like *Patlabor 2* move between these two categories goes a long way toward helping us identify the specific powers (and blind spots) of anime like Oshii's.

The Phenomenology of Anime's Body: Medium or Mechanism?

Sobchack applies her observations about technologically mediated experience and alienation to the experience of watching film in her essay "The Scene of the Screen: Envisioning Photographic, Cinematic, and Electronic Presence." It argues that while still photography fixes events in a way that prevents us from entering back into them, the advent of motion pictures allowed us to record not just a frozen experience or perception, but the ongoing act and process of looking. Cinema "made visible *for the very first time* not just the objective world, but the very structure and process of subjective, embodied vision."[25] For Sobchack, this gives rise to a sense that cinematic film is a perceiving subject that orders space and time for itself.

But with the advent of electronic technology, from television and videotape to computer graphics and personal electronics, film's ordering of space and time gives way to dispersal and discontinuity, "an alternative and absolute electronic world of immaterialized . . . experience" that "incorporates the spectator/user uniquely in a spatially decentered, weakly temporalized, and quasi-disembodied (or diffusely embodied) state." This is figured in terms of the discontinuous methods of representation, transmission, and experience in electronic media: from the pixels, bits, and packets of digital video and computer graphics to the frantic pace of the images in the dominant television or Internet aesthetic, a style that Sobchack (following Jameson) associates with a sequence of intense, present instants rather than a coherent linear narrative. The result for the spectator is a "dizzying sense of bodily freedom (and freedom from the body)."[26]

So while cinematic film and electronic film are both kinds of virtual sensation, cinematic films reinforce the significance of human bodily experience, while electronic films undermine the sense of the body. And where does anime fit on this spectrum? I have argued that *Patlabor 2* expresses the increasing mediation of electronics, portraying the screens that get between the characters and their experience of the world. But to rephrase a question I have already asked repeatedly above, is the anime itself one more such screen, refracting or distorting the world in a way that cinematic film does not? In other words, do *Patlabor 2* and other anime belong to the realm of the electronic or the cinematic?

In some ways anime seems to be a quintessential example of Sobchack's electronic media: it is more likely to be seen on television, DVD, or as a digital download than in the theater. As for its style, there is a ready stereotype of anime that matches Sobchack's description of rapidly changing, intensely present but disconnected images. As we saw in chapter 1, several critics described *Akira* in exactly this way. Chapter 1 also showed that it is possible to connect Jameson's aesthetic flattening (which Sobchack associates with the flattened screen space of late twentieth-century science-fiction films) to the two-dimensional quality of anime. But Oshii's *Patlabor* films immediately violate some of these stereotypes: their pacing, for example, can be glacial, both the movement of the plot and the physical movements of the figures, which are often depicted in lingering close-ups and static tableaux. Many anime use this kind of limited animation (something we'll examine further in chapter 6); but while limited animation seems to render some anime even flatter, Oshii harnesses it to convey a sense of thoughtfulness and narrative depth.

Ultimately, the advantage of Sobchack's phenomenology is that it allows us to go beyond these general qualitative descriptions of postmodern aesthetics (like Jameson's) and theorize the coherence or incoherence of the visual film experience in a more extensive and rigorous way, using the idea of embodiment. Sobchack's book *The Address of the Eye* develops this theory of the "film's body," drawing on an existential phenomenology associated with Maurice Merleau-Ponty, which grounds the subject in bodily (specifically visual) experience. Sobchack describes how "the act of seeing is entwined intimately with the act of being, how seeing *incarnates* being."[27] And since pre-electronic, cinematic film is not only a *seen object* but a representation of the experience of vision (a *seeing subject* in its own right), it also has a body, which consists partly of the material and technology that make up the film and partly of an imagined body that the spectator assigns it. In the way that cinema is filmed, edited, and composed,

> discontiguous spaces and discontinuous times are gathered together in a coherence ("scenes") whose reflection and signification constitute the significance of what can be called conscious experience. And (as with the spectator) that coherence is accomplished by the lived body. The camera its perceptive organ, the projector its expressive organ, the screen its discrete and material occupation of worldly space, the cinema exists as a visible performance of the perceptive and expressive structure of lived-body experience.[28]

Sobchack argues that cinema is a variant of embodied technology because it portrays an act of vision that the spectator experiences as if from within another body—the body of the film itself. The film's body is not directly visible, but the spectator can posit it or fill it in by comparing the film's vision with his or her own and extrapolating a body that belongs to that filmed vision.[29] For us to imagine the film's body, however, the way in which the film views the world must have a "coherence" that allows us to relate its vision to our own. This is not a matter of realism in a naive sense: a film should not try to mimic a human being's viewpoint literally, since its own body is never identical to a human body in shape or function. But the film's vision must have a unity that allows us to imagine a coherent body for it. In the electronic (as opposed to cinematic) regime, the film's act of seeing loses this coherence as the image becomes subject to all the subdivision and manipulation possible with electronic and digital media. Divided into channels, frames, and pixels, images are rewound and replayed, slowed down and speeded up. Extrapolating from Sobchack, we might say that if this electronic vision does have a body, it is a networked (not even mechanical) body that we can no longer relate to our human one.

In Sobchack's scheme, then, the alienated, technologized body portrayed in the plot of mecha anime might be doubled in our own *experience* of watching these films, an experience that might alienate us from our normal senses. But what of *Patlabor 2* specifically? The question of whether Oshii's film is electronic or cinematic (and our earlier question about whether it can critique the electronic) both boil down to the question of whether the film's body has coherence. This in turn is a question of *how it looks* (how it watches and how it appears), and how close that is to the way *we* look.

Asking these phenomenological questions of *Patlabor 2* yields an interesting result: Oshii's film does try to portray the dismemberment of the electronic body (the labors, the media, Tsuge's war). But to do that it must also try to shed its own electronic suit or skin. To this end, the film imitates or simulates *both* the unified cinematic body *and* its electronic dissolution, resulting in the film's characteristic oscillation between cinematic and electronic vision.

In Oshii's film, we see events unfold on monitors, in viewfinders, through goggles we are forced to don. And through the process Sobchack describes, viewers try to posit a body that sees things in this way. Frequently we can: the technologically-mediated views we see are not the disembodied torrent of images Sobchack identifies with the electronic; instead, they are essentially human visions, partly transformed. This vision is analogous to the bodies of the labors themselves: with their massive hydraulics and complex software, the labors' bodies are suspended between the mechanical and computer ages, ages that Sobchack associates with the cinematic and electronic, respectively. The film at these points has a similar kind of body: neither wholly electronic nor wholly cinematic; vaguely human, even charmingly old-fashioned, yet also tangibly different.

At other points, however, the film's body approaches a less localized, more distributed body that resembles Sobchack's electronic regime. These are the moments when Oshii portrays the view not through the eyes of the electromechanical labors but through the electronic lens of the mass media, a networked body with sensors everywhere. For example, the aftermath of Tsuge's attack on the Yokohama Bay Bridge is revealed as a series of television news reports on different international networks, including a flickering videotape of the incident in which key frames are blown up and re-run endlessly, a tape loop repeated again and again until it becomes unreal. (And in fact, as the story unfolds, the tape is revealed to be a fake, no more reliable than the other mediated sensations portrayed in the film.) It is a channel-flipping sequence that suggests Sobchack's disconnected, present instants and Ueno's inescapable simulacrum, where "the same incident is repeated endlessly." So it is actually when the mediated view departs from the fictional scenario of the giant robots and approaches our own everyday bodily experience of watching television that the film's body begins to lose coherence.

Other shots through the media's eyes are accomplished not by showing the film's spectators an image of a television screen but by placing them in the position of the screens themselves. When martial law is declared, there are several shots of rapt citizens watching the announcement on television; only gradually does it dawn on us that we are watching these people from the television's perspective (Figure 19). These shots recall Jean Baudrillard's catchphrase for the controlling influence of media and the equivalence of the worlds inside and outside the TV set: "you are the screen, and the TV watches you."[30] These scenes are the ones that associate the film most clearly with the electronic: by forcing us to look from the perspective of the monitor, or the mass media itself, they suggest a viewing body that is radically different from the human, not only in its shape and optics but in its logic and its concerns.

The question remains: what does the film have to contrast with these electronic views? Is it possible to generate a more natural view to accentuate the artificiality of the mediated ones? Sobchack points out that in twentieth-century American science-fiction films, the electronics and screens are often foils for the human actors, who are made to represent a world of authentic experience.[31] But in *Patlabor 2*, the humans remain the least real-looking element in the frame. In visual terms, the contrast with the film's many monitors is provided not by human faces and bodies but by exterior landscapes and cityscapes, which are rendered in striking detail. This style of realism is something Oshii developed further in his later films, reproducing effects of low light and reflected light that are visible to the eye but difficult to capture with optical cameras: complex multiple reflections at night, for example, or the glowing quality of snow falling in the dark. These provide the ground against which the other scenes become apparent as mediated or virtual.

Oshii also has a complementary strategy: he makes the video screens appear less real or less immediate by introducing flickering, banding, or overexposure effects—for example in the TV news footage of the damaged Bay Bridge or whenever a television or monitor appears on screen (Figures 17, 19, and 20). This kind of flickering and banding shows up in older live-action films when a television appears, because the television screen refreshes its image at a rate different from the rate the camera captures successive frames on film. The phenomenon is called "aliasing," and has a more familiar variant in the famous wagon wheel effect, where spinning wheels appear to turn slowly or backwards on film because the frame rate is close to their rate of rotation. But in animated film, there is no reason for these effects to occur: the television monitor in the frame is animated as well, so it can appear any way Oshii wants. In fact, he has introduced these effects to make the screens appear to have been filmed with a conventional motion-picture camera.[32] This *virtual* aliasing is an effort to trick us into recalling an earlier technology. It is a simulated gap in perspective (i.e., frame rate) that Oshii uses to create a larger sense of critical perspective, simulating the cinematic in order to critique the electronic.

A related strategy is to simulate lens distortion in the animated

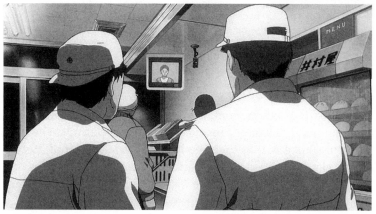

FIGURE 19. The first image of this convenience store turns out to be from the perspective of the television, as revealed in the next shot. At the same time, the fisheye effect simulates filming with a real camera.

image, for example in a scene where Oshii blurs a wall of monitors in the background in order to duplicate a television news camera's shallow depth of field, or in several shots where he introduces a fisheye effect (Figure 19). The latter is one of the director's trademark shots. Oshii says only that the effect represents "the world from a different viewpoint."[33] The situation here is complex: some of these fisheye shots represent the disembodied way that monitors and media see us, but on the other hand these shots simultaneously simulate an optical cinematic regime in a way that

FIGURE 20. Flicker, banding, strobing, and other forms of virtual aliasing emphasize the mediated quality of television footage in the film. There are several layers of mediation simulated in this image of a television announcer: everything behind her is blurred to simulate a news camera's shallow depth of field, then the whole image is made to flicker, as if Oshii had pointed a real camera at a television screen. The doubly mediated images on the background monitors strobe even more dramatically. (See also Figures 17 and 19.)

gives the film a coherent analog body, a perspective from which to mount its attack on the incoherence of the electronic. The final irony, of course, is that the glass lenses that form part of this coherent cinematic body are themselves simulated by the animators, leading us to ask if the critique itself is not a virtual one. Oshii's reply might be "Yes. Is there any other kind?"

To sum up, if *Patlabor 2* comes in a context of renewed Japanese debates about how to develop Japan's global political role beyond the restrictions or contradictions of the earlier postwar period, the anime also portrays a dilemma: the dilemma of wanting to connect with the real world by critiquing the distortions or omissions of the mass media, while realizing that there is no way of fully escaping these filters. We may speak of a "global political reality," but we cannot perceive or experience the global outside the mass media. And certainly anime, part of the popular media itself, is a mediated view. The fate of the human body in an increasingly technologized environment—the other crisis portrayed in the film—is simply another version of the same story: the inability of the individual to reach beyond his or her monitors.

The plot of *Patlabor 2* makes clear this bind between politics and representation, but the plot does not really suggest a solution: the conclusion of the story remains ambiguous. However, I think a visual reading guided by Sobchack's phenomenology suggests a more productive critique: a way of *simulating reality*, and acknowledging that this is a simulation, as a first step to thinking through the effects of technological mediation. In the way it mixes or alternates between the two, *Patlabor 2* never lets us lapse into a naive view of unmediated realism, and reminds us we have to remain agile enough to shift our perspective and "outflank," in Jameson's terms, the discourses that surround us.[34]

Oshii himself makes some interesting comments on the importance of this alternation between immersion and critical distance, in a discussion of the film's soundtrack. "I think creating a sense of immersion in film is just one tool, and does not constitute a bedrock principle that's always needed. . . . The audience is situated in an extremely privileged position from where they watch the film. . . . If you pursue immediacy too much, you rob the audience of their privileged, godlike position."[35] This echoes Arakawa's speech about a world where "everyone is like a god. Omniscient, all seeing, but unable to touch any of it from where they sit." And yet these same gods (we ourselves) will see to it that "someday we'll be punished for our lies." This circular image of a god reduced to human terms, fearing and promising its own punishment, seems to encapsulate the bind of *Patlabor 2*, but also the hope that critique of a discourse can emerge from within the discourse itself.

Live Ghosts

This chapter has compared anime with live-action film through the lens of Sobchack's film theory. Another way of conducting this comparison would be to juxtapose Oshii's anime directly with his own live-action films. But this is complicated by the fact that just as *Patlabor 2* combines elements of the cinematic and the electronic within itself, Oshii's live-action films are also hybrids. *Stray Dog: Kerberos Panzer Cops* (*Keruberosu: Jigoku no banken*, 1991) and *The Red Spectacles* are two live-action military thrillers in Oshii's "Kerberos Saga." Both of these live-action films have exaggerated, experimental visual styles that seem to draw on manga and anime's dynamic graphic elements. These pair with *Jin-Roh: The Wolf Brigade* (*Jinrō*, 1999), an anime set in the Kerberos world, scripted by Oshii and directed by Okiura Hiroyuki. *Jin-Roh* uses traditional cel animation but minimizes fantastic elements and seems to want to be read as a live-action film. Some of Oshii's later films, like *Avalon* (*Avaron*, 2001), *Assault Girls* (*Asaruto gaaruzu*, 2009), and *Garm Wars: The Last Druid* (*Garumu wōzu*, 2014) use a combination of live-action footage, computer graphics, and digital post-processing to blur the visual line between anime and live action.

If one goal of this book is to compare anime with other media to discover what it can and cannot do, Oshii seems to be exploring the same question as a filmmaker. Anime has great potential, he says, but most directors hew to a relatively small set of established conventions. So what do you do, he asks, "when you want to expand the range of anime as expression? . . . One solution is to go out and do different work in a different environment (in my case, live action movies), and via the new way of seeing which results from the experience bring new standards back to anime." Oshii says the results can surpass live-action film, which has few surprises left: the live-action "film medium as a creative frontier has gone about as far as it can go. . . . From this perspective, anime may still possess a larger potential to impact the audience, as long as it still carries around more conventions [i.e. devices] than live action."[36]

Some of Oshii's live-action experiments are more successful than others, but one that is of particular interest for our purposes is a live-action version of *Patlabor* he directed more recently. *The Next Generation Patlabor* starts with a thirteen-part series in 2014 (released almost simultaneously in theaters, on cable television, and for home video), followed by a full-length movie: *Shuto kessen / Gray Ghost* in 2015. This series is set years after *Patlabor 2* and follows an entirely new generation of characters. But that notwithstanding, *Gray Ghost* feels like a virtual remake of *Patlabor 2*, with a plot, structure, characters, and many specific scenes that closely mirror the 1993 anime. Captain Gotō as been replaced by Captain Gotōda, and pilot Izumi Noa by a similar character, Izumino Akira. There is also a new generation of plotters identified as Tsuge sympathizers, and their plan unfolds almost exactly like Tsuge's, starting with a stolen aircraft and a missile attack on a Tokyo bridge, building to a helicopter assault that cripples police headquarters and destroys the Section 2 station house. There is even a similar climax, in which the labor's automatic systems fail, forcing Izumino to climb out of her cockpit and aim her weapon manually. The new element in this film is the "gray ghost" of the title, a cutting-edge attack helicopter covered with video screens that project images of its own background, rendering it invisible—in other words, a symbolic incarnation of the media's slipperiness and threat.

Throughout the film, Oshii uses live-action and digital effects to recreate many specific shots from *Patlabor 2*. One of these is a meeting at an aquarium between Gotō and his shadowy government contact Arakawa (now Gotōda and *his* shadowy government contact Takahata) (Figure 21). In *Patlabor 2*, the wall of the aquarium is one more glass screen that works like all the others: it displays an alternative reality, an uncanny underwater double of our world that helps us step back and see our side of the glass as equally artificial or constructed. So to see this shot again in *Gray Ghost* is to glimpse the double's own double, to press further into Oshii's house of mirrors. If in *Patlabor 2* we were still occasionally tempted to speak of the anime reflecting life, here is an even clearer expression of the opposite idea, that live action and our live actions play out according to the scripts or models of the mass media. This is what postmodern theorist Jean Baudrillard identifies as the final stage of simulation, "the generation by models of a real without origin or reality: a hyperreal."[37]

And one final irony: in *Patlabor 2*, even as the aquarium scene portrays another kind of screen, it has a visual realism that contrasts with the digital displays elsewhere in the anime. It is an example of the anime's stylized realism, an image one could see with the naked eye that would be difficult to capture on live film. (Consider the challenges of lighting the tank and figures, of coordinating the movements of the actors and the fish.) But the 2014 film executes this shot flawlessly, almost certainly by resorting to computer graphics. This shows how far we've travelled since 1993. The image looks real, but what I have been calling "live action" turns out to be just a different form of animation: digital animation. It is

FIGURE 21. Oshii's live-action *Next Generation Patlabor* film *Shuto kessen /
Gray Ghost* recreates several scenes from *Patlabor 2,* like this meeting in an
aquarium. Lighting and composition effects that could only be achieved by
anime in 1993 can now be incorporated into live-action films using digital
animation. *Gray Ghost* still from the Japanese special edition Blu-ray disc
(Happinet, 2015).

only the parallels with *Patlabor 2* that make us notice these effects:
the gap between reality and representation that the anime worked
so hard to expose would fall in *Gray Ghost*'s blind spot, were it not
for the self-conscious way that the two works mirror one another.

Oshii's next film after *Patlabor 2* was the 1995 anime *Kōkaku
kidōtai / Ghost in the Shell,* and like *Gray Ghost, Ghost in the Shell*
is haunted by earlier works. In this case, the works date from two
centuries earlier, and their medium is classical puppet theater.
This is the comparison taken up in chapter 3.

3

Puppet Voices, Cyborg Souls

Ghost in the Shell and Classical Japanese Theater

If his work on the *Patlabor* franchise represented a breakthrough for Oshii in Japan, the anime film that followed, 1995's *Kōkaku kidōtai / Ghost in the Shell,* represented an international turning point for the director. In *Ghost in the Shell,* the geopolitics of films like *Patlabor 2* are largely displaced by gender politics, with results that fascinated not only anime fans but also Western academic critics, who were drawn to Oshii's evocative, provocative text.

Based on a manga by Shirō Masamune, *Ghost in the Shell* is set in a near future where advanced robotics, prosthetics, and electronic networks have blurred the lines between information, technology, and the human body. The female protagonist, Kusanagi Motoko, is a cyborg secret operative whose body and brain are a fusion of human and machine. When an interviewer asked Oshii what drew him to animate Shirō's manga and its hybrid protagonist, the director replied, "It was mostly my interest in the cyborg. . . . I didn't yet have it in me to portray a real flesh-and-blood heroine."[1] In other words, it was difficult to portray a real woman realistically in anime, but he was attracted by the opportunity to depict an artificial one.

This comment suggests the edgy and sometimes disturbing power of *Ghost in the Shell,* which traces the same tensions we see in Oshii's other films, between technology's power to extend or enhance the human and its tendency to alienate us from ourselves. But *Ghost in the Shell's* entanglement between technology and biology is more intimate—more individual and personal but also distinctly sexual. The plot and visual structure of Oshii's film seem divided between a voyeuristic obsession with the heroine's physical body and the promise of discarding that body to enter a world of pure data. In the film's violent and affecting climax, Kusanagi's cyborg body first transforms heroically and then tears itself apart. A portion of her consciousness escapes her ruined body by uploading itself to the net, which leaves her stricken partner bending over her severed head and wondering if any trace of her physical self remains.

Does a scene like this portray Kusanagi as a euphorically powerful and flexible new posthuman (even feminist) subject, or as an objectified doll? The cultural critic Donna Haraway posited the cyborg as a feminist icon that is split in precisely this way: its transgressive combination of mechanical, organic, and electronic can challenge the dichotomy between natural and artificial or individual and network, promising to free the subject from imposed categories of biology, gender, and race. But at the same time Haraway admits the challenges that this image poses to individual integrity. There is a fear that this posthuman redefinition of the subject will end up dehumanizing us all.

Several critics have read *Ghost in the Shell* through the lens of Haraway's cyborg feminism, and some have linked this split between the dehumanizing and liberatory power of technology to the way the film wavers between endorsing and transcending fixed gender roles. We could relate this to anime's power to move us back and forth between accepting a represented reality and questioning or interrogating the representation itself—the oscillation traced throughout this book. But *Ghost in the Shell* accomplishes this in a very different way from Oshii's previous film. *Patlabor 2* juxtaposed two different *visual* worlds: a physical world (of landscapes, faces, and bodies) and a virtual world (of electronic readouts). *Ghost in the Shell* remains visually focused on the body and is much more reluctant to let these kinds of digital texts intrude.

The opening scene, for example, shows a three-dimensional, computer-generated map of the city that recalls the displays of *Patlabor 2*, but almost immediately it cuts to a conventional view of the skyline—moving out of the digital world and into the physical one, where it largely remains for the rest of the film. This is followed shortly afterward by the film's opening credit sequence, which depicts Kusanagi's construction with lingering shots of her

naked body as it floats through the liquid-filled conduits of a fu-
turistic assembly line. These scenes alternate with screens of computer code that represent the textual world, code that resolves itself
into the names of the film's makers, Kusanagi's authors. As body
and text alternate, it is the naked female body that remains the
undeniable focus of attention. The result is strikingly similar to
the opening sequence of *Read or Die,* which used the same visual
tropes (clearing away text and then projecting it on female nudes)
in a way that seemed to sweep away the world of the text and replace it with the female form (Figures 2 and 22). (A 2008 update
of the anime, *Ghost in the Shell 2.0,* alters this opening sequence
in ways that may shift that balance, but here and throughout this
chapter, I am working from the original film.)[2]

If the credits juxtapose the body with literal text, the bulk of
Ghost in the Shell replaces this with a different but analogous oscillation that remains visually focused on Kusanagi's body but
portrays it as alternately real and unreal, living and artificial. To
realize this, one need only consider how different the violent ending sequence described above would look and feel if a real actress
were to play the role of Kusanagi as she is stripped, dismembered,

FIGURE 22. Kusanagi's cyborg body, assembled over the course of the opening
credits, competes with the credit text for the viewer's attention. This and other
Ghost in the Shell stills are from the twenty-fifth anniversary Blu-ray disc
(Anchor Bay, 2014).

beheaded, and finally uploaded to the net. Inevitably, it would look too fake to be truly believable and paradoxically feel too real to be entertaining. The anime has a way of making us experience this body as simultaneously more and less real than a live actress.[3]

We could say we regard Kusanagi as a child regards its doll—as something alternately alive and inert. The plot of the film periodically makes this point by comparing the shell of the cyborg body with a puppet, manipulated or inhabited by a ghost or a soul. In this chapter I would like to pursue this metaphor further by comparing Oshii's visuals more specifically with the classical Japanese puppet theater, which can help us see the anime with new eyes.

Japanese puppet theater (ningyō jōruri in Japanese) developed amid the cultural flowering of the Edo period (1603–1868), one of many popular art forms associated with the growth of urban mass culture. Government seclusion policies in this period isolated Japan from Western cultural influences, so the result was a series of vibrant prose, poetic, and dramatic forms that were radically different from Western counterparts—from kabuki theater to haiku poetry and woodblock prints. In the case of the puppet theater, these differences included the unique dramatic qualities of the plays, which combined psychological realism with striking poetic and stage effects; the virtuosic quality of the vocal performance, in which a single chanter would often voice several puppets at once; and above all the unique manipulation of the puppets, each operated with extraordinary grace by three people standing in plain view on stage.

The results have fascinated modern Western audiences and stimulated critics in interesting ways. "The puppet is like a ghost," writes Paul Claudel, and for decades various Western critics viewing the Japanese puppet theater have been fascinated by the same questions of duality and dichotomy that Haraway and Oshii raise.[4] Commentators from Claudel to Susan Sontag note a movement in the puppet theater between the real and the unreal, the unified and dispersed subject, the violent deconstruction of the body and a tender regard for it. Seen in the light of these readings, the ambivalent status of the heroine's mechanical body in Oshii's film can be traced to the ways that anime bodies, like the bodies of puppets, are performing and performed.

Donna Haraway and the Ambivalent Body

Donna Haraway's 1985 essay "A Cyborg Manifesto: Science, Technology, and Socialist Feminism in the Late Twentieth Century" defines the cyborg as a fusion of human and animal, biological and mechanical, and individual and network, a fusion that blurs the boundaries between those categories. Haraway discusses the cyborg in two interrelated ways, as "a creature of social reality as well as a creature of fiction."[5] In the first case, the cyborg is a real phenomenon that shows us our relationship to technology. Cyborgs have come into being all around us, through actual technologies from prosthetics to genetic engineering that blur the line between natural beings and created machines, or through the ways our individual bodies have become subsumed in commercial and government information networks that now govern our collective fate—what Haraway calls the "informatics of domination." While earlier feminist discourses may have opposed this with the dream of a Natural world free from technology's monstrous encroachments, Haraway rejects this division between Natural and artificial, instead positing the cyborg as a mixed figure who can show us how we are changed but also enabled by technology.

At the same time, Haraway's cyborg is also an abstract metaphor or fictional "myth" for rethinking the concept of the individual subject, particularly in the context of feminist theory. The image of the cyborg in fiction undermines the idea of the natural body in ways that encourage us to question the idea of a natural or universal human subject—an idea Haraway says feminism must overcome if it is to embrace the heterogeneous experiences of different races, genders, classes, and individuals. The critical term often associated with this is the "posthuman." Haraway writes that there are "great riches for feminists in explicitly embracing the possibilities inherent in the breakdown of clean distinctions between organism and machine and similar distinctions structuring the Western self. It is the simultaneity of breakdowns that cracks the matrices of domination and opens geometric possibilities."[6] Ultimately the myth of the cyborg alludes to an escape from the bounded individual body altogether, into a network of genetic or electronic language or information. While the assumption of the individual into the collective and the absorption of the body into discourse are often viewed as a threat to individual dignity and agency, Haraway's manifesto refigures this as the ability and opportunity to build new kinds of networks or collectives for increased political agency and cooperation across lines of gender, culture, language, race, and class.

In this way "A Cyborg Manifesto" appropriates a figure of individual dehumanization and refashions it into a posthuman emblem of collective political liberation. Haraway is aware of the risks here and aware that the cyborg's seductive power is never entirely benign. ("The main trouble with cyborgs, of course, is that they are the illegitimate offspring of militarism and patriarchal capitalism, not to mention state socialism. But illegitimate offspring are often exceedingly unfaithful to their origins.") For Haraway, though, the political, scientific, and philosophical shifts that the cyborg represents—the unhealthy growth of commercial and military networks on the one hand, and the healthy skepticism of the natural or universal subject on the other—are both too advanced to deny. We are "in the belly of the monster," she comments in an interview, and we must "contest for the discourse from within."[7]

The ambivalence *Ghost in the Shell* displays towards Kusanagi's cyborg body seems to reflect the split quality of Haraway's cyborg, which alternately represents patriarchal oppression and feminist liberation. Kusanagi is both a strong heroine who has become powerful by internalizing technology, and a technological object possessed by others. The specter that humans will be owned by the networks (Haraway's "informatics of domination") has literally come true in the story: "the major" *(shōsa)*—as Kusanagi is known through most of the film—works for "Section 9," the security service of an unnamed future state, and she undertakes covert missions that pit her against other sections, governments, and organizations on a confused political battlefield. Her body and mind belong to the state, and she cannot leave Section 9 without surrendering that body and large classified chunks of her memory.

Perhaps as a result, the major treats her own body as a thing apart—something alien or inconsequential. In an interview, the director comments that the otherness or the burden of the major's alien body is figured in terms of its weight. Kusanagi can leap tall buildings in a single bound—one of many images of flight in the anime—but her armored skeleton is so heavy that she leaves impressions in the concrete when she lands. Her hobby of scuba diving is a dangerous one not because she is threatened by rust or short circuit (the banes of less modern robots), but because her body would sink like lead if her flotation suit ever failed. This self-destructive pastime becomes an emblem of her contempt for her own form and her desire for an oblivion that transcends it. "I wanted to portray the restrictions of this body," says Oshii. "That was what you might call the aim of this work."[8]

In the climax described above, the very mass and power of the major's body seem to be its undoing: as she struggles to tear the hatch off an armored tank, her synthetic muscles bulge and swell until she assumes body-builder proportions, exerting such enormous forces that she rips off her own arm (Figure 23). Portrayed in studied slow motion and accompanied by Kawai Kenji's eerily low-key score, the major's dismemberment has a violent but curiously affectless quality that highlights her disregard for her own body: the scene might be interpreted as her own deliberate, Harawayan transcendence of the limited physical form, or her victimization at other hands.

In the background of this disregard for the physical body is the film's suggestion that perhaps the self can be abstracted from the body and located in thought and memory, or in language itself. But the reduction of the self to disembodied information produces both the freedoms and the threats that Haraway predicts. The major can send her consciousness out into the virtual world of the data network through a jack in the back of her neck, but others can enter her thoughts through the same doorway, and minds as well as memories can be manipulated over the network. The criminal genius that the major pursues throughout the film turns out to be a disembodied piece of intelligent software nicknamed the Puppet Master (Ningyōtsukai) for its ability to hack into the cyborg bodies and brains of its victims, implanting artificial memories that will make them do its bidding.

In this context, the core of the major's self is reduced to her

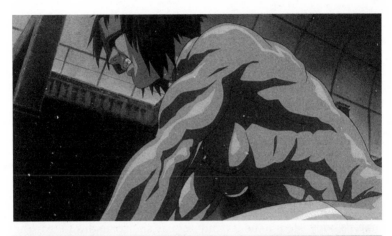

FIGURE 23. In the climax of *Ghost in the Shell,* Kusanagi strains to pry open the hatch of an armored tank, transforming dramatically and then tearing her cyborg body apart.

"ghost," an imprint of her original personality deep in her brain, presumably beyond artificial duplication and out of the network's reach. In the final scene where she battles the tank, Kusanagi's body is destroyed except for her head and brain, which her partner spirits away so as to free her from her old body and from Section 9. And in another sense she escapes embodiment altogether: just before the final denouement she chooses to unite with the Puppet Master's electronic consciousness, leading to an alternative existence in which all or part of her floats free on the net.

The formal visual aspects of *Ghost in the Shell* echo the ambivalence of the plot. While the story describes the transcendence of the major's mechanical shell, the film's visuals show an obsessive interest in the major's human shape or shapeliness, an interest that suggests the gendered body is not necessarily transcended by technology but possibly objectified and commodified to a greater degree. The major possesses not only superhuman strength but the superhuman proportions common to manga and anime heroines, and her artificially voluptuous (or voluptuously artificial) form is the visual center of the film. At several key points she uses an optical camouflage technology built into her skin to render herself invisible, but to do this she must first take off her clothes, leaving her momentarily visible and nude. In terms of the spectator's experience, the major is an object possessed not only by Section 9 but by and through the technology of animation, a high-tech pinup girl for the theater audience, like the seminude cyborgs that strike Vargas-like poses on the covers of Shirō's manga.[9]

Feminist Readings of *Ghost in the Shell*

In terms of academic criticism in English, there has probably been more written about *Ghost in the Shell* and its 2004 sequel, *Innocence,* than any other anime film or franchise to date, making the 1995 film a turning point not only for Oshii's recognition in the West but for anime's recognition by the academy. Many of these articles reference Haraway: the match between the divided quality of Oshii's protagonist and Haraway's cyborg seemed to make the comparison irresistible. But in keeping with that divided quality, some interpretations read Kusanagi as a progressive character who bears out the liberatory possibilities of Haraway's cyborg, while others see the opposite.

Sharalyn Orbaugh sees some feminist, posthuman potential in the way that *Ghost in the Shell* upsets notions of a unitary subject—the singular, bounded, male body that emblemizes modern subjectivity. For Orbaugh, the anime represents "the paradoxical *hope* that the one power that can finally oppose the various forces of evil is precisely the eruption of the abject femininity—permeability/penetrability—that is repressed in techno-patriarchal society." In contrast, Carl Silvio argues that the film's voyeuristic male gaze ultimately undermines its radical possibilities, concluding that while the film "seems to espouse a political agenda that is in keeping with feminist theorizations of the cyborg, it covertly reworks this agenda into an endorsement of conventional configurations of sexual difference." Susan Napier starts from a consideration of Haraway and technology's dissolution of the human but argues that the film ultimately seeks a remedy in a kind of technoreligious transcendence—a "new technological world and the possibility of different kinds of spiritual connections," "a union of technology and the spirit."[10] We could say this represents a clear break from Haraway, who adamantly opposes any narrative (spiritual or technological) that promises we can transcend the body completely. For Haraway, these narratives of transcendence authorize a disregard for the physical suffering all around us in order to focus unproductively on a hypothetical reality beyond this one.[11]

Each of these readings is interesting and compelling. Taken together, I think they give an excellent picture of the tensions inherent in *Ghost in the Shell*. Here, though, I would like to approach the comparison between Oshii's film and Haraway's essay from a slightly different direction. There is a blind spot in some Harawayan readings of film and fiction, particularly the readings of prose science fiction that Haraway undertakes herself. Her textual examples range from immunology textbooks to feminist sciencefiction novels, but she tends to focus on narratives and plots, as if they described real people and experiences we were intended to relate to our own lives. Her tendency is to treat these texts as entirely realistic or immersive and to ignore all the ways in which the style of a text can render its characters deliberately artificial, impossible, unreal.[12]

Readings like this are often convincing but predictable. For example, this approach will inevitably have difficulty locating feminist potential in a text like *Ghost in the Shell*, which casually inflicts violence on an apparently female body. But here I would like to argue that treating Kusanagi as a living subject misses the ways her body will always fall inside quotation marks; she is a virtual or performed subject that is real, unreal, and hyperreal from the outset. Indeed, anime's potential lies precisely therein.

Tatsumi Takayuki's work on Haraway suggests an approach that could recover this notion of performance in the context of the cyborg. In a pair of striking essays that accompanied the Japanese publication of Haraway's manifesto, Tatsumi discusses cyberpunk science fiction (which is characterized not only by intimate unions between human and machine but also by violent fantasies of female superbodies like Kusanagi's), alongside feminist science-fiction author Alice Sheldon (who wrote under both male and female pseudonyms), Roland Barthes's structuralist reading of Balzac in his book *S/Z*, and David Henry Hwang's stage play *M. Butterfly*, based on a true story about the sexual relationship between a French diplomat and a Beijing opera singer/Chinese spy in the "role" of a woman. Tatsumi connects these diverse texts through the idea that the power of technology to redraw lines of gender or culture lies in the power of performance, whether it is the layers of cultural and gender performance in Hwang's drama, Sheldon's literary personas, or the tour-de-force textual performance of *S/Z*. By focusing on performance, Tatsumi is able to discover, behind cyberpunk's sexism, the promise of bodily changes at a fundamental (gender and cultural) level. In what follows I will substitute the puppet theater for Hwang's play, and Barthes's *Empire of Signs* for *S/Z*, in order to refocus attention on anime's layers of language and performance, and to discover the same promise or possibility in Oshii's film.[13]

Barthes and other Western interpreters of the puppet theater have been concerned with two aspects of the puppet's performed body that have important parallels in anime. The first of these is the way that the puppet's voice and motive force seem to come both from without and from within. For Barthes and others, the puppet represents language and action that are simultaneously embodied and disembodied—a theatrical sign that wavers between pure language and speaking subject in a way that makes us rethink the apparent split between body and language. The second parallel is the light or floating quality of the puppets and the way it conveys both vulnerability and liberty: a mobile independence or freedom, but also a sense of being subject to the gusting winds (or heavy hand) of fate. These observations on the puppet's movements also apply to animation, and they not only cast the major's heavy body in a new light but also transform our reading of her violent fate.

Chikamatsu and the Puppet Theater

In his book comparing anime with classical Japanese drama, Stevie Suan describes their common "mixture of unreality and realism." Suan focuses on the visual and narrative artificiality of both media, juxtaposed with the spectator's ability to invest in them as almost real. Suan's book covers several Japanese theatrical genres, but he has a particular interest in theories of medieval nō theater and its highly stylized but moving combination of costume, music, chanting, and dance.[14] However, we can find a theory of artificiality and engagement similar to Suan's in a three-hundred-year-old description of the early modern puppet theater, or *ningyō jōruri*, from its most famous playwright Chikamatsu Monzaemon (1653–1724).

In a monologue recorded by Hozumi Ikan in *Naniwa miyage* (Souvenir from Naniwa, 1738), Chikamatsu describes the combination of detachment and concern we feel toward the puppet's mechanical body: "Because *jōruri* is performed in theatres that operate in close competition with those of the kabuki, which is the art of living actors, the author must impart to lifeless wooden puppets a variety of emotions, and attempt in this way to capture the interest of the audience."[15] Chikamatsu argues here that emotion or pathos is the central dramatic element of the puppet theater, and that the artificial can often move the audience more effectively than the strictly realistic. For example, Chikamatsu's many "love suicide" plays *(shinjūmono)* elicit the audience's sympathy for two puppet lovers who kill themselves to escape the conflict between their passion for one another and the social responsibilities that keep them apart. Chikamatsu suggests that what makes the puppets sympathetic in roles like these is that the playwright can invest inanimate things with more emotion and more humanity than a real person or actor could express. In effect, we identify more with the artificial than with the real.

If this interplay of identification and artificiality sounds like the argument we have been making about anime, the parallels stem in part from the fact that both anime and puppet theater are essentially popular media. Although the latter is a rarified classical art form in Japan today, in Chikamatsu's time it was part of a highly visual, highly popular, and highly commercial urban artistic culture. Chikamatsu's comment about the need to compete with the kabuki theater reveals precisely why it was necessary to "capture the interest" of seventeenth- or eighteenth-century consumers, and both anime and the puppet theater have captivated audiences in similar ways, with a combination of melodramatic human interest and violent physical excitement, emphasized by special effects. Chikamatsu's *sewamono* (domestic plays like the love suicides described above) concentrate on the emotional interest of urban residents' everyday lives, but his historical plays (*jidaimono*) emphasize exotic locales, superhuman characters, and elaborate stagecraft. Chikamatsu's most popular *jidaimono*, *The Battles of Coxinga* (*Kokusen'ya gassen*, 1715), features a protagonist right out of Haraway: a half-Japanese, half-Chinese hero who wields magic and technology in a series of far-flung, epic battles. After cataloging the visual effects that appear in *Coxinga* (including a wrestling match with a tiger and a magical cloud bridge that disperses beneath the feet of the hero's pursuers), Donald Keene notes that the play was one of many in which Chikamatsu responded to increasing pressure from theater manager Takeda Izumo to incorporate complicated stage machinery.[16]

As time went on, the technology of the puppets became even more developed, and by the early eighteenth century each puppet was manipulated by three operators working together to impart incredible nuance to its movements. This is the mature puppet familiar from puppet theater performances given today: while one operator moves the puppet's lower body, a second controls the left arm, while the senior operator manipulates the right arm and head. A system of cords and baleen springs inside the head allows operators to change the expression of the puppets, some of which can open and close their eyes and mouths, look askance, and even raise a single eyebrow. Certain special puppets can even perform sudden transformations, like the *gabu* puppet that turns from a young woman into a demon by sprouting horns and sharp teeth.

Yūda Yoshio writes that automated mechanisms or *karakuri* were originally separate from the puppets, used only in stage machinery or in robot dolls that performed between acts. But the machinery eventually found its way into the puppets' own bodies.[17]

This *internalization* of technology is the central trope of the cyborg, and the key step in blurring the line between bodies and tools or between humans and machines.

Of course we could also see the complex of puppeteers and puppet as a cyborg-like or mecha-like hybrid of human and technology. Even in early performances, puppeteers sometimes performed in full view of the audience, and as the operation of the puppets became more complex, the puppeteers increasingly moved out from behind the screens that had concealed them, further highlighting the puppets' hybrid quality and the act of manipulation itself. This continues in the puppet theater today, where the operators' only concealment is the black clothing that formally signifies their absence.

This brew of violent action, emotional (frequently romantic) drama, artificial actors, and extravagant special effects is something the puppet theater shares with anime. But beyond the general parallels between these two popular dramatic media, *Ghost in the Shell* also incorporates some more explicit references to the puppet theater. Kusanagi's final union with the Puppet Master is figured in terms of sex, death, and rebirth, as a kind of love suicide very much like Chikamatsu's. The Puppet Master proposes the union because it desires the qualities of embodiment—expressed as individuality and fragility. In return it promises Kusanagi an unbounded existence on the net. The deal is phrased in terms of self-destruction and sexual commingling: "After our union," the Puppet Master says to Kusanagi, "the new you may release hybrids of me into the net as needed, in the same way a human passes on its genes. And I too will achieve death." The compromise between worldly embodiment and transcendence resembles the idea in Chikamatsu's love suicides that the lovers can transcend their worldly obligations and bodily desires through death and yet remain spiritually, even physically connected—that they can die and "be reborn on one lotus."[18] In the climax of *Ghost in the Shell*, Kusanagi's partner Batō makes the comparison explicit, telling her "I'm not going to be involved in a love suicide with that thing" (*Soitsu to shinjūsuru ki wa nee zo*).

Visually, too, the scene suggests a love suicide's combination of sex and violent death: the major's body—naked, limbless, and

FIGURE 24. The scene where Kusanagi is connected to the Puppet Master resembles one of Chikamatsu's love suicides, in which the lovers bind themselves to one another and travel together into the next world.

nearly ruined by her encounter with the tank—is laid next to another robot body into which the Puppet Master has temporarily downloaded itself, a body that is also damaged and limbless, also naked, and (a twist) also female. The two figures are connected by a series of data wires that recall the sash or cord that traditionally binds dying lovers so that they will remain joined in the next life. Motionless, shattered, open-eyed and staring, they look already dead (Figure 24).[19]

Uncanny Parallels

Given these parallels between *Ghost in the Shell* and the puppet theater, perhaps Chikamatsu's observations on the emotional appeal of the puppets can explain the poignancy of the artificial or mechanical body in anime. Chikamatsu's full argument is that the dramatic quality of the puppets, like the cyborgs, depends on their striking suspension between living and nonliving. He illustrates the possibility of imparting life to the inanimate puppets by describing a scene from *The Tale of Genji*, in which some courtiers are tending an orange tree after a heavy snowfall. When the snow suddenly drops from the branches of an adjacent pine tree, the pine is described as having shaken off its own burden in jealousy. "This was a stroke of the pen which gave life to the unconscious tree," says Chikamatsu. "From this model I learned how to put life into my *jōruri*."[20]

The treatise refers to the puppets alternately as "*ningyō*" ("doll" or "human form") and "*deku*" ("fragments of wood"), and here the analogy with the wood of the tree is a careful one. The flailing limbs of the pine, like those of the puppet, are moved by an outside force that only appears to come from within. Yet, the comparison with the "unconscious" *(kokoronaki)* living tree suggests that the puppets are not dead either. What Keene has translated as "put life into" is *kaigen* or "eye opening," a term that refers to the act of adding eyes to a carved or painted Buddhist figure to endow the inanimate work of art with a soul. And this idea that a lifeless puppet could be invested with a soul has precedents in Japanese religious practices that use puppets and mechanical dolls.[21]

But while Chikamatsu may be alluding here to traditions of spirit incarnation, elsewhere in this treatise he locates the effectiveness of the puppets precisely in their artificiality: "It is because female puppets express things that could never come from a real woman's mouth," he says, "that the true emotions are revealed." He also tells the story of a court lady who has a doll fashioned in the image of her absent lover—a perfect replica from "the number of teeth in the mouth" to "the pores of his skin." But the very resemblance becomes frightening to the lady, and even her feelings for the real man cool. Chikamatsu concludes:

> In view of this we can see that if one makes an exact copy of a living being, even if it happened to be Yang Kuei-fei, one will become disgusted with it. If when one paints an image or carves it of wood there are, in the name of artistic license, some stylized parts in a work otherwise resembling the real form; this is, after all, what people love in art.[22]

Today we would describe the court lady's doll as "uncanny." In his 1906 essay "On the Psychology of the Uncanny," Ernst Jentsch identifies the uncanny with the disorientation caused by uncertainty about whether something (such as a doll or automaton) is living or not. Building on Jentsch, Sigmund Freud's well-known essay "The

'Uncanny'" focuses on the doll's role as a double, something that speaks both to Chikamatsu's doll lover and to *Ghost in the Shell*, where the threat to the major's subjectivity includes the idea that she is mechanically reproduced, one in a series. (In one scene Kusanagi's doubts about her individuality manifest themselves in glimpses of doppelgängers, including a shop-window mannequin that shares her face.) For Freud, these doubled figures represent a self divided by repressed memories or superstitions. One represents the id's anxiety-ridden connection with repressed memories or banished superstitions, and the other what Freud would later call the super-ego's efforts to control or overcome them. The unsettling appearance of our own doppelgänger represents the return of the fears (or fearful self) we had repressed.

Produced for an audience with a large adolescent contingent, anime like Oshii's is surely susceptible to a critical approach that focuses on anxiety and repression, particularly sexual anxiety. The next chapter explores psychoanalytic theories and the idea that anime might reveal the social and sexual anxieties of the culture that consumes it. But in that chapter as in this one, we will find that simple applications of Freud tend to fall short because of the limits they place on ambiguity—not just the question of whether Kusanagi's character is human or machine but also the question of whether the viewer experiences the figure on stage or screen as real or virtual. When Freud's essay turns to literature, his explanation of the uncanny assumes the reader's psychological identification with a character in the text: for the reader as well as the character, the puppet double must represent a real thought or memory that has been suppressed or overcome. Like Haraway, Freud here devotes little energy to the gap the reader or viewer might perceive between reality and fiction; but as we will see, this is precisely the gap in which the puppet moves.

Friedrich Kittler suggests that Freud's scientific image of the individual constitutes its own kind of uncanny double, in a way that limits the reader's agency even more decisively. He argues that whereas nineteenth-century readers could still imagine or picture themselves in the text, the science of psychoanalysis, the technology of film, and other progressively more elaborate tools of reproduction have all defined the individual with a precision and power that leave us no freedom to construct ourselves. Speaking of film, Kittler says, "It is not the soul that is real, but the celluloid." So we might identify with characters in earlier fiction, but starting with Freud and film, the text identifies us.[23]

Kittler's technological uncanny may resonate with Haraway's informatics of domination and Kusanagi's fear that she is not only seen and known by the network but manufactured by it. Yet, the viewer of *Ghost in the Shell* surely does not feel defined by this film. Kittler asserts that film images of individual bodies are more precise than written ones, but as discussed in chapter 2, simple notions of visual realism are not very convincing when applied to anime. Oshii's characters are, like puppets, a complicated combination of realistic and abstract. For example, in the sequence described above where Kusanagi encounters her doubles, her own face is drawn more schematically, becoming an abbreviated mask (Figure 25). Oshii's animated bodies are certainly not so realistic that they define how we see ourselves; rather, they are layered theatrical signs in which character, puppet actor, and language all occupy separate strata that we can perceive simultaneously. What we require is a reading of the puppets that locates their uncanny (lively but nonliving) quality in this layering or striation, and it is for this that we turn now to Roland Barthes.

FIGURE 25. In a scene where she is confronted with her own artificiality, Kusanagi's face appears as an abstract mask.

Lovable Bodies, Layered Souls: The Puppet Theater in Western Criticism

Chikamatsu's most famous dictum is that "art is something that lies in the slender margin between the real and the unreal."[24] But for later critics writing on the puppet theater, art does not so much dwell in a narrow gap between realism and unrealism as veer back and forth between extreme versions of each. For these critics, the pathos of the puppets depends on their ability to be simultaneously much more than human and much less. This tendency to swing between extremes seems analogous to *Ghost in the Shell*, which moves through exultation, desire, indifference, and hostility as it alternately worships, scorns, envies, and destroys the major's cyborg body.

Barthes's reading of the puppet theater comes in "A Lesson in Writing" ("Leçon d'écriture," 1968), later revised and incorporated into *The Empire of Signs* (*L'Empire des signes*, 1970). His interpretation of bunraku (the descendent of Chikamatsu's *ningyō jōruri* that is preserved and performed in Japan today) hinges on two features of the performance that have fascinated a number of Western critics: the fact that each puppet is manipulated by three human puppeteers who remain visible on stage, while the voices of all the puppets are performed by a single chanter. For Barthes, this visible separation of the puppet's body from its voice and its motive force shatters the illusions of the Western theater, laying bare the layers of the theatrical sign and destroying the illusion of a whole subject presented on the Western stage. The dichotomies that constitute the classical Western subject (dichotomies like inside and outside, body and soul, God and human) are now replaced with new articulations of body, voice, and will that expose the layers of signification and self. Speaking of this dissociation as a kind of Brechtian alienation or "distance," Barthes says:

> that distance is made explicable by *Bunraku*, which allows us
> to see how it can function: by the discontinuity of the codes, by
> this caesura imposed on the various features of representation,
> so that the copy elaborated on the stage is not destroyed but
> somehow broken, striated, withdrawn from that metonymic

contagion of voice and gesture, body and soul, which entraps our actors.[25]

The divide between body and voice is already foregrounded by the ventriloquistic medium of animation, and Oshii emphasizes that divide by occasionally mismatching bodies and voices, for example making characters speak without moving their lips to express the idea that they are communicating over the network. In the final scene, the Puppet Master occupies a ruined female robot body, but speaks in a male voice, sometimes through Kusanagi's mouth. The film's sound director Wakabayashi Kazuhiro describes how he emphasized these effects by using a spatializer to delocalize sounds, making them seem to come from everywhere and nowhere at once.[26]

As an example of the importance of sound for locating or dispersing the film's subjects, consider the opening scene, where we move in and out of the network aurally as well as visually. We see a three-dimensional, computer-generated map of the city that transitions to a conventionally animated cityscape. Then we watch Kusanagi assassinate a foreign diplomat by diving off the roof of a building, hanging tethered outside his window, and firing through the glass. She escapes the pursuing security forces by triggering the camouflage that renders her nude body invisible as she drops away from the building. Seen from above, her falling body seems to fade into the pattern of city streets below, streets that look like the paths on a printed circuit board. The analogy is completed by a transition to a circuit diagram that resolves itself into the film's title, beginning the opening credit sequence.

The dramatic visuals make it easy to miss various aural components that reinforce a disjunction between body and voice in order to portray the networked self. The opening digital map is accompanied by a collage of overlapping radio voices in Japanese and English. As we zoom in on two blinking symbols that represent helicopters over the city, the sudden roar of their rotors announces the transition to a conventional naked-eye view. Kusanagi converses with her team over the network, without moving her lips, in a voice that has this delocalized quality, and her disembodied voice sounds briefly inside the diplomat's mind just before the bullets strike him, a final invasion announcing his death. Finally, in the opening credits that follow, the idea that the major's body is human and inhuman is supported by Kawai Kenji's brilliant score, which employs a choir of keening voices that sound both recognizably human and disturbingly alien.

Here attention to the film's voices, à la Barthes, shows how they capture very precisely the combination of embodiment and disembodiment that the major represents. Oshii expresses this by saying that the technique of traveling voices is intended to make the abstract idea of the network more palpable, "to express things like computers and the net in a way that would be recognizable to people living in present-day Japan." But the flip side of this is the way that the abstract network erodes our palpable sense of self.[27] This is finally not far from Barthes's strategy of using the puppets to express the idea that the language composing us is just as important as our bodies—that we are all in some sense disembodied beings moving within its discursive network. A marketing tag for the English version of the film describes the Puppet Master in the same way Barthes (or Haraway) might describe us: "It found a voice. . . . Now it needs a body."

Barthes's attempt to undermine transparent representation by breaking the literary or theatrical sign apart into its distinct components is the defining move of structuralist criticism, but he takes a further step we could identify with the poststructuralist criticism that followed. This next move identifies a challenge to Western dichotomies not only in the puppet's division but in its unity as well. Despite the "striation" of the puppet into what Barthes terms the "three writings" of voice, body, and action, he argues that the puppet eventually achieves a wholeness or unity lacking in both the Western marionette and the live actor/actress. The Western actor or actress tries to lay claim to a wholeness based on organic (biological) unity but ends up as a fragmented series of parts and gestures on stage. In contrast the puppet makes no claims to wholeness but emerges more graceful and more perfect than the human, which for Barthes is the final defeat for the putative organic unity of the actor's human body.

Everything which we attribute to the total body and which is denied to our actors, everything covered by the idea of an organic, "living" unity, the little man of *Bunraku* recuperates and expresses without any deception: . . . in short the very qualities which the dreams of ancient theology granted to the redeemed body, i.e., impassivity, clarity, agility, subtlety, this is what the *Bunraku* achieves, this is how it converts the body-as-fetish into the lovable body, this is how it rejects the antinomy of animate/inanimate and dismisses the concept which is hidden behind all animation of matter and which is, quite simply, "the soul."[28]

Barthes's curious term "lovable" *(aimable)* hints at his divided attitude toward the puppets, expressing sympathy with a degree of detachment.[29] It encapsulates the oscillation in Barthes's reading, which resists the realism of the puppets but can still fall momentarily back into the illusion of life they present. While Barthes's argument may seem abstract, this oscillation is based on a concrete impression that confronts many spectators at the puppet theater as well as many spectators of anime: at first one is interested in the manipulation of the puppets or animated figures—the puppeteers' or animators' technique. But these manipulations are forgotten much more quickly than one would expect. One stops seeing them and instead becomes absorbed in the actions of the puppets or figures themselves.

The oscillation between signifier and signified that is present in any stage production is something that is emphasized and exploited by the bunraku operators, who cause the puppets to perform complex physical actions that sometimes make them appear lifelike but at other times interrupt the illusion by self-consciously showcasing the puppeteers' skills. When Oshichi climbs the ladder of a fire tower in the climax of the *Yaoya Oshichi* plays, it is an acrobatic feat that requires similarly acrobatic skill from the manipulators, and the scene is greeted by applause directed at the puppeteers. I noted that the three operators work in full view but with a conventional invisibility imparted by their black clothing; two also wear black hoods, but the principal operator's face is visible, an acknowledgment of his skill and presence. (In some performances I've even seen the principal operators perform in colorful kimono.)

In all these ways and in many more, the puppeteers move back and forth between the psychological background and the forefront of the audience's attention. Likewise, animation conceals and then foregrounds the performance with a similar alternation: just as we are becoming wrapped up in the characters and their story, the animated quality of the bodies or landscape will come to the fore in a way that reminds us momentarily of the illusion.

Enriching this oscillation between realism and visible artistry in the puppet theater is its complex exchange with the live theater of kabuki, with which it shares not only plots and texts (Chikamatsu composed for both stages) but sometimes even the style of movement: the scene of Oshichi climbing the fire tower was so popular that in the kabuki production today the human actor performs with a characteristic jerking motion called *ningyō-buri* that is designed to mimic (but actually exaggerates) the motions of a puppet. Oshii's work also exhibits this kind of exchange between media: the character design for Kusanagi was adapted from the character in Shirō's manga, but it also influenced the look of the heroine in Oshii's next, live-action movie, *Avalon* (*Avaron*, 2001). *Avalon* also features a plot about simulated experience and virtual bodies, plus a lead actress who looks startlingly like her cartoon predecessor Kusanagi.

Finally there is a gender dynamic to this oscillation, given that women in kabuki theater are conventionally played by specialized male actors (*onnagata*), just as the female dolls in the national puppet theater are manipulated and voiced by male performers.[30] The spectator can move back and forth between (1) a feeling of immersion in the illusion, (2) a sense of disjunction between actor and character, (3) an appreciation of the performer's technical expertise in conveying that illusion, and (4) a sense that the technique itself exposes a stereotyped discourse of femininity. We can feel the same dynamic in Kusanagi, whose look was created by male character designer Okiura Hiroyuki, with perfectly exaggerated female proportions.

All this exposes the construction of gender (the layers of discourse and performance that constitute it), but Barthes's idea that puppet theater undermines conventional notions of a "soul" goes even further. It is the rejection of an inner core or essence that separates a human being from the material reality (world, body, language, philosophy) that supposedly lies outside. In other words, "soul" is Barthes's shorthand for the entire model of subjectivity that radical structuralism and poststructuralism call into question. We encountered a version of these ideas in chapters 1 and 2, in postmodern theories that the acceleration and expansion of language in the mass media have made it increasingly difficult to think of ourselves as political subjects separate from that media—the idea that we are no longer individual media consumers with individual choice and political agency, but that now our thoughts and our very ways of conceiving ourselves are formed by powerful political discourses all around us.

Barthes's work suggests we can take this a step further. Radical poststructuralism (the foundation for theories of postmodernism and for Haraway's posthuman feminism) generalizes this argument beyond a critique of mass media or political discourses, to make an argument about the fundamental relationship of all human subjects to language. In this model the subject (the self) is formed in and by language. The subject has no inside, because that would imply a core that exists before language and uses it as a transparent tool to communicate with some other stable soul outside itself. To conceive radical poststructuralism's claim that language defines and uses us, we might think of ourselves as nodes in a network of language (electronic or otherwise) that connects us with one another across our own blurry boundaries. When I speak to you (when you read me), how much of my language is my own and how much is borrowed or inherited from elsewhere? In what way does my language then become a part of you? And outside of language, what tools do either of us have to define, understand, or think ourselves?

The French dramatist Jean Louis Barrault says the puppet "believes" in its operator "as we in God. . . . In the most simple way in the world, this is metaphysical theater." But Barthes and later critics have read the puppet theater as a rejection of the metaphysical model in which each soul remains individual and distinct from an outside reality represented by God above. Another French playwright, Paul Claudel, notes that while the Western marionette operator stands over the puppet in a way that might suggest just such a god, the bunraku puppet is surrounded by a cloud of manipulators, chanter, and audience for which the puppet becomes like a central "collective soul." This shared soul or communal consciousness is not metaphysical; in poststructuralist fashion it is forged from language. "It is something that detaches itself from the chanter's script and borrows its language; we are no longer in the presence of interpreters, but of the text itself." "The puppet is not an actor who speaks," concludes Claudel, "but speech that acts."[31]

If Claudel transforms the subject from something metaphysical into something textual by redefining the soul as a text, other critics perform a similar operation using the concept of fate. The idea that characters' destinies are fixed from the outset is a defining feature of puppet plays, many of which have titles (like *Love Suicides at Amijima*) that describe their outcomes. But "fate" can be conceived in different ways: as a metaphysical ordering of the universe (God's plan, your destiny); as socially created inevitability (your place in society, your lot in life); or in poststructuralist terms as your indebtedness to the language that composes you.

"The three operators sum up the essence of what it is to be a god," writes Susan Sontag, and they govern the puppet's fate. But Sontag's gods and fates are both defined by the theatrical text. "The audience watches the operators observing the puppet, primal spectators to the drama they animate. . . . What the audience sees is that to act is to be moved. (And simultaneously, observed.) What is enacted is the submission to a fate." So for Sontag, fate is ultimately an act, and the operator-gods are playing their own role (which is why at "some moments the operators seem like the puppet's servants, at other moments its captors").[32] The spectators, too, are captive gods, elevated and imprisoned by the language of the performance. Everyone in the audience is, to borrow a line from *Patlabor 2*, "like a god. Omniscient, all seeing, but unable to touch any of it from where they sit."

Naoki Sakai gives the most linguistically and historically informed reading of the puppets' struggle against fate, equating it with the distinction between quoted and narrative language in the text of the play. Sakai sees Chikamatsu's *jōruri* as part of a moment around 1700 when texts are just beginning to "stratify" language into artificial layers of quoted speech and third-person narration, a division that begins to distinguish interior psychology from an external world and construct (the myth of) a unified modern subject. In a reading that covers not just the performance conventions but the grammar, intonation, and music of the text, Sakai relates this play between direct and indirect speech to the play between the immediate drama of the moment (which he identifies with a sense that the puppets are alive) and what amounts to a sense of fate or something already accomplished, associated with a narration that replaces the subject's own speech after his or her death. As a brief sketch of Sakai's complex argument, we might say that the puppets can be perceived as alive, independent, and individual speaking subjects only by defining themselves against the externalized background of a fate that is represented by death or narration.[33]

Some readers may prefer Sakai's historically and linguistically informed reading to the more impressionistic interpretations of Barthes, Sontag, et al., who use their own creative takes on the puppet theater as a kind of foil to make their readers see contemporary Western culture in a different way. (Barthes wrote that his inability to understand Japanese was liberating, freeing language of all its conventional meanings, allowing him "to 'entertain' the idea of an unheard-of symbolic system, one altogether detached from our own."[34]) In the context of this chapter, though, Barthes's reading may be as productive as Sakai's. I am not arguing here for (or against) a causal continuity—that anime is the way it is because early Japanese drama was the way it was. Critics like Karatani Kōjin have made related arguments, suggesting that Japan looks particularly postmodern to us because the concept of the modern subject was absent from the seventeenth century, took only weak hold in the nineteenth, and was readily discarded at the end of the twentieth. Those causal arguments require a more rigorous examination of the classical texts and contexts than we have time for here. Without that careful work, they tend to devolve into essentialist stereotypes about Japanese and Western culture that lead only to predictable conclusions.[35] What I *am* suggesting here is that we look at the puppet theater as a way of seeing anime with new eyes—eyes that could view the major as a flexible subject whose outlines are defined in uncertain or unexpected ways.

To that end, let us revisit the final scenes of *Ghost in the Shell*—particularly the major's subjectivity or objectification in the final violent conclusion—in light of the lessons suggested by the puppet theater. What is the fate of the mechanical body? And does the self reside equally in the body, the ghost that inhabits it, or the voice? We will find that the violence of *Ghost in the Shell* has specific analogues in the puppet theater, and that it should be considered in light of the fact that the major, like the puppets, oscillates between being more and less present than flesh. The result is that the violence is more and less real; in Sontag's formulation it is both multiplied and displaced.[36] At the same time, although the major's violent fate is in some sense prewritten, she gains a freedom from the fact that, like any fiction, her fate is not conclusively fixed.

Weighty Matters

As described above, in the film's climax the major's body is violently dismembered and finally made irrelevant after she accepts the Puppet Master's proposal to merge her consciousness with his code and ascend to the net. This scene appears divided in the same way as the rest of the film: in terms of the body, we can view it either as the transcendence of the awkward, gendered body, or as a bit of violent pornography in which a female superbody is exercised and casually snuffed. Mirroring this is a divide between the Puppet Master's slow, extended monologue on transcendence and the scenes of frantic physical action that bracket it. And finally, in terms of the major's fate or her place in society, it is possible to see the final union either as an escape from the restrictions of Section 9 or as a reinscription of gender roles through the sexual metaphor that defines that union. Susan Napier articulates some of these more pessimistic readings when she writes: "Ultimately, Kusanagi's strength and agility seem hollow, underlined by the many dependent, vulnerable, and damaged modes in which the viewer sees her. Furthermore, the fact that the supposedly sexless Puppet Master speaks in a somewhat masculine voice and essentially invites Kusanagi to perform a kind of 'wedding' with him seems to emphasize Kusanagi's dependent feminine status."[37]

The question of social and gender roles suggests more parallels with the puppet theater. In Chikamatsu's love suicide plays, for example, the violent outcome is conventionally viewed not as destiny but as the result of conflict between individual desire and social expectations (*ninjō* versus *giri*). For example, in *Love Suicides at Amijima* (*Shinjū ten no Amijima*, 1721), the married merchant Jihei and his prostitute lover Koharu are pulled between the desire to be together and the conflicting duties imposed by their various social and gender roles.[38] Kusanagi likewise faces a choice between the needs of her humanity and the needs of society, including the duties she is expected to fulfill as Section 9's agent and the Puppet Master's chosen partner. Destiny is refigured as the inevitability of the political conspiracies that enfold her, and society is replaced by the data network and its eternal surveillance.

But the puppets often escape their gender roles by transforming themselves, physically or socially. The major's muscular metamorphosis in the final scene, for example, recalls the *gabu* puppet that changes from a beautiful woman to a demon. In the plays that use this puppet, the metamorphosis can be read as a kind of terrible empowerment that crosses social and bodily barriers, allowing the woman to take a revenge that is not possible or permitted in her feminine form. In *Hidakagawa iriaizakura* (Dusk at the Hidaka River, 1759), a woman pursues the lover who spurned her, transforming into a serpent to swim the river that separates them. More realistic plays often turn on disguised or confused identity, leading up to dramatic transformations in which a hero's (or victim's) true origins are revealed.[39]

Even death in the puppet theater can be viewed as a social transformation and a form of agency. Suicide releases Jihei and Koharu from their obligations to others and atones for their failures, while constituting a final consummation of their love, a hope that they will be reborn together. After Kusanagi's body is destroyed, her partner Batō steals off with her brain and transplants it into a new body, letting Section 9 assume that she is dead. The destruction of her body becomes a physical and social transfiguration that allows her to escape and fulfill her duty as an agent. At the same time, her rebirth with the Puppet Master, understood as a final act of *ninjō*, is both the end of her humanity and the fulfillment of her human desires.

Yet, the parallels between violence in anime and puppet theater go beyond plots. Much of the puppet theater repertoire turns on murder, revenge, self-sacrifice, and even child sacrifice, but even more striking is the way this violence is represented—graphically, as in anime, with no shortage of gruesome special effects. (This is in marked contrast with the live-action kabuki theater, where combat is depicted with minimal physical contact, as a beautifully stylized dance.) Keene points out a number of examples in *The Battles of Coxinga*, including one scene in which the villain gouges out his own eye and offers it to an emissary as a sign of allegiance. When a cursed sword sends its owner on a killing spree in *Iseondo koi no netaba* (The blood-thirsty sword, 1838), the severed limbs of the puppet victims are strewn in all directions, leading up to a moment where the decapitated head of a small child flies across the stage. The twentieth-century author Tanizaki Jun'ichirō writes about a struggle from *Morning Glory Diary* (*Asagao nikki*, 1823) in which "the heads and feet of the two puppets clack against one [an]other, hard enough to shatter." Chikamatsu's play *The Woman-Killer and the Hell of Oil* (*Onnagoroshi to abura jigoku*, 1721) climaxes with a murder in an oil shop, the victim struggling to escape her assassin across a floor slick with spilled oil. The puppeteers make both puppets slip and slide across the stage for several minutes as the murderer hacks her to death. And in the Awaji tradition, when the heroine of *Tamamo no Mae asahi no tamoto* (Lady Tamamo no Mae, 1806) is killed by a fox, the puppet spills red batting from its torso and the fox chews on the simulated guts. Tanizaki writes that the first time he watched a puppet performance, he fled the theater in fright.[40]

And formally, how is this violence depicted? As the examples from *Morning Glory Diary* and *The Woman-Killer and the Hell of Oil* both suggest, an important element is the puppets' combination of momentum and speed. The puppets are heavy or solid enough to convey a sense of physical consequences that a hand puppet or a marionette could not, but also light enough to be thrown about the stage with a violence that would tear a human actor apart. Tanizaki discusses violence in the same way that Barthes and Sontag discuss pathos, suggesting that the artificial bodies exaggerate the violence but simultaneously hold it at a distance. "Even scenes of cruelty when performed by puppets create a peculiarly uncanny atmosphere which no living person could convey," he writes, contributing to an effect "at once childlike and deeply moving."[41] Sontag says, "Sometimes the puppet seems to be reposing solidly on the operators or to be borne placidly aloft by them; other times to be in perpetual, hapless flight," and her words capture the puppets' complex mix of freedom and vulnerability. For Sontag, this play of light and heavy is part of the oscillation between realism and unrealism whereby emotions are magnified and then set aside. Her characterization of bunraku as a combination of "heightened, purified emotionality" and "mythic impersonality" is completely analogous to the affectless violence of *Ghost in the Shell*.[42]

Oshii notes that "no matter how acrobatic a person is, a human being's body will never be able to create a sense of rhythm like that of an anime character," and we see the same combination of heaviness and lightness in the violent climax of *Ghost in the Shell*.[43] The weightiness of the body that Oshii associates with unwieldiness is now highlighted and juxtaposed with images of floating and flight. As she executes a series of gymnastic leaps that finally land her on top of the enemy tank, the path of Kusanagi's invisible body through space is indicated by a series of faint traces, as if she were nothing more than a breath of air. But as she strains to pry open the tank's hatch with her bare hands, her body becomes visible and her muscles bulge impossibly, magnifying her mass. The strain finally pulls her apart in what I earlier called an affectless slow-motion shot. As her limbs are ripped from their sockets, her formerly light body drops from the tank like a rag doll or a dead weight.

Her devastated body is destroyed a short time later by a sniper firing from an enemy helicopter, a coup-de-grace that comes just after she has merged with the Puppet Master. In the moment before the final bullet strikes, the merged major/Puppet Master hybrid sees the black avian helicopter overhead transformed into the image of a hovering angel. Oshii says angels represent "what lies on the other side" of technological evolution.[44] Here the Christian image pairs with a Biblical quote from 1 Corinthians that the Puppet Master cites earlier in the film: "For now we see through a glass, darkly; but then face to face."

At one level, both the image and the verse suggest a rebirth or evolution that transcends the weighty physical body, a floating, disembodied existence on the net. Haraway fears that narratives of technological and religious transcendence are a way of evading our concrete social responsibilities here and now—"a way of participating in the God trick. A way of denying mortality."[45] But a compelling and interesting feminist reading of *Ghost in the Shell* must consider the formal reasons that the violence of anime, like that of the puppet theater, is so exaggerated and affectless at the same time: it is precisely because the major's body is both less and more immediate or "lovable" than the human body. In the face of what Barthes called the "sensuous abstraction" of the puppet, the treatment of the figure becomes, in Barrault's words, both "indulgent and severe."[46]

This suggests that the play of heavy and light in the anime's climax can be read as more than simply a careless desire to cast off the weighty body through transcendence. The major's lightness signifies a more complex combination of fragility, mobility, and unreality. She is "light" in more ways than one, since she is finally just an image drawn on celluloid (on an anime cel, on a reel of film). At one point in the film Oshii makes this connection by having Batō refer to the cyborgs' plastic bodies as "celluloid dolls" (*seruroido ningyō*). Luminescent and evanescent, Kusanagi is subject to any manipulation. Her body may be treated lightly. But we also realize that her image never had a body behind it.

Virtual Journeys and Final Destinations: The *Michiyuki* and *Ghost in the Shell*

While Sontag sees the light or heavy body as an indicator of the puppet's vulnerability or fate, we have already seen that Claudel and Sakai shift attention to the idea of the self or soul as text. If the puppet's soul is a soul of language, in what sense are the major's death and rebirth not bodily experiences but acts of writing or rewriting her soul or fate? In Chikamatsu's love suicide plays, this act of self-authoring or self-narration comes in a part of the play called the *michiyuki*. This is the segment that precedes the concluding suicides and shows the lovers traveling to their place of death. The *michiyuki* is an emblem of death's transformation but also its unreality, a poetic passage that describes each station on the lovers' journey in a highly metaphoric way. While Chikamatsu's texts are characterized throughout by wordplay, allusive language, and creative ambiguity about whose voice is sounding at any given time, the *michiyuki* represents the climax of these literary fireworks. Yūda Yoshio writes that these sections were often regarded as separate parts of the performance, where the plot faded into the background and the skill of the performers came to the fore. Other critics have argued that the *michiyuki* represents the verbal rehearsal of the lovers' death and rebirth or redemption.[47] Together, these facts suggest that the *michiyuki* can highlight the performed aspect of the death scene and the role language plays in the lovers' transformation, expressing their power to author their own story or history even as they submit to their fate. In the *michiyuki* of *Shinjū kasaneizutsu* (Love suicides at the sunken well, 1707), the two lovers even pass through the theater district and imagine (or perceive) themselves on stage, the hero and heroine of their own drama.[48]

Classical Japanese dramatic theory describes the *michiyuki* in terms of a three-part dramatic structure, indicated by the Japanese terms "*jo*," "*ha*," and "*kyū*" (roughly "introduction," "break," and "acceleration"). This structure repeats itself several times in the course of a play; if the *ha* segment is a dramatic break or peak in the action, the *michiyuki* is an example of a *kyū* section—a quick, entertaining denouement that follows that break. Stevie Suan argues that anime has the same *jo–ha–kyū* structure: for example, a scene may begin by introducing its characters, then build toward a twist or conflict, and finally resolve it in an exciting way, then reset with the introduction to the next scene. Suan associates anime's *kyū* segments with a climax in artistry—a sense of "spectacle" or "aesthetic display" that works like the *michiyuki* to break us momentarily out of the drama, before the next *jo* segment introduces us back into the story. Suan identifies this movement back and forth between tension and release as a "push-pull" structure, similar to the oscillation I've identified between immersion and distance.[49]

The final union in *Ghost in the Shell* is preceded by a section analogous to the *michiyuki*, in which the Puppet Master explains his proposed union to the major. In an ambiguous voice that sounds like the Puppet Master but issues from Kusanagi's mouth, it leads her on a figurative walk through time, arguing for a version of evolutionary history in which humans and machines are virtually indistinguishable. Sandwiched between action scenes, the long monologue and its static visuals might seem like one more flip-flop in the anime's alternation between word and image, or body and voice.[50] But through analogy with the puppet theater, we can regard the words of the Puppet Master (itself a piece of code, a being of language) as a kind of *michiyuki*, highlighting the power of words alone to bring about the pair's transformation. A moment after the Puppet Master finishes describing this union with Kusanagi, it is accomplished. Its speech has rewritten them both.

In *Ghost in the Shell*, the *michiyuki* and "lovers' suicide" are followed by a concluding scene that finally resolves this back and forth between word and image or body and voice. Kusanagi wakes up in Batō's safe house. After her brain survives the sniper attack seemingly by chance, Batō rescues it and transplants it into a new chassis, but the only thing he can find on short notice is a cyborg body with the shape and voice of a little girl. The newly young body that represents Kusanagi's rebirth is again subject to a double reading: her escape from her playboy proportions might signify an escape from imposed gender categories, or the doll-like body of the little girl could be seen as a tamed, infantilized version of the female subject.

For help in choosing between these two alternatives, consider one final time the two elements highlighted in our readings of the puppet theater, voice and weight. At first, the new Kusanagi speaks in the high-pitched voice of her child body. But when Batō asks her what is left of the original Kusanagi, she answers in her familiar husky alto. She is neither Kusanagi nor the Puppet Master, but some combination of the two, alive both in body and on the net. Barthes and others saw the puppets' shared voice as a sign of the decentered self, but Kusanagi is able to regain her old voice, seemingly gathering it up again from across the net. Her face is also virtually lit in such a way that it appears passive and mask-like at the beginning of the scene, and gradually becomes more human and more like her old face. But it is the voice more than anything that signals a retention of her old self and a bodily wholeness, while the power to change voices shows she can find herself in new places or transform herself in new ways. In this new (old) voice, she recites more of the Biblical passage that we heard earlier in the film: "When I was a child, I spake as a child . . . but when I grew up, I put away childish things." In this verse from 1 Corinthians that equates selfhood with speech, the Japanese translation is inclusive; where many English Bibles have "when I became a man," Kusanagi says "*hito to narite*": "when I became an adult" or even "when I became human."

The dynamic of weight and weightlessness is also transformed in this final scene, as Kusanagi finally achieves the freedom signified by lightness without the vulnerability, the ephemerality, or the rejection of the body that comes with it in the rest of the film. When she has finished her speech to Batō, she goes outside the house and stands on a cliff overlooking the city. The city looks like it did in the film's opening sequence, when we saw her falling and blending into the pattern of city streets. But in this final scene, instead of fading into the urban network, she remains silhouetted against it. Instead of being blown away or falling victim to forces around her, she now stands firmly at the head of them, transcendent but grounded as well.

If Kusanagi is a puppet whose voice, weight, and story reflect a division between unified and decentered subjectivity, or fate and freedom, then this final scene also represents her as an independent subject—independent in the sense of being both sufficient and free. She is whole, but she retains an openness that allows her to define herself. But because the film's conclusion provides an optimistic sense of closure precisely by leaving Kusanagi's character open, there remains a lingering sense of suspense or anticipation around the question of what she will make of herself. Nine years later Oshii provided a kind of answer, in a sequel that picks up where the first story left off, in the body of a child.

Ghost in the Shell 2: Innocence

Set some time after the first film, *Ghost in the Shell 2: Innocence* (*Inosensu*, 2004) follows Kusanagi's old partners Batō and Togusa. (Kusanagi herself has disappeared, leaving Batō to wonder if there is anything like her old self still wandering the city or the net.) The two detectives are attempting to solve a series of murders committed by female androids, called "gynoids." These are not cyborg amalgams of human and machine but robots made to resemble humans. The gynoids' electronic brains lack the "ghosts" that mark human personalities, but a company named Locus Solus has developed an advanced "Hadaly" model that acts virtually human, even in the bedroom, allowing the Hadalys to serve their owners as sexual surrogates. When the Hadaly gynoids begin malfunctioning and killing their unsavory masters, Batō and Togusa are assigned to investigate.

Eventually Batō discovers that Locus Solus has been illegally copying or "ghost dubbing" the minds of kidnapped girls into the brains of the androids. This is what makes them seem so human, but the process eventually kills the children. The murders were caused by a programmer at Locus Solus who attempted to put a stop to the ghost dubbing by rewriting the gynoid safety protocols that prevent them from harming their owners. His hope was that the resulting violent incidents would bring authorities to investigate, that the ghost dubbing would be discovered, and that the girls would be rescued.

Who exactly is "innocent" in *Innocence*? It is not the children. Oshii leaves open the question of whether the captive girls, the programmer, or the gynoids themselves initiate the violence, but in any case the little girl that Batō rescues at the end of the film has no concern for the gynoids' victims. "What was I supposed to do?" she cries "I didn't want to become a doll!" In response, Batō suggests angrily that the real victims are the gynoid dolls who never asked to become human. This connects to a conversation earlier in the film, between Togusa, Batō, and a forensic scientist who examines the rogue gynoids. She argues that the distinction between human and nonhuman is arbitrary, and as evidence she offers the example of children: "If by person we mean someone with a completely formed ego who acts in accordance with their own will, then children are conventionally excluded." Children, the scientist argues, are no more or less human than the dolls they play with. When Togusa asks the scientist her name, she replies: "Haraway."[51]

As this suggests, *Innocence* extends the ideas of Oshii's earlier films but also transforms them. A full discussion of this complex film would require an additional chapter, so I will leave it to the reader to discover and interpret the ways in which the tropes of the first film are developed in the second. But here I will offer a brief reading of *Innocence* to bring some broad issues from the last two chapters into focus.

The first *Ghost in the Shell* film suggested that as human as Kusanagi seems, she is in fact a kind of doll, and it communicated that idea by making her animated mechanical body seem both more and less than a real person. The second film blurs the same lines between human and nonhuman, but now by suggesting that as artificial as the gynoids look, they are alive by any reasonable definition of life. The gynoids in *Innocence* lack truly human bodies. They are inevitably seen in damaged or incomplete states— their faces expressionless, their movements a combination of awkward lurching motions and weirdly balletic martial arts, their skins removed or their bodies disassembled to reveal strangely proportioned skeletons modeled on ball-jointed mannequins (Figure 26).

Innocence thus abandons the earlier film's oscillation between the reality and the unreality of the visible female body, making the

FIGURE 26. In *Innocence,* the bodies of the gynoids are portrayed as awkward, damaged, or grotesque. (See also Figure 27.) All *Innocence* stills are from the Funimation Blu-ray disc (2017).

bodies portrayed in the film wholly artificial; instead it turns toward an oscillation between the physical body and the electronic network. Like *Patlabor 2*, *Innocence* moves back and forth between an immediate physical view that represents one world, and a digital overlay of information that represents another. But in *Patlabor 2*'s media critique, the network was essentially a foil for the real bodies of the human characters. In contrast, *Innocence* suggests that the characters' humanity (their realness) resides not inside their bodies but in the outer network of signals and language that they inhabit. For example, in the course of the film we learn that Kusanagi is now a powerful but wholly disembodied consciousness, floating in the net. Near the end of the film, she appropriates a body in order to fight by Batō's side, but to do so she has to download a fragment of herself temporarily into one of the gynoids and manipulate it awkwardly, like a puppet. The gynoid's face and mouth remain motionless, even when Kusanagi speaks, but Kusanagi is still compelling for the sound of her disembodied voice. "The emotions in the film are intense," summarizes Sharalyn Orbaugh, "but they do not show on the surface of bodies; they are always outside any enclosed, autonomous subject, always moving, transferable."[52]

In other words, as *Innocence* oscillates between the physical world and the network, both seem to have equal weight or reality. The clearest and cleverest example comes in the climax. Aided by the gynoid puppet under Kusanagi's control, Batō invades Locus Solus's production facility, where the two of them battle an army of rogue gynoids. The heroes fight their way to a locked computer access terminal, which Kusanagi pulls open, tearing off her gynoid puppet's arm in the process. Then she connects to the facility's network and begins to hack their system. The action that follows alternates between Batō, holding off the gynoids with the last of his ammunition, and abstract images of the code Kusanagi is running within the Locus Solus system in an effort to shut down the gynoids before Batō and her borrowed body are overrun. The code is represented only as a series of moving colored bars in a three-dimensional display, but the changing patterns manage to convey clearly the idea that Kusanagi's code is writing over and taking

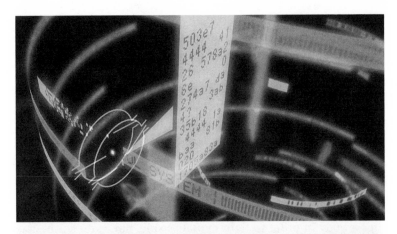

FIGURE 27. In the climax of *Innocence,* Oshii uses abstract graphics to portray a war of code as Kusanagi hacks the Locus Solus computer. Meanwhile Batō fights a more concrete battle against the gynoids. At left in the second figure is Kusanagi, trapped in the limited, expressionless body of a gynoid she controls as a puppet.

over the enemy system. In a visual feat, Oshii manages to make this depiction of competing computer language as suspenseful in its own way as the juxtaposed scenes of Batō's pitched physical battle with the gynoids (Figure 27).

In *Innocence,* the ubiquity and solidity of the network (and the idea that our true selves reside there) bring with them a sense that the network cannot be escaped. For example, the opening scene of the first *Ghost in the Shell* film brought us out of the network into a physical world, transitioning visually and aurally from an electronic representation of the city to an unmediated view. But *Innocence* reverses that: a shot of a surveillance helicopter above the city cuts to a digital representation of the city, and then to the interior of Batō's car weaving through city streets, with that same digital map of the city displayed inside the car. When Batō gets out to investigate a crime scene (the latest gynoid rampage), we may feel we are finally and firmly in the physical world, but then Oshii switches to a point-of-view shot through Batō's cyborg eyes, and we watch as digital information about his surroundings superimposes itself repeatedly on his (on our) vision. The same effect is repeated periodically throughout the film.

Patlabor 2 exhibited this same oscillation between the electronic and the unmediated view, but as the previous chapter argued, the two are juxtaposed in such a way that we may believe the mediation can be stripped away. The unmediated view may be constantly interrupted, but it remains an anchor, an option. This led to a paradox in that *Patlabor 2*'s supposedly unmediated views (faces, bodies, and particularly landscapes) were also animated, a part of the simulation of the anime itself. But this is an irony that *Patlabor 2* did not encourage the viewer to dwell upon. In fact, it actively disguised the irony by using animation to simulate the view from a physical camera. The first *Ghost in the Shell* film introduces a change: the simultaneous realism and unrealism of Kusanagi's body moves our attention back and forth between immersion and distance in a way that makes us conscious of the mediation and artificiality of the film itself—just as the bodies of the puppet move us back and forth between a concern for character and consideration of the medium we are watching. In *Innocence*, Oshii takes this development one step further, accomplishing this oscillation not with the major's animated body but with the entire look and structure of the film—what we might call the anime's own body.

How does *Innocence* accomplish this? This anime calls attention to its own performance in several different ways, but all of them boil down to gestures that remind us of the work of the filmmakers (the puppeteers). One of the most effective is the use of computer animation, which is so obvious, even ostentatious, that it constantly draws our attention to the film's visual surface and its construction, reminding us of the electronic filter that is the anime itself. In the opening scene described above, when Batō gets out of his car, we are just about to relax into the story and the world of the film's diegesis when we see a moving pattern of neon reflected in the hood and windshield of the car, a piece of digital animation so intricate that it draws our attention back to the film's creators or the process of creation (Figure 28). This is the same dynamic we feel in the most virtuosic moments of the puppet theater, when the skill of the puppeteer causes us to believe in the illusion at one moment and then in the next moment ask, "how did they do that?"[53]

There is an equivalent gesture in the dialogue, much of which consists of direct quotations or close paraphrases from literary texts, a gesture that calls attention to the anime's textuality. Characters repeat verbatim language from Plato, Confucius, Buddha, and the Bible; a range of French literature and philosophy; Japanese poetry and prose from the seventeenth to the twentieth centuries; plus Milton, Gogol, Max Weber, and others. Oshii said in an interview "When lines of the dialogue are severed from the plot, they become details within the film. Ideally I would have liked to

FIGURE 28. In this scene from *Innocence*, the complex moving reflections on the hood and windshield of Batō's car call our attention to the film's virtuosic computer graphics in a way that lifts us momentarily out of the story.

construct the dialogue completely from quoted material."[54] These quotations sound like anything but natural dialogue, and they appear in quotation marks in the subtitles, but the characters recite them without attribution, making it unclear whether the characters know that their own language is woven from other texts. Steven Brown argues that this expresses the intertextuality of the subject itself, which "becomes a tissue of citations"; but he also notes that Oshii's citations, like the puppet chanter, call attention to "the ventriloquism of the director or screenplay writers" and "the performative aspect of anime itself."[55]

Finally, *Innocence* performs the same trick with the plot, by calling attention to the constructedness of the story. A key element of the plot is the idea that because the characters' cyber-brains are connected to the network, they can be reprogrammed with visual and sensory hallucinations. More than once during the film, the action is interrupted and we are informed that scenes we've just been watching are actually false images planted in the brains of a specific character: we the viewers have been trapped in their viewpoint and their delusions. With this, more than anything, Oshii reminds us that we are always trapped behind the filter of the film itself. In the most elaborate such sequence, Batō and Togusa visit a hacker named Kim in his fantastic mansion, and instead of moving forward, the film keeps returning to the moment when they enter the building, repeating the same dialogue and actions until finally Batō realizes their brains are being hacked by Kim and breaks himself (and us) out of the illusory loop. The mansion features some of the most elaborate graphics in the film, surreal objects and images digitally rendered with hallucinogenic vividness. The conceit is that the mansion itself is a giant *karakuri* or moving machine, like a doll or a music box; but the mansion is also a metaphor for the anime itself, a virtual reality labyrinth that Oshii moves us through according to his own whims.

One might object that eventually the film ends, and we leave the theater, or turn off the DVD player. But consider the ways that *Innocence* repeats specific sequences from the first *Ghost in the Shell* film—the helicopter in the opening scene, the moment when Kusanagi tears off her arm, or any of several other winking repetitions. This is the same trick Oshii pulled off with *Patlabor 2* and its live-action simulacrum, *Gray Ghost*. Taken together, Oshii's films mirror the structure of Kim's mansion: the audience escapes one dream only to fall into another.

In *Innocence*, these three uncanny motifs of the dream, the puppet, and the child are linked in a way that Freud might have predicted. They all speak to our anxieties about control, when our puppets or our dreaming children come alive like the gynoids or come awake like the ghost-dubbed little girl and overthrow us. At the same time, our anxieties of powerlessness manifest themselves in a fear of returning to childlike helplessness or being reduced to a puppet ourselves, a fear that we are trapped in a dream or an illusion from which we cannot escape. In the context of popular-culture criticism, the hallucination we cannot exit may ultimately be popular culture itself. So it is not surprising that puppets, unending dreams, and dreaming children are motifs that transcend *Innocence* and appear in a wide range of other anime. We will see some examples in the chapters that follow.

4

The Forgetful Phallus and the Otaku's Third Eye

3x3 Eyes and Anime's Audience

The last chapter referred in passing to a scene from the puppet play *Hidakagawa iriaizakura*, in which a spurned woman pursues a monk who has rejected her advances. She chases him as far as the banks of the Hidaka River only to find that he has escaped to the opposite shore. With no way to cross, she flings herself into the water, where her rage and passion transform her into a giant serpent capable of swimming the river and continuing the chase.

The story is derived from the legend of the Dōjōji temple, a medieval tale that has been adapted over and over for popular visual media, from early picture scrolls to a sixteenth-century nō play, eighteenth-century puppet and kabuki theater, and even a virtuosic stop-motion animation version by Kawamoto Kihachirō. No matter the medium, the woman's climactic transformation is always portrayed with impressive visual effects. In the puppet theater, for example, the movements of the swimming puppet slowly become more serpentine as the transformation progresses, while the trick puppet head used for the role sprouts horns and fangs.[1] The scene inevitably draws applause from the audience, but what are they cheering? Are they rooting for the man, hoping for his narrow escape? Or are they applauding the woman's hidden power and frantic determination, which supernaturally transcend the social restrictions imposed on her and allow her to take revenge? Or finally, are they clapping for the visual effects that seem to push story and character momentarily into the background, the dynamic associated with puppet theater and anime in the previous chapter?

Anime is filled with similar figures and similar dynamics, often in the form of cute young girls who transform into powerful demons or mighty warriors when betrayed or threatened. A number of critics have suggested that these split figures represent the sexual fantasies and anxieties of their largely adolescent audience, a conclusion that might be bolstered by the snakes, demonic worms, and other phallic transformations in the Dōjōji legend and its popular descendants. But the question posed above—what is the audience cheering?—should direct our attention once again to the complex ways these figures or performances are received by the spectator. As a popular medium, anime is sometimes regarded as a reflection of social attitudes and anxieties about things like gender roles, or as part of a popular discourse that reinforces those attitudes. Likewise, anime's consumers are sometimes regarded as its victims, lured into these attitudes and ideas by the force of the media. Like the previous chapter, this one turns partly on the motif of the puppet, but this time as a figure not only for the animated actors (both more and less than real) but also for the spectator or consumer, who is invited to identify with the puppet as a figure that does not belong entirely to itself, a figure caught and manipulated by the text. We can thus revisit the question that the Introduction posed about *Read or Die*: does anime sometimes reflect viewers' anxiety about becoming lost in the fictional worlds of anime itself, and can we read ourselves out of that dilemma? If previous chapters compared anime with other media, the implicit comparison of this chapter is between anime and the possibility or impossibility of *unmediated* experience—the experience of a reality apart from media or before it.

Some of the theories that have addressed this most explicitly are theoretical descriptions of anime fans, or "otaku," and these are the other focus of this chapter. In answer to the question, "what is the audience cheering for?" some of these theories insist that the audience itself does not know: that the cute girls who transform into menacing demons reflect subconscious anxieties about sexual authority or sexual performance, for example. But I will argue that ultimately these transformations permit the audience to see itself, which allows these series to suggest or carry out a surprisingly layered interrogation of the way anime is received.

This ability to see or consider oneself in the act of looking is the perspective I associate with a "third eye," a motif that appears both figuratively and literally in the anime discussed below.

The issues of gender and power introduced in chapter 3 are taken up here in a new context: *Vampire Princess Miyu* (*Vanpaia Miyu*, 1988–89) and *3x3 Eyes* (written the same way in Japanese and pronounced "*Sazan aizu*," 1991–92 and 1995–96). Both of these are short OVA horror series by directors who specialize in weekly television anime and direct-to-video series. If the goal is to talk about anime audiences, it seems wise to balance art house films by auteur directors like Ōtomo and Oshii with some titles that are closer to the weekly mainstream of television broadcast anime. These early, relatively low-budget titles certainly can't equal *Innocence* or even *Read or Die* in terms of their visual sophistication. On the other hand, *3x3 Eyes* has an intricate plot that unfolds in seven episodes released over several years. Even more interesting than the story is the way the story is structured, particularly the rhythm the series develops between and within episodes.

The Otaku's Third Eye

In an early survey of transforming female bodies across a range of anime genres (from comedy to horror and pornography), Susan Napier argues that there is something liberated or liberatory about these strong female images, a reflection of women's growing power in Japanese society; but at the same time, she sees anxiety about these changes reflected as well, and notes that many anime series try to reign in these powerful female figures in the end: the evil ones are killed, while the "good" ones eventually transform back into nurturing mothers, harmless little girls, or helpless victims.

One of Napier's most interesting examples is *Wicked City* (*Yōjū toshi*, 1987), a sexually explicit anime horror film by Kawajiri Yoshiaki, who brings a brilliant sense of graphic design to popular and even schlock genres. *Wicked City* concerns a pair of supernatural security agents, the suave human Taki Reizaburō and his beautiful demon partner Makie, who team up to protect the world from rogue devils. The latter include some striking female demons with weaponized sexualities, including a beautiful hostess who transforms into a giant spider during sex with Taki and nearly emasculates him with a toothed vagina (Figure 29). Another demon has a chest that opens into a giant vulva and engulfs Taki whole. Napier notes that these powerful female bodies are juxtaposed with weak male figures who, like the fleeing monk in the Dōjōji legend, seem bewildered or overwhelmed by women's potent sexuality. "Women's bodies in these scenes are clearly powerful," writes Napier. "These anime depict the female body as being in touch with intense, even magical, forces capable of overwhelming male-dominated reality." But for Napier this is undercut by the fact that the strong women turn out to be evil, while the good ones turn out to be weak: originally powerful and threatening, Makie must eventually be rescued, married, and impregnated by Taki as the fulfillment of an ancient pact that promises to unite humanity and demonkind. "*Wicked City* thus uses the image of female metamorphosis to inscribe itself back into the patriarchal order," Napier concludes. "The collectivity is threatened by a series of fantastic others, but ultimately order is restored by the reassuring image of Makie's beautiful body serving its most traditional function."[2]

Some critics have invoked readings that resemble Napier's to argue that anime horror reflects a "male fear of women's sexual power," while others have linked this with a widely held stereotype of anime otaku as immature male viewers with limited social skills, boys who prefer the simplicity of fictional fantasy girlfriends to the complications of real-live women.[3] Napier herself does not draw too many conclusions about the psychology of the individual viewer—she prefers to address gender anxiety at a more abstract social level. But she does reference the work of Barbara Creed, a psychoanalytic critic who interprets American horror films at the level of individual psychologies and neuroses.

For example, Creed notes that many of the "monstrous-feminine" images in Hollywood horror films are female characters that castrate their male victims. Creed begins from Freud's account of the male Oedipus complex, in which the adolescent boy sees himself in competition with the father for the mother's affection, until the threat of discipline (perceived as the threat of castration) convinces the son to bow to the father's sexual authority. If the father represents the castrator, the child perceives the

FIGURE 29. *Wicked City* features a series of female demons with supernatural sexual powers. Here Taki's beautiful bedmate transforms into a spider woman who nearly emasculates him. From the Urban Vision special edition DVD (2000).

mother as castrated herself. Post-Freudian psychoanalysis might refigure castration anxiety less as a fear of literal dismemberment and more as a figurative encounter with authority, but to one degree or another that authority remains in the father's hands, and the woman is subjected to it. But Creed inverts Freud's argument, contending that in the subconscious it is often the woman who occupies the role of castrator and possesses authority, sometimes figured in horror films by the vagina dentata—a toothed vagina like the one that appears in *Wicked City*. For Creed, the female castrator usurps male prerogatives and also cuts off the source of male authority at its root, in some sense overturning the gendered system of psychoanalysis itself.

Interpretations like these have been pathbreaking for the way they stake out possibilities of reading these popular genres of anime and horror. But some of these readings also seem caught in the same dilemma as the audience for the Dōjōji drama: one is never quite sure whether to cheer for these feminine monsters, who are both powerful and debased. On the one hand they are distortions of the feminine created from male fear and prejudice, distortions that seem to perpetuate those prejudices as they propagate through the mass media. On the other hand, the violence perpetrated by these monstrous females also wreaks a satisfyingly cathartic revenge on the male social or psychoanalytic order that created them.

Why do these readings remain so divided or ambivalent? I think one reason is that they see the films as operating largely undetected on an audience that consumes them uncritically. By arguing that these films work out subconscious anxieties, these readings suggest that the films' spectators are apt to confuse their own feelings toward real women with the fantasies on screen: viewers supposedly respond to images of the monstrous feminine because they fear that women are indeed monstrous, and after seeing these images repeated they begin to believe their own worst fears. In these kinds of readings anime certainly does not encourage any deep examination of these fantasies (except perhaps when it is read by the critic). Anime simply manipulates its viewers like puppets.

It is true that some anime represent the fears and anxieties of adolescent male viewers in a way that seems embarrassingly clear, but as I have been arguing throughout this book, some of the most interesting anime have an ability to call the viewer's attention continually back to the particular qualities of the representation itself, and to the ways that it is rarely transparent. Given that, it should be possible to find in some of these anime an interrogation of how these monstrous fantasies are constructed to begin with, and what it means to have these fantasies. From there we might posit that some of the films' viewers are deliberately working through these issues—including the issue of their own manipulation by the text and media at large. This will lead us in turn to theories of fandom that define otaku not as fans who are trapped in fiction by their inability to distinguish it from reality, but as just the reverse: critically minded fans who have the ability to step back and consider anime's effect on themselves.

Napier considers this in an appendix to the readings discussed above, where she suggests that, for Western fans at least, there is indeed a "heightened self-consciousness to watching anime," enabled by a sense of distance that comes from these fantastic genres, from Western fans' position outside Japanese culture, and from the gap between animation and live action. Napier calls this higher critical perspective the "fifth look," contrasting it with the look of the actor, the look of the camera, the spectator's look at the screen, and Paul Willemen's fourth look, grounded in psychoanalytic film theory, wherein the spectator engaged in voyeuristic looking becomes uncomfortably aware that there is another, more abstract or anonymous gaze directed at himself.[4] Taking my cue from these critics, I would like to propose something similar, perhaps somewhere between Napier's optimistic and broadly defined fifth look, and Willemen's more specifically and negatively framed fourth.[5] Borrowing from a titular and visual motif in the anime that is the focus of this chapter, I will label this critical perspective "the otaku's third eye."

In Hindu and Buddhist philosophy and iconography, the third eye (often portrayed in the center of the forehead) is a motif that signifies a broadened or transcendent perspective. I use it here to suggest something analogous: an awareness or consciousness that is not focused on the television or film screen, but that allows the spectator to stand apart from him or herself and consider that self in the act of watching. Earlier chapters identified an oscillation between immersion in a work and a critical perspective that could step back and ask how the formal language of anime produces meaning. This chapter asks if we can take a further step back and ask how anime shapes our own psychology, and vice versa. Can certain anime promote that kind of self-conscious viewing, where we can look at ourselves?

To address this I would like to examine the motifs of manipulation and fantasy in some short series, *3x3 Eyes* and *Vampire Princess Miyu*. Both feature teenage heroines who alternate between schoolgirl cuteness and demonic strength, as well as male characters who transform inversely, going from heroes who pursue or rescue the apparently weak heroines to sexually inexperienced adolescents who are baffled by the transformed women's physical and sexual power. And yet, on top of these transparent fantasies and wish fulfillments (things calculated to manipulate adolescent male and female viewers and consumers), these films also have elements that foreground representation and wish fulfillment itself. These include dream demons who wrap their subjects in empty fantasies, enemies in the guise of puppets and puppeteers, and even an authorial demon who imprisons his targets within a book. Finally, the split female characters can be read using theories of the otaku that go beyond Freud, refiguring psychoanalytic notions like castration anxiety in ways that regain some measure of authority for the women characters and the viewer.

A First Look at *3x3 Eyes*

Based on the early volumes of a long-running manga series by Takada Yūzō, the anime version of *3x3 Eyes* consists of two OVA series released directly to video. The initial series consisted of four episodes released from 1991 to 1992 (titled simply *3x3 Eyes* in Japanese, released as *3x3 Eyes: Immortals* in English). The second series was *3x3 Eyes: Legend of the Divine Demon* (*3x3 Eyes: Seima densetsu*), with three episodes released in 1995 and 1996. The first series was directed by Nishio Daisuke, known for directing various installments of the *Dragon Ball* franchise, and the second by Takenouchi Kazuhisa. The early episodes introduce the characters: a Japanese high school student named Fujii Yakumo and a three-hundred-year-old supernatural creature from Tibet who appears in the guise of a teenage girl named Pai. Pai is the appealing schoolgirl common to anime, innocently cute and naïvely cheerful. But in times of danger, a third eye opens on her forehead and she awakens to her true (or alternate) identity as a demon goddess called Sanjiyan. Pai seems to have only a dim awareness or interest in her other side, which is for all intents a separate personality. Besides a deeper, more masculine voice and fearsome psychic powers, Sanjiyan also has a cruel streak and a dismissive scorn for humans, though she remains a force for good in the supernatural battles that follow (Figure 30).

Yakumo is transformed into Pai's "Wu" (or Ū), a minion and guardian who remains unkillable as long as Pai lives. Yakumo thus gains a dual personality to match the heroine's, and shifts awkwardly between being bodyguard to the violent Sanjiyan and carrying on a halting teenage courtship with the innocent Pai.

FIGURE 30. In *3x3 Eyes,* the innocent teenage girl Pai periodically transforms into the fearsome supernatural creature Sanjiyan, though Pai herself seems unaware of this power. All *3x3 Eyes* stills are from the Pioneer collector's edition DVDs (2000).

3x3 Eyes is associated with a variety of anime sometimes called the "magical girlfriend" genre, and it combines a powerful female goddess with a passive childlike girl in just the way Napier describes. One can certainly see this in terms of adolescent anxiety that alternates between fantasies of empowerment and sexual uncertainty—what critics of these genres have seen as "representations of male sexual passivity . . . which are simultaneously seductive and terrifying" or the "graphic enactment of adolescent sexual anxiety and guilt."[6]

If we delve a little more deeply into the plot of *3x3 Eyes*, we find no shortage of elements that seem to reflect adolescent apprehensions about adult sexuality. As the first series opens, Yakumo is sixteen and has been abandoned by both parents. The absent father is an eccentric ethnologist who left Japan four years ago to travel to Tibet, where he discovered Pai/Sanjiyan, apparently the last of her race. The father vowed to find the supernatural artifact that would allow her to become human, but realizing he will die before he can fulfill his promise, he tells Pai to seek out Yakumo in Tokyo. Yakumo is called upon to replace his father as Pai's protector, but his masculine identity is continually in question. Pai finds him dressed in women's clothing, working as a host at a gay bar in Tokyo but also protesting that he is not gay. In fact, he quickly falls for Pai, but he is no match for her alternate personality Sanjiyan, who is depicted with the fangs that Barbara Creed identifies with the castrating vagina dentata. And Yakumo is continually called on to protect the girls and women of the series from an array of incredibly phallic demons against which he must measure himself and compete.

In the climax of the first series, for example, Yakumo enters a demonic temple to rescue a young girlfriend, Mei Shin, who is tied almost naked to a sacrificial altar and molested by a demon who possesses a barbed tale, an elongated ram-like skull, and a probing tongue several meters long. Forced into a sexual competition with this phallic father, Yakumo first cuts off its tongue and then stabs it in the skull (with a spear), but the demon pierces Yakumo's right arm with a tentacle that grants it control of the arm, whereupon it tries to force Yakumo to eviscerate the girl with a huge sword (Figure 31).

FIGURE 31. In *3x3 Eyes*, Yakumo's girlfriend Mei is captured and readied for a sexualized sacrifice at the hands of a lascivious demon. The sword that menaces her is held by Yakumo himself: the demon's phallic tail has penetrated Yakumo's arm and is now controlling it.

For a critic inclined toward Freudian readings, this scene presents such an embarrassment of riches that it is hard to know where to begin. It is tempting to invoke some version of Freud's male Oedipus complex, in which the son develops his own sense of sexuality and sexual guilt in terms of a phallic competition with the father, who (in the child's mind) possesses a penis and simultaneously threatens the son with castration. Eventually the child internalizes the father's authority as a kind of self-control and develops his own adult sexual identity. Today Freud's narratives of sexual development inevitably sound a little farfetched, but the Oedipal complex and castration anxiety are, more broadly and intuitively, just ways of expressing the individual's evolution from a close, almost indivisible relationship between mother and child to another stage: an awareness of links between sexual and anatomical difference and a recognition of the distinction between received family relationships and sexual ones that demand competition, initiative, and self-awareness.[7]

We need not stick slavishly to Freud here, but it is hard to avoid reading 3x3 Eyes along these general lines. There is a love plot running through the first series that involves Yakumo and Mei Shin, so the image of him standing over her naked bound form holding a sword, battling the demonic rapist but also confronting the fact that the demon is inside him, forcing him to impale her—it is virtually impossible not to see this as a combination of adolescent eagerness, anxiety, and guilt over sexual urges and sexual activity. As the scene continues, Yakumo cuts off his own demon-controlled right hand in order to prevent himself from stabbing the girl—internalizing or taking on the role of castrator as an exercise in self-control, exactly the way Freud predicts.[8] Later, however, Yakumo reclaims this phallus, using his regenerative powers to draw his severed hand across the room with the sword still in it, and then wielding the hand and blade telekinetically to kill the demon before reattaching the hand to his arm. With the Oedipal father slain and his masculinity reclaimed and controlled, Yakumo saves the day and goes home with the girl.

In fact, the phallic symbolism in this scene is so easy to read that one might ask if it does not produce a sense of irony, even parody—as if the director, animators, and complicit spectators were deliberately baiting their critics. Instead of waiting for critical analysis to expose the neuroses at the heart of this fantasy, are viewers perhaps taking a sardonic or open-eyed view of fantasy and sexual fantasy, including the way it is marketed and consumed, and the way they are constituted by it? If the first *3x3 Eyes* series raises these questions implicitly, the second series turns much more explicitly and ambitiously to questions of representation, fantasy, and manipulation, while these phallic figures get a distinctive new twist. But addressing questions about audience response requires not just a closer look at the anime but a closer look at the audience itself. So before turning back to *3x3 Eyes,* let's consider some theories of the otaku that support or refute this notion of a self-conscious, even self-critical audience.

The Serial Killer versus the Ota-King: Okada Toshio

In Japan, the word "otaku" canonically denotes male fans who have an obsessive interest and encyclopedic knowledge of anime or other hobby- or media-oriented subcultures. Like "geek" or "nerd," the connotations of the term vary widely. At the positive end of the spectrum are images of the otaku as charmingly shy but admirably earnest tastemakers at the cutting edge of popular or consumer culture. But the term is often used pejoratively in Japan to suggest not only an unhealthy interest in an unworthy subject but also a lack of social skills, a sexual immaturity, and a detachment from reality that prevents the otaku from participating in society and forming authentic relationships. In this stereotype, otaku are unable to form relationships with real women and have only virtual connections with cute characters—solitary, masturbatory activities that consist of things like watching these characters in anime, collecting them in the form of plastic models, or interacting virtually with them in computer games that simulate dating or sex.

In Japanese, "otaku" is originally a deferential second-person pronoun, "you." From its use among fans of popular media, it was eventually applied to those fans by others as a blanket term, with some of the pejorative connotations outlined above. The term entered the popular lexicon and took on its most negative associations following an infamous Japanese serial murder case in 1989. Four little girls ranging in age from four to seven were abducted, killed, and dismembered by a twenty-seven-year-old Tokyo man named Miyazaki Tsutomu. Using images from Miyazaki's bedroom that showed hundreds of videotapes and manga devoted to horror and little-girl themes, the media wove a single syndrome that linked his enthusiasm for these media, his social and physical isolation, and an amorality that seemed explicable only as a profound detachment from reality. Miyazaki was cast as the demonic transformation of the maladjusted otaku male.

However, around the turn of the millennium, the rising popularity of Japanese popular culture around the world was accompanied by a reexamination, rehabilitation, or even a romanticization of fandom's image. Anime audiences and marketers in Japan and beyond reclaimed the word "otaku" and spun it into something more positive or more social. At the same time, the distinct but overlapping world of female fans has gained more attention, and critics in Japan and the West have produced a range of nuanced studies of the audience for Japanese popular culture, from a range of disciplinary perspectives.[9] I will not attempt to summarize all that work here, but I would like to discuss three foundational Japanese theories of the otaku that turn on the tropes introduced above: psychology, sexuality, and eye or vision.

A pivotal figure in the evolution of this discourse is Okada Toshio, an anime producer turned cultural critic who at one point claimed for himself the position of public spokesman for otaku culture, or in his words "Ota-King" (otakingu). Okada was one of the founders of Gainax, the legendary anime studio that arguably grew out of otaku culture and in turn helped define it in the 1980s and 1990s. In the mid-1990s, he garnered attention for teaching a course on the otaku at prestigious Tokyo University and publishing *Otakugaku nyūmon* (Introduction to otakuology, 1996), a book that defines otaku by the visual skill or acumen they bring to reading popular media. "Otaku are a new species," Okada declares, "born in the twentieth century, a century of images, and they have an eye that demonstrates an incredibly evolved sensitivity to these images." Okada has his own version of "the otaku's 3 eyes" (*otaku no mitsu no me*), which he labels "an eye for style (*iki*)," "an eye for technique (*takumi*)," and "the eye of a connoisseur (*tsū*)." The first of these corresponds to an ability to distinguish and appreciate the formal visual styles of different creators—for example a familiarity with the distinctive visual trademarks of certain Hollywood directors, or an ability to see how the character designs in a given anime series change over time, under different lead animators. The "eye for technique" and the "eye of a connoisseur" constitute an understanding of the technical and behind-the-scenes processes involved in producing visual media, which allows the otaku to appreciate particular visual effects and even home in on tiny errors or inconsistencies that a casual viewer would overlook.[10]

Okada's otaku is a kind of critic, but one with a narrow agenda, concerned particularly with mechanical details surrounding the text's production. The interpretive ideal for Okada's otaku seems to be something like the "making of" documentaries or staff commentaries now included as DVD extras. On one hand, this approach to anime and manga suggests a metatextual perspective on anime's construction and consumption that involves stepping back from the text: Okada's otaku are not simply immersed in the fiction but are able to view it at a distance, and they can identify the kinds of specific details that might lead to interesting readings of a visual text.

And yet, the scheme of Okada's book seems to regard these backstage details as the goal or endpoint of the reading rather than the beginning. Knowing that 3x3 Eyes resembles the Dōjōji story may be interesting, but on its own it is little more than background information. What is genuinely interesting is to take this as a starting point for considering how these texts work in the world—how popular culture thinks through gender roles using tropes from fantasy and horror, for example. To bring this back to the oscillation we have been talking about throughout this book, oscillation alone is never enough; yet, the ability to move instinctively back and forth between the worlds inside and outside the text can help us to that next stage, a critical perspective that enables us to read and evaluate a work in a wider context.[11]

Saitō Tamaki's Beautiful Fighting Girls

For a portrait of otaku that invokes critical theory to construct a more complex model of reading and language than we find in

Okada, we can turn to Japanese psychiatrist and cultural critic Saitō Tamaki, who uses a psychoanalytic framework to argue that otaku are more sophisticated than other readers in their understanding of the blurry boundary between reality and representation in postmodern society.

In his canonical book *Beautiful Fighting Girl* (*Sentō bishōjo no seishin bunseki*, 2000), Saitō argues that the otaku's tendency to become lost in the world of the text is the product not of myopia but of an intuitive and ultimately savvy understanding of the ways that reality is always mediated, both by electronic media and by sensation and the psyche itself. It is this higher perspective that causes the otaku to "regard reality itself as a species of fantasy." "In that sense," says Saitō, "otaku are definitely not 'confusing fantasy and reality,' but neither do they place much importance on the opposition between the two. . . . This does not mean that they are swallowed up in the world of a text they love, but that they take a posture of open-eyed enthusiasm toward it."[12] Like Okada, Saitō identifies different layers of fictionality and metafictionality in anime and describes the otaku's ability to move back and forth between them.

> Manga and anime both contain multiple imaginary layers: the world depicted in the text, the personal circumstances of the author that the text may also describe, the backstage world of the work's production, and marketing questions of where it circulates and how it is received. When enjoying a work, the *otaku* takes pleasure in straddling all the levels of these layered contexts. Adapting a term from classical psychiatry, I call this "multiply oriented."[13]

"Multiply oriented" conventionally refers to delusional patients, but Saitō spins it positively here, to make his point that the multiple layers of fictionality in manga or anime are not so different from the layers of our everyday lived reality: we all take on different roles in different situations, and in some ways those roles multiply with the multiplication of media we use to interact. "From within our increasingly mediatized environment, it is already difficult to draw a clear line between reality and fiction," says Saitō. "It is no longer a matter of deciding whether we are seeing one or the other, but of judging which level of fiction something represents."[14] Saitō inherits a poststructuralist or postmodern suspicion of the effects of the mass media on language, and he sees otaku as intelligently parsing the different layers of language, without believing wholly in any one.

But at the same time that Saitō's otaku are savvy about slippery meanings, they manage to avoid nihilism—what Saitō characterizes as a destructive fantasy that nothing exists beyond information. Amid the shifting realities of postmodern society, otaku are grounded or anchored by their emotional investment in these fictional texts and particularly the "beautiful fighting girls" that feature in them. Saitō characterizes that investment very explicitly as a sexual one. What finally defines the otaku for Saitō is their sexual attraction to drawn characters, the ability to be aroused by anime. "It is *sex* that keeps resisting to the end the fictionalization and relativization brought on by the fantasies of an informationalized society," Saitō writes. "Sexuality has never been portrayed as a complete fiction, and it is unlikely that it ever will be." This is an extraordinary reversal of the discourse on otaku: while their sexual attraction to fictional characters formerly amounted to a disconnection from reality, now it is the rest of us who are cut off from reality and otaku who find a way back: anime's beautiful fighting girls reopen "a pathway to reality for people whose exposure to the media space has caused them to seclude themselves in the information fantasy."[15]

To more fully understand Saitō's argument (including the significance of the beautiful fighting girl and the parallels with anime like *3x3 Eyes*) it is helpful to understand his psychoanalytical framework, which draws heavily on the twentieth-century French psychoanalyst Jacques Lacan. Lacan reconfigured Freudian concepts like the Oedipus complex and castration anxiety so that they now referred not (or not only) to the development of sexuality and people as sexual subjects but to the development of language and people as subjects of language. When Saitō speaks about layers of fiction or reality, for example, he is working from Lacan's division of the human psyche into three parts—referred to as the Imaginary, the Symbolic, and the Real. Saitō summarizes:

The Symbolic is for the most part synonymous with the system of language. It is external to the subject and referred to as the "Other." That language is other to us means that it is a transcendental entity positioned outside the subject. . . . The Imaginary is the realm of images and representations, and . . . is located inside the subject. It is here that "meaning" and "experiences" are possible.[16]

As for the Real, it is what exists apart from the subject and language, meaning that it can never be accessed or experienced directly. What we think of as everyday reality is not the Real, but just what individuals in society choose to regard as our shared reality by consensus. ("It is the fiction that is shared most widely.") Likewise, the Imaginary realms of other people (their experience) is never directly accessible to us. In a relationship with another person, even or especially an intimate relationship, we may think that we know and love their inner essence, but that is an illusion or delusion—a situation Saitō sums up by quoting Lacan's provocative dictum "there is no sexual relation."[17]

It is in this context that Saitō suggests that a relationship with a fictional character is not dissimilar to a relationship with a real person: both involve the projection of our own experiences and emotions onto a blank slate. An otaku who senses this has become a kind of intuitive Lacanian (and in fact, Saitō repeatedly notes the overlap between otaku and psychiatrists). Saitō implies that the relationship with the fictional character might be productive and fulfilling in its own way, and that when the otaku goes on to relationships with actual women, he will have a more sophisticated sense of what a relationship is and isn't.

For Saitō, this explains the nature of beautiful fighting girls like Pai/Sanjiyan—their blank or confused identities, their lack of any clear internal motivation. While he does not give a reading of *3x3 Eyes,* he does mention it in his lineage of the beautiful fighting girl, and it is easy to see why: the heroine appears vacuously empty when she is Pai, only to become a complicated tangle of personalities when Sanjiyan takes the stage.[18] For Saitō, this is because such figures are designed as a blank slate onto which otaku can project their desires, or perhaps a kaleidoscope in which they pick out appealing patterns.

In psychoanalytic terms, Saitō says that characters like Pai/ Sanjiyan are "phallic girls," a term that reconfigures Freud's Oedipal complex and castration anxiety along Lacanian lines. As we've said, Freud emphasized that as the male child becomes conscious of his own sexuality, he learns socialization or self-control by internalizing what he perceives as the father's authority. If Freud's link between paternal sexual authority and the threat of castration seems exceedingly literal, Lacan makes it extremely abstract: the father is replaced by the "Name of the Father," a function associated with language, signification, and the Symbolic. Freud's penis is translated into Lacan's "phallus": an abstract multivalent symbol connected with authority (what the child thinks the father has), desire (what the child thinks the mother wants), and wholeness (what the child thinks he wants to possess). But just as language never expresses the Real and just as we never connect perfectly with another, the phallus is a symbol for an authority, a wholeness, or an object of desire that we can never obtain. By extension, it then becomes a symbol for that impossibility or lack itself. The lack of the phallus, "symbolic castration," is not just a child's fear but the state of all subjects once they pass out of infancy and enter the Symbolic Order by becoming individual, language-using subjects.[19]

In the realm of both meaning and sexuality, Saitō's phallic girl is a fantasy that becomes identified with this symbol of what we must desire but can never attain, which is why she lacks any firm grounding of her own. "In other words," says Saitō, "by being placed in a completely empty position she acquires the functions of a truly ideal phallus and drives the narrative forward on that basis. Our desire, moreover, is awakened by her emptiness."[20]

Earlier we said that a stock Freudian reading of *3x3 Eyes* might interpret its phallic imagery, rape imagery, castration imagery, etcetera more or less literally, as an expression of male fans' excitement, anxiety, and uncertainty about their own sexuality. Theories like Saitō's and Creed's do not necessarily negate that anxiety and uncertainty, but they do recast it as something much more self-aware. If the phallus is a symbol for representation itself, then Yakumo's struggle with the phallic demon for control of his own sword is ultimately a struggle for control of language—for control of how sexuality is represented or understood, including how we see and understand ourselves. The exaggerated quality of these scenes helps generate that ironic distance: in Saitō's formulation it is a way for otaku "to comically objectify the self that experiences this attraction," in order to put "distance between themselves and their own sexuality."[21]

By now the reader will have noticed that while Saitō characterizes the otaku's mode of reading as radically different, it resembles the combination of immersion and distance that I have been arguing we all experience to one degree or another. Saitō's idea that only a select few people can be aroused by drawn images seems highly suspect to me. (Japan has a vibrant tradition of woodblock print pornography that predates photography and film, for example.) But on the other hand, surely many of us who have watched sexually charged anime (that is, virtually any anime) have experienced a sense of disjunction in realizing that while the bodies definitely look less real, our feelings of arousal (or the feelings that are aroused) are little different than with live-action media.

So going beyond Saitō, I would suggest that just as violence against the anime body can feel both highly exaggerated and highly abstracted when compared with live action (as we saw in the previous chapter), eroticized anime bodies can feel simultaneously more and less present for many spectators, not just for a particular population of enthusiasts. I would like to use "otaku" not to indicate a separate group or even a separate way of reading but to describe a potential in any viewer and any viewing—the potential to have that third eye open as we become aware of the artifice or artificiality, and become able to see ourselves watching the text. This awareness can be genuinely productive (for considering how our ideas of gender are enmeshed with our systems of representation, for example), and it is an awareness that anime can provoke in many viewers. The idea of the otaku, then, is interesting to the degree that there is some otaku in all of us; true to its origins as a pronoun of address, the otaku is "you."[22]

Another Look at 3x3 Eyes

It turns out that we can indeed discover in 3x3 Eyes something that encourages the spectator to look at him or herself, particularly in the second of the two series, *3x3 Eyes: Legend of the Divine Demon*. Made four years after the first series, the story also picks up four years later, which encourages viewers to identify with Yakumo and his growth. The first series ends with a battle between Pai/Sanjiyan and her nemesis Beneres. The outcome of that battle is unclear, but Pai/Sanjiyan disappears, and Yakumo embarks on a search that takes him across Asia. When the second series opens, Yakumo is now twenty and still searching. Returning to Japan, he learns her whereabouts when he sees a picture of her in a sketchy magazine. This moment of self-referentiality is a clue that the second series will deal more explicitly with the issue of the audience's position and desire.

Pai/Sanjiyan's third eye has been sealed by an evil charm that takes the form of a scale-like covering on her forehead, robbing her of her memory and preventing Sanjiyan's emergence. She is now living as an ordinary high school girl and adopted daughter of a kindly old couple named Ayanokōji. "Ayanokōji Pai" has no knowledge of her origins or her true nature. The otaku viewer's stand-in Yakumo (more powerful and more mature than he was four years ago) is charged with jogging her memory and sorting out the different levels of reality and fantasy.

Saitō associates the beautiful fighting girl's open-ended fictionality with exactly this kind of blank past. She has no past memory or trauma that might serve as internal motivation, making her an open text. He also notes that anime and manga feature large numbers of simple characters, creating "a structure that resembles a patient with multiple personalities."[23] In *3x3 Eyes* we find several of these characters combined into one: Pai/Sanjiyan/Ayanokōji Pai. And eventually more personalities are revealed inside her: after her defeat in the battle that ends the first series, her enemy Beneres overlaid her personality with the personality of his snake servant Hōwasho (or Hōashiwo), hence the scaly shield that covers her third eye. The snake's identity was supposed to replace her own and take over her body. But because of the complicated combination of identities already present inside her, this overlay instead produced the schoolgirl personality of Ayanokōji Pai, who can remember neither her past as Pai/Sanjiyan, nor his(?) past as Hōwasho. Pai/Sanjiyan/Ayanokōji Pai/Hōwasho's final dilemma is whether to remember his or her real pasts and surrender the fictional ones, and in the process risk turning again from a little girl into a demon or an "ugly monstrous snake." (Ultimately she chooses to break the seal on her memory and discover "the truth" about herself, presumably which of her different personalities will finally prevail. But in fact, none of the personalities is any truer than the other, and in the final scene she has been further divided, split into two different bodies with two personalities each.)

This mixing of personalities and putative genders (girlish Pai, butch Sanjiyan, male Hōwasho) has the effect of confusing or relativizing the conventional gender identities and sexual anxieties seen in the first series—of making us stand back and question the original representations. Saitō's formulation for this flexible fictionality is that the beautiful fighting girl "becomes identified with the phallus," and we see this strikingly literalized here, as Pai/Sanjiyan/Ayanokōji Pai trades identities with the snake/phallus Hōwasho.[24]

In sum, Saitō helps us reach beyond oversimplified Freudian readings that see anime as a thinly veiled, nearly literal expression of sexual anxieties and instead appreciate it for the layered complexity of its visual and narrative language. Just as Lacan reconfigured Freud in the light of structuralism and phenomenology, Saitō's psychoanalysis of the otaku combines different bodies of theory that this book has examined so far: postmodern and posthuman theories about the ambiguity of language and the complexity of subjectivity in modern media society, phenomenological investigations of how the subject defines itself vis-à-vis other subjects at a fundamental psychological and perceptual level, and finally the feminist idea that genders are not finite natural categories but flexible identities that combine heterogeneous discursive elements.

Of course, in other ways Saitō's Lacanianism tends to reaffirm gender dichotomies and essentialisms: although the Lacanian phallus is not a penis, the act of signification that it represents does retain a male quality, and the fundamental blankness or lack that makes the beautiful fighting girl an ideal object of unattainable desire is feminine. Lacan helped redefine male and female genders as constructions unlinked from biological sex, but it is nevertheless the full "male" position that desires and signifies, the empty "feminine" one that is signified and desired. This is the Lacanian logic that Barbara Creed tries to overthrow with her focus on the vagina dentata and other feminine castrators: if castration establishes the Symbolic Order and the phallus represents it, the castrator usurps the paternal role (the role of instituting the system of signification) at the same time she defies it or cuts it off. Gender roles are explored further in chapter 5, in the theoretical work of Judith Butler and the anime of Kon Satoshi. Butler and Kon arguably replace the essentialism of psychoanalysis and the feminine stereotypes of genre film with the possibility of a more flexible gender that is performed.

Azuma Hiroki's Database Animals

A more pessimistic counterpoint to Saitō is Azuma Hiroki's theory of otaku as "database animals." Azuma is a philosopher and cultural theorist known for his work on poststructuralism, postmodernism, and popular culture. While Saitō suggested that the otaku's frank attraction to fictional subjects represents an intuitive understanding of the layered quality of all desire and all subjects, Azuma sees otaku desire as an unthinking, automatic response. Adapting Alexandre Kojève's notion of "animalization," Azuma argues that if human desire requires some negotiation or interaction with an Other, postmodern consumer society is characterized instead by animal needs that can be satisfied instantly, automatically, solitarily. Otaku interest and arousal are so mechanical that they can be triggered by stock female characters remixed from a database of visual tropes to which otaku have become programmed to respond—huge eyes, maid uniforms, cat ears, neon hair.[25]

Narrative now takes a back seat to character design. Here Azuma draws on Jean-François Lyotard's idea of the decline of grand narratives, introduced in chapter 1. Lyotard suggests that the universal "grand narratives" of civilization and progress that provided meaning in the eighteenth and nineteenth centuries have become more and more suspect, harder and harder to believe. Today they have been replaced by a series of more modest, more contingent "little narratives" that provide shape and meaning in limited or local contexts. Azuma argues that a decline of narrative in anime is part of this shift: Oshii Mamoru's progressive efforts to rewrite real-world political narratives, and even anime that constructed their own artificial worlds and histories (like the decades-long *Gundam* franchise), have now been supplanted by anime that exist less to tell a story than simply to display their characters.

For Azuma, the grand narrative has been replaced by the "grand nonnarrative" of the database, the only master text driving cultural production. Yet our attraction to a grand structure remains, manifesting itself in the otaku's desire to understand the database by categorizing all the possible combinations and permutations it can generate. Azuma devotes particular attention to computer games, especially the dating simulations called "novel games" *(noberu geemu)*, where players attempt to forge a virtual sexual relationship with one of several female characters. Otaku playing these games exist simultaneously in two different states, says Azuma. They suspend disbelief to experience the current play-through as their character's romantic fate or destiny, but at another level they realize that this is only one ending in the game database that they are trying to reconstruct (typically by playing the game multiple times to reach every possible scripted ending). Azuma writes:

> Modern individuals traced a path back from small narratives to a grand narrative. . . . However, postmodern individuals let the two levels, small narratives and a grand nonnarrative, coexist separately without necessarily connecting them. To put it more clearly, they learn the technique of living without connecting the deeply emotional experience of a work (a small narrative) to a worldview (a grand narrative). Borrowing from psychoanalysis, I call this schism *dissociative*.[26]

While Saitō or I might emphasize the sense of perspective in this two-layer structure—the ability to go back and forth between immersion in one narrative and an awareness of how different narratives are constructed—Azuma sees it negatively, as a kind of partial memory loss, dissociative schism, or even something like "multiple personality disorder."[27]

If my idea of "the otaku's third eye" was meant to suggest a higher perspective that lets one see oneself in the act of seeing, Azuma is skeptical that otaku can ever achieve this perspective. His own theory of the otaku's eye comes in an essay on Murakami Takashi's Superflat art—introduced in chapter 1 as an example of how a flat picture plane can suppress visual hierarchies (like distance and recession) in a way that might imply a loss of higher perspective. Azuma invokes Lacan to read Murakami's painting series *In the Deep DOB*. Each of these paintings is populated with multiple stretched and distorted images of a character whose body is covered with anime-like eyes. Azuma suggests that these multiple flattened eyes, seeming to look everywhere and nowhere, signify the multiple perspectives of the postmodern: potentially productive or creative but without any kind of order or hierarchy. The otaku's three eyes have become thirty or three hundred, seeing everything and nothing at once.[28]

Azuma's otaku experience one little narrative after another, caught between an act of forgetting that will let them start fresh with a new iteration, and an act of memory that might allow them to reconstruct the overall reality of the database. This is very similar to the situation of the characters and viewers of *3x3 Eyes*, which is characterized by this kind of repetition and forgetting at every level. Some of this is traceable simply to the formulaic quality of texts that Azuma associates with database culture. (In virtually every episode of *3x3 Eyes*, a domestic scene emphasizing teamwork and friendship is interrupted when Pai's demonic enemies catch up with her, forcing Yakumo to battle them. As Sanjiyan's Wu, Yakumo is also immortal, so the battles are gruesomely repetitive, with Yakumo repeatedly cut, crushed, and impaled, but never killed. Finally Sanjiyan awakens to kill the enemy, then everyone returns home to another domestic interlude, and the whole thing repeats.) But what is more interesting, particularly in connection with Azuma's diagnosis, is the extent to which this repetition is supported by the plot trope of amnesia.

Within each episode, the domestic interludes are sustained by the characters' implausible ability to forget the occult horrors they have been subjected to, sometimes just moments before, in order to settle down for a party or a shopping trip. On a broader scale, Pai/Sanjiyan comes into herself at the end of the first series and

declares her love for Yakumo, only to have her memory sealed by
Beneres so that everything (the escalating confrontations with her
enemies, the slow realization of her power, Yakumo's awkward
courtship) can begin again in the second series. And finally there
is a plot that spans both series, in which Pai attempts to recover
the three-hundred-year-old memories of her life as "Parvati," the
life she lived before the extinction of her race.[29]

In Azuma's account, we otaku watch each episode and then forget everything so we can watch the next identical one without a
loss of interest. But what does it mean when the amnesia and fragmentation that Azuma associates with the postmodern are foregrounded in the plot and structure of the anime itself? Pai (along
with a legion of other dreaming, amnesiac, child heroes and heroines across a wide range of anime) provides a portrait of this postmodern subject that we viewers can stand back from and observe.
For Azuma, it takes a savvy critic to open our eyes to this; but the
way 3x3 Eyes exaggerates these themes of amnesia and doubling
seems to offer virtually any viewer a critical perspective on his or
her relation to popular culture. Seeing ourselves in Pai, we may be
reminded of our own forgetfulness.

In 3x3 Eyes, the struggle against that forgetfulness is played out
using the now familiar figure of the puppet. Several times I have
suggested the puppet as a figure for the split bodies of anime, suspended between real and unreal. But they can also represent the
viewer: to the extent that otaku are involuntarily aroused by these
mediated subjects and manipulated as consumers, the puppet can
become a figure for the spectator.

In a pivotal scene from the second series, Yakumo battles this
sense of manipulation and fictionality literally, in a combat with
a series of demons shaped like dolls and puppets. The Ayanokōji
family that adopts amnesiac Pai are doll makers, and Yakumo discovers that the dolls in the house are possessed. They are led by a
life-size ball-torso mannequin that looks very much like the per-
verse doll bodies of Oshii's Innocence (Figure 32). She has the uncanny combination of sexual realism and stylization we have previously associated with the puppet. (She is composed of blocks
of carved wood, for example, but the way the pieces fit together
clearly suggests sexual details.) This figure could easily be read in

Freudian terms, to represent a frightening sexual world in which women are familiar but somehow monstrous, uncanny. But what is more interesting is the way the puppets represent amnesia and control. They signify the fact that Pai and her adoptive parents are puppets themselves, their memories manipulated by the same forces that control the dolls. In the climactic battle, the dolls take control of Pai's friends and parents and force them to fight against Yakumo. In fact, several episodes of the series contain scenes like this, in which good characters are inhabited or penetrated by demons and become their puppets.

By doing battle with these puppet- and doll-bodied monsters, Yakumo struggles to free Pai/Sanjiyan from the fiction that controls her, the false identity of Ayanokōji Pai. In Freud's essay "The Uncanny," dolls are disturbing because they double us: they represent a self divided against itself by thoughts or memories that we had repressed but which then return to haunt us. And these thoughts could certainly be sexual: Freud's essay mentions infantile fears

FIGURE 32. *3x3 Eyes: Legend of the Divine Demon* features a puppet demon whose body is a combination of grotesque stylization and anatomically correct detail.

and fantasies about abjection and castration, for example. But the explicit way the anime relates the puppets to sex and memory suggests that what might have been repressed or unconscious in Freud is now being battled in the open. In other words, scenes like this promise to open a third eye on the text, and force a recognition and response to the viewer's own manipulation by these media.

Vampire Princess Miyu

3x3 Eyes is not the only horror series that turns on female/monster hybrids, phallic transformations, lost memories, or puppet imagery that foregrounds audience, simulation, and control. We see these individual elements across a wide range of anime and manga. For example, all of them are combined in *Vampire Princess Miyu*, an evocative four-part OVA series directed by Hirano Toshiki and released in 1988–89.[30] The title character is a vampire in the body of a little girl. Part human and part monster, Miyu is charged with hunting down supernatural creatures called *shinma* who have strayed into the human sphere. This casts her as humans' protector, but she also hunts humans herself, and both Napier and Saitō cite her as an archetypal combination of beauty plus danger or power.[31] Miyu is in turn hunted by a female exorcist named Himiko, who feels a predictable mix of fear and attraction for her quarry.

Yet *Vampire Princess Miyu* is less about the battle between good and evil than about the contest between delusion and reality. Several of the *shinma* act by wrapping their victims in some kind of fantasy. In episode one, "Ancient Kyoto" ("Ayakashi no miyako"), Himiko is called to an eerie mansion where a man and a woman ask her in a strangely expressionless tone to perform an exorcism on their daughter. The girl has fallen into a coma they believe to be spirit related. It transpires that the girl is possessed by a vampire-like *shinma* that goes out every day to exsanguinate female victims, something which has attracted Miyu's attention as well. But when Himiko and Miyu finally join forces to exorcise the *shinma*, it reveals itself to be a giant worm-like incarnation of Baku, a demon of Japanese folklore who feeds on human dreams. After the girl's family was in a car accident, she received a blood transfusion from her dying mother in order to be saved. Guilt-ridden over the death of her parents and believing herself a vampire already, the girl trades her soul to Baku in return for an unending dream in which her mother and father are still alive. (The oddly wooden parents Himiko meets are images projected from within this dream.) Using the girl's energy and her vampiric delusion, the Baku *shinma* has been going out at night in the body of the girl to suck the blood of other victims.

Many of the *shinma* Miyu battles act in similar ways, and Miyu herself is not really any different. When she drinks the blood of a victim (usually a beautiful young girl or boy) her quarry falls into a liminal state between life and death, escaping their pain to live on in a condition like catatonia, apparently reliving their fondest memories over and over. Miyu and the *shinma* both seek out hopeless and despondent victims who willingly choose their "gift" of oblivion. And virtually all of the major characters, human and demon, are chasing after lost loves and lost memories. In the final episode Himiko herself recovers a lost memory of being bitten by Miyu as a child. The blood of the vampire is also within her, suggesting that some or all of her life (and the series) might be a delusion.

In some episodes of the OVA and manga, these dreams are associated explicitly with literary fiction, directly engaging the accusation that these texts bewitch their audience and substitute empty sexual fantasies for real relationships. For example, in an episode of the manga titled "The Sleeping Girls in the Picture Book," a *shinma* in the shape of a handsome boy imprisons his girlfriends on the pages of an illustrated storybook. The most striking example of this in the anime is a *shinma* called Ranka, whose costume and theme music associate her with the traditional Japanese theater, and who turns her lover victims into puppets. In an episode titled "Banquet of the Marionettes" ("Ayatsuri no utage"), Ranka and Miyu compete for the soul and the affections of yet another weak but exquisite boy who might constitute a stand-in for the otaku viewer. In the final showdown, Ranka transforms her body into a puppet's, and the boy chooses Ranka over Miyu, allowing himself to become a puppet as well so that he can join her (Figure 33). It is hard to think of a more literal image of the otaku fan withdrawing from reality to pursue a fictional relationship. As the episode concludes, Ranka and the boy dance a traditional Japanese

FIGURE 33. The demon Ranka in *Vampire Princess Miyu* not only takes the form of a puppet but transforms her victims into puppets as well. As for the beautiful boy, he goes willingly into her arms. From the Animeigo DVD (2001).

dance that consciously recalls classical theater, and the episode ends with a curtain (it bears the characteristic orange, green, and black pattern of the kabuki and puppet theaters) falling across the screen. The episode thus foregrounds the issue of representation and makes us ask ourselves whether we, too, will become lost in fiction.

The examples of these patterns go on. *Blood: The Last Vampire* (2000) similarly turns on a cute, vicious vampire in the body of a young girl. She is a pastiche of anime fetishes (or Azuma's database elements): a schoolgirl in braids and a sailor suit, wielding a samurai sword. And as the *Blood* franchise develops through one series after another, she repeatedly falls into a state of amnesia that allows the story to reset and repeat. In the most recent iteration, the repetition becomes so implausible and artificial that it can be explained only by revealing that the heroine's life is a staged production (complete with television cameras) engineered by an evil producer *cum* puppeteer.

We will revisit some of these issues when we take a detailed look at the *Blood* franchise in chapter 6. For now, we might ask why these tropes are so prevalent in anime, or why we are drawn to notice them. Certainly there are practical explanations related to the economics of anime production. The demon girl, the phallic transformation, the dreaming heroine, and the puppet victim are all tested devices that allow a single series to be renewed and extended indefinitely. If a character becomes boring, she can be transformed into someone else (in a past life if not this one). If she resolves her conflicts, her memory can be reset and a new series can begin from square one. And if these repeated patterns become too stereotyped or too implausible, they can be revealed as a dream or staged construction, in a way that shifts the action up a level to a new set of characters, the puppeteers.

But at the same time, all of these motifs generate interesting effects that go beyond extending their franchises. The psychoanalytic theories discussed above point out that these tropes share an ability to destabilize and relativize conventional gender identities and gender roles—by opposing them, virtualizing them, parodying them through exaggeration, or mixing them indiscriminately together.[32] The results make these anime interesting to many contemporary critics, who sense that this free play with gender and sexual norms can make us consider how arbitrary these norms are to start with.

3x3 Eyes is interesting for the way it combines and sorts several of these different psychoanalytical frameworks: Pai/Sanjiyan/Parvati/Ayanokōji Pai/Hōwasho might embody Freud's repressed memory or anxiety—a hidden meaning. But more interestingly, she is also Saitō's beautiful fighting phallic girl, pure fiction and pure lack, identified with any and all significations according to the fantasies of her fans. Justifiably, one of those fantasies is a feminist one of tilting or toppling Saitō's psychoanalytic structure itself: in a reading like Barbara Creed's, Sanjiyan is the feminine castrator, wielding and severing the putatively male power of signification. Finally, all these multiple identities can be linked together by Azuma's idea of dissociation and amnesia. But in my own variation on Azuma, this kind of character does not unthinkingly and unquestioningly reflect a fragmented postmodern subject but foregrounds and even critiques this contemporary schizophrenia for the viewer.

While Azuma suggests that otaku are fans who have lost critical perspective, Saitō says, "All otaku have something that should probably be called a critical drive. . . . Their talk does not stop at the work itself but also extends to include their own relationship to it." "In fact," Saitō writes, "a fan who has forgotten his or her critical perspective is not an otaku."[33] I have tried to stake out a third position, one that associates otaku not with a defined group of subjects but with a mode of reading that moves back and forth between sincere absorption and a true critical perspective, a mode of reading associated particularly if not exclusively with anime and its viewers.

If the readings above have taken the colorful (sometimes garish) fantasies of anime horror and reinterpreted them as metaphors for aspects of ordinary human psychology, then the next chapter inverts that. The anime films of Kon Satoshi invariably start out in the world of realism, which is then rendered fantastic by the complex psychologies of his characters. In spite of this inversion, the key motifs from the present chapter are repeated in Kon's work. Many of his anime depict male otaku paired with beautiful women who change shape to match the dreams of the audience and protagonist. We are prodded to ask whether the women characters exist like Saitō's phallic girls, entirely for the pleasure of the otaku characters and otaku audience, or whether these characters can gain control of their shifting personas to achieve some sort of agency and depth. The repetitive structure we see in a series like 3x3 Eyes is raised an order of magnitude: as Kon's heroines move through the nested fictional worlds created by media and their own psychologies, they often seem unable or unwilling to escape, condemned to repeat the same roles over and over. Finally, several of these heroines are actresses, and Kon uses this metafictional framing to engage questions about anime itself.

5

Anime in Drag

Stage Performance and Staged Performance
in *Millennium Actress*

The previous chapter centered on anime's audience and the accusation that anime encourages a confusion of fantasy with reality, or a retreat from realistic relationships into fictional ones. I suggested that there is a self-conscious attention to these issues in many anime (in the way that otaku or fans are portrayed, for example) and that this offers the spectator some perspective on his or her own situation. These readings focused largely on plots and plot structures, but we might ask how a visually innovative director could harness anime's formal qualities to address these themes of fantasy, fandom, and consumption. For an answer to this question, we will look to the work of Kon Satoshi, whose plots and visual editing both blur the line between fantasy and reality. For critical perspective we turn from the psychoanalysis of chapter 4 to queer theory, specifically Judith Butler's foundational reading of drag performance. The chapter concludes with a comparison between anime and modern experimental theater, focusing on a stage adaptation of Kon's anime *Millennium Actress* in which all the roles are played by women.

Kon Satoshi

Kon Satoshi was born in 1963, about ten years later than Ōtomo Katsuhiro or Oshii Mamoru. Like Ōtomo, he started out as a manga artist, and during his early career he worked on manga and anime projects with both Ōtomo and Oshii, including backgrounds and layouts for *Patlabor 2* and a screenplay for *Magnetic Rose* (*Kanojo no omoide*, 1995), a jaw-dropping virtual reality thriller directed by Morimoto Kōji and loosely based on an Ōtomo manga.[1]

Kon's own manga from this early period has a visual style like Ōtomo's but a very different sensibility. For example, his brilliant but unfinished title *Opus* (1995–96) is a manga about an artist, Nagai Chikara, who is sucked into the world of the manga he is drawing (titled *Resonance*) and forced to interact with his own characters, who now realize that their world is a fiction. The hero of *Resonance* discovers that he is to be killed off in the final installment and refuses his fate, breaking into the real world to steal the half-finished page that depicts his own death. The plot twists and narrative tricks multiply from there.

Kon's anime have similar themes and similarly complex textures. His directorial debut *Perfect Blue* (*Paafekuto burū*, 1997) is about a pop singer, Kirigoe Mima, who is obsessively stalked by a crazed fan. As she climbs the media ladder from B-list idol to TV actress and becomes progressively sexualized by the media, her stalker intervenes to "protect" her by murdering those who are responsible for her objectification—first a lecherous photographer who cajoles her into doing a nude magazine spread, then the scriptwriter who makes her character the target of a graphic rape scene in the TV series she has landed. But things quickly become more complicated: Mima's TV series is a police procedural with a plot about a woman who invents an imagined stalker in order to cover up murders she commits herself. As the violence mounts, Mima begins to experience dreams and hallucinations that blur distinctions between the person, the idol, the idol playing at being an actress, and the (schizophrenic) role the actress plays. Eventually it is revealed that the stalker himself is a kind of projection or puppet—not of Mima but of someone else, another Mima double hidden in plain sight within the story, someone who sees herself as the real star and Mima as the impostor.

Perfect Blue was a remarkable debut. But within a few years Kon had upped the ante on this layering of identity with *Paprika* (*Papurika*, 2006), a near-future science-fiction story about a psychotherapist who can take on a virtual alter ego, "Paprika," and enter patients' dreams in order to treat their neuroses. Paprika's latest patient is a police inspector who is also a film buff, and his

dreams take the form of scenes from well-known Hollywood movies. As he and Paprika scour his dreams for clues to the source of
his neurosis, they also find themselves tracking a real-world criminal who has hijacked the dream-reading technology to invade people's dreams and drive them insane. Gradually the technology to
penetrate the dream world erodes the wall between dream and
reality: first it is just the criminal's targets who become unable
to distinguish their dreams from their waking lives, but eventually the technology malfunctions and allows phantoms from one
person's dream to materialize in everyone's waking reality, to the
point where dreams threaten to overwrite reality entirely.

This confusion of identities in Kon's plots is interesting, but the
real hallmark of Kon's films is the way this layering and confusion
play out at the visual level. For those who have never seen one of
Kon's films, it is hard to describe all the tricks he uses to make the
spectator think they are seeing one thing before he reveals it to be
something else. The way Kon's films are edited often makes it unclear which frame we occupy at any given moment—for example,
whether a given scene in Perfect Blue is Mima's real life, her TV show,
a dream sequence, or the delusion of a third party looking on.

In the opening shot of Perfect Blue, we see a team of helmeted
heroes in matching space suits fire their ray guns at a flamboyant
villain. They look like the heroes of the popular live-action TV series Super Sentai (familiar to U.S. viewers in its repackaged form,
Power Rangers). But then the shot widens to reveal that the "heroes"
are costumed actors on a stage putting on a show in a public park.
Next we see the audience, many of whom are filming the action,
and then we follow a group of boys out of the park and hear them
say "It looked better on TV," "Pretty cheap, huh?" Only then does
the film introduce Mima by having her idol group take the stage.

Both visually and narratively, this opening shot announces an
intention Kon stated explicitly elsewhere, to eschew anime's stock
fantasies in favor of different topics. "The anime industry restricts
itself," Kon commented in one interview. "They say anime is un-
limited, but so much of it is cute girls, robots, and explosions." If
anything and everything is possible, Kon concluded, there should
be room for more realistic stories as well.[2] Yet Kon ceaselessly capi-
talizes on animation's flattening effect to layer different kinds of

remediation cleverly together and confuse the viewer about what is real (in the context of the story's diegesis) and what is represented. The joke in this opening scene is that this is not a typical anime space opera, but also that we don't know that the ray guns are supposed to be special effects until the camera pulls back, and that we have no way of knowing the special effects are unrealistic or cheap until an animated character informs us.

And this is an exceedingly simple example by Kon's standards. The director employs a wide range of other visual techniques to lure viewers into one reality and then suddenly shift them into another, revealing the action to be a simulation, a media quotation, a hallucination, or a dream. Kon also combines these different narrative frames in unpredictable ways, transitioning from one to another in rapid sequence so that the action progresses dizzyingly from one frame to another. Andrew Osmond and Tony Zhou both call attention to the way Kon cuts between images that are compositionally similar but that belong to completely different scenes—what is called a match cut.[3] This technique allows Kon to cut rapidly between very different scenes and maintain a sense of *visual* continuity even as the action or *narrative logic* becomes radically discontinuous.

Kon's stories and editing can be interpreted as an expression of the poststructuralist or postmodern idea that real life is not radically different from the constructed narratives of fiction—that often what we regard as reality is nothing more than a constructed text. But one of Kon's trademarks is that his metafictional experimentation with visuals and narratives is paired with very plot-driven genre stories: romances, dramas, thrillers, and other potboilers that keep the viewer conventionally absorbed in the narrative and the characters. Kon's work thereby provides one of the clearest examples so far of anime's oscillation between transparency or immersion and opacity or distance. Beyond this, Kon's style also allows us to revisit and extend our discussion of some key themes from chapters 2, 3, and 4: the issues of embodied consciousness and vision we saw in Oshii's work, anime's self-critical portrayal of the otaku fan as one who might reject conventional distinctions between fiction and reality, and the related trope of dreaming and forgetting.

Millennium Actress

The text taken up in this chapter is Kon's second film, *Millennium Actress* (*Sennen joyū*, 2001), a biography of a fictional twentieth-century film actress, Fujiwara Chiyoko, who starred in dozens of films from the 1930s through the 1960s, but quit suddenly for un-explained reasons at the peak of her career. Or rather, in classic Kon fashion, it is a film about a director who is himself a die-hard fan of the actress, and who brings a cameraman to her house to film an interview for a documentary about her life (Figure 34). During the interview we see memories of her life intercut with scenes from her various films in various genres. These film scenes themselves recapitulate the history or variety of twentieth-century Japan's live-action cinema, displaying all the different historical settings and genres that compose it. But what is common across all these period films, early modern melodramas, thrillers, and science-fiction films is that Chiyoko is always the romantic lead, and all the romantic plots mirror the central love affair of her real life outside the films.

FIGURE 34. *Millennium Actress* is framed as a documentary interview between Chiyoko and the otaku-like director Tachibana. A documentary about the making of *Millennium Actress* (on the Dreamworks DVD) reveals that Kon based visual details of this scene on an interview he himself had recently taped with a (third) documentary crew that came to film him. Kon was fond of such synchronicity, one more way that the director created layers within layers in his work. All *Millennium Actress* stills are from the Bandai Japanese-language Blu-ray disc (2014).

The love affair begins like this: as a young girl living through Japan's increasingly militaristic 1930s, she bumps into a man on the street one day, a revolutionary fleeing from the secret police. Chiyoko rescues the revolutionary by tending his wounds and concealing him in the family storehouse. He is a painter, and he is carrying an unfinished painting and a key on a chain around his neck, a key he tells her will open "the most important thing in the world." He promises to find her when peace comes to Japan, and take her to his homeland in the north, where he will complete the painting. He disappears the next day, leaving behind the key and a portrait of Chiyoko he has painted on the storeroom wall. Though she searches her entire life, she never finds him again.

Chiyoko reveals in the interview that her film career has been part of this search: she hoped he might see one of her films and track her down. The plot of each movie inevitably features a strong heroine (lady in waiting, warrior, ninja, geisha, nurse, teacher, scientist, astronaut, etcetera), and each of these heroines is on a quest to find or rescue a lost love (Figure 35). As Chiyoko describes her biography and her film roles to the documentary director, Kon's script and seamless cutting blend the different films together, and blend these in turn with scenes from Chiyoko's life. The director character Tachibana and his cameraman are visibly present not only at the interview, but also within the movie scenes and the scenes of Chiyoko's memories, as if they had actually been present filming decades ago. (If this sounds disorienting, it is, and the cameraman gives voice to our own confusion by continually asking whether he is currently in a film or a memory.)

Consider an example from near the beginning of the anime that shows how some of these elements fit together. When the painter flees from Chiyoko's house just ahead of the secret police, she runs all the way to the train station to see him one final time, but running along the platform she trips and falls just as the train pulls away. "I will find you," she declares. The cameraman then appears on the platform, filming, at which point Tachibana says "I saw this scene fifty-three times in the theater and cried each time." "When did this become a movie?" asks the cameraman, and as the girl on the platform raises her head, Kon cross-fades to the seventy-five-year-old Chiyoko raising her head in the same way, as she looks up

FIGURE 35. Movie pamphlets scattered across Chiyoko's living room table display the range of her roles. *Millennium Actress* remediates many other media within itself, not only film but video, painting, photographs, and print sources.

from the coffee table at the interview and says "That's how I got into movies." The table is covered with film pamphlets, including one with a cover image matching the train station scene we've just witnessed (and under that are pamphlets for other films, previews of scenes we'll see later in Kon's film). We cut to Tachibana saying, "Is that how you got started?" and watch the cameraman do a double take as he realizes that Tachibana is holding the hat worn by the girl on the platform; he has somehow carried it out of the flashback or the film into the present reality of the interview. The seventy-five-year-old Chiyoko explains that the first role she was offered was for a film made in Manchuria, the place the painter had said he was going. Then the film's perspective rotates around her head in conjunction with another cross-fade match cut that transforms her back into the girl on the train platform, who says "Manchuria . . . that's it!" while a boat horn inexplicably blows in the background. The girl on the train platform stands up, and there is a third match cut to the young Chiyoko rising from a deep bow as she stands in front of the ocean liner that will take her to Manchuria to film her first role. After some brief dialogue Tachibana appears beside her on the dock and asks if she actually went to Manchuria looking for the painter, and the young Chiyoko breaks character and voices words we understand are actually spoken by the seventy-five-year-old interviewee decades later: "That was it. I actually didn't care at all about making movies."

If I add that these transitions (from the moment Chiyoko trips on the platform to this ironic final line) all take place within eighty seconds, it should give a sense of the baroquely metafictional texture of Kon's film. And from here Kon only increases the pace. The film's most iconic scenes show Chiyoko traveling in search of the painter—by horse, train, boat, car, truck, bus, rocket ship, or most often, as in the scene above, running on foot. As the film progresses, these journeys become more and more kaleidoscopic. In a scene that marks the transition from her samurai-era period films to early modern ones, Chiyoko travels on horseback, then by carriage, rickshaw, and bicycle past a series of stylized backdrops that resemble nineteenth-century woodblock prints. And in the film's climax, she rushes from Tokyo to Hokkaido in a seven-and-a-half minute sequence that consists of more than a hundred and thirty-five different cuts or transitions, intercutting different forms of transportation with running and travel flashbacks from throughout her life and her films.

Kon also raises the stakes by having the director Tachibana appear in the film scenes in costume, playing various supporting characters who rescue the heroine from danger. At first we read this as an otaku-like overidentification or delusion on the part of Tachibana, who is so captivated by Chiyoko that he seems to hallucinate himself in the role of her protector. But as the interview progresses, a youthful version of the director suddenly appears in Chiyoko's flashbacks, revealing that he and Chiyoko actually do have a real history together. He was a young, unnoticed assistant director at the studio where she made her films; there was a day when an earthquake collapsed a set and he saved her life; and he has the key originally given to her by the painter, which he found on set the day she quit the studio and which he has kept for decades as a memento. (The key is the means by which he gets access to the famously reclusive star: he returns it to her at the beginning of the interview, though it is only at the end of the film that we understand where he got it.) So what appears to be Tachibana's otaku fantasy turns out to be reality, or as real as anything in Kon's film.

In this way *Millennium Actress* repeatedly immerses us in the story and then pulls us out of it with self-conscious cinematic devices, only to plunge us into another story and start the whole process over again. (The devices are so intricate that one can discover new ones on every viewing, so that even after repeated screenings the film can still keep us balanced between these two poles.) This oscillation between absorption and distance is also figured concretely in two different sets of questions the film generates for spectators. On the one hand, we are drawn forward by the plot and our desire to solve the narrative mysteries of Chiyoko's life: Who is the painter? Will the two of them ever be reunited? What is the answer to the riddle of the key, which is said to open "the most important thing in the world"? And maybe most centrally, why does Chiyoko sustain this apparently fruitless search over so many years?

On the other hand, for other spectators the desire will be to track down the film's intertextual references. Kon's many visual quotations from classic Japanese cinema prompt a kind of scavenger hunt to locate the original sources. For example, the overall plot about a chance meeting and years-long search recalls the 1950s radio and film series *Kimi no na wa* (What is your name?), and Melek Ortabasi points out that a poster for one of Chiyoko's movies, seen briefly in the background, is patterned on images from those films. Other critics note that Tachibana's supporting roles as a ninja, trucker, and rickshaw driver bear a striking resemblance to the protagonists of the real Japanese films *Rickshaw Man* (*Muhōmatsu no isshō*, 1958), *Torakku yarō* (Truckers, 1975–79), and the *Kurama tengu* series.[4] (When we see the pamphlets for Chiyoko's films spread out on her table during the interview, we can read parts of the titles, and they frequently resemble the titles of these and other real-life models.) Chiyoko's life story strongly recalls the legendary film star Hara Setsuko, who acted in more than seventy films from the 1930s to the 1960s, most famously as the luminous heroine of several films by master director Ozu Yasujirō. Then at the height of her popularity in 1963, Hara suddenly quit acting and disappeared abruptly from public view. Identifying these parallels gives us the satisfying feeling of having solved a little puzzle each time, even if it does not shed much light on larger questions about Chiyoko's character.

The gap between those two sets of concerns might be expressed in a question: is *Millennium Actress* a story about individual characters we care about, or is it only ever a film about film?[5] The challenge, I think, is to bring together both sets of questions, and ask whether the film's metatextual commentary on film itself can be related to its questions about life's purpose. There is one figure in the film that unites these diegetic and metadiegetic questions, a figure that floats between film reference and character: it is a specter of an old woman at a spinning wheel that haunts Chiyoko throughout the film and that seems to lie at the origin of her perpetual quest.

Specter, Spectator, Spirit: Interpreting *Millennium Actress*

This ghost first appears in a scene from Chiyoko's film *Ayakashi no shiro* (Castle of the specter), in which she plays a samurai wife in a besieged fortress. When her lord dies, she is determined to kill herself and follow him, but at that moment the specter appears and tricks her into drinking a cup of tea that extends her life for a thousand years, postponing the lovers' reunion for a millennium. Asked its motive, the specter says only: "I hate you, I hate you more than I can endure. And you're dearer, dearer to me than I can stand. One day you will see."

If this curse is the source of Chiyoko's endless quest, what does the specter actually represent? One answer, though not the only one, is provided by the final scenes of the anime, which suggest that the specter is an aged version of Chiyoko herself, and that it represents the actress's fear of growing old. Chiyoko explains that in the same way she started making films in hopes that the painter would see her and find her, her sudden decision to quit in her forties stemmed from a fear that he would see her as an old woman. And looking back, we notice a couple of other points in the anime where the specter's face appears in glass surfaces, replacing or overlapping Chiyoko's reflection at moments when Chiyoko is feeling her own age or mortality (Figure 36).

William Gardner argues that mirrors in Kon's films are intersubjective sites where an individual's self-image combines with the expectations of others. In *Perfect Blue*, for example, when the

FIGURE 36. These point-of-view shots from Chiyoko's perspective start with her mother urging her to marry before she is too old. As the scene progresses, her mother changes to her co-star Eiko, and we realize we are now watching Chiyoko film a scene from one of her movies. Meanwhile Chiyoko's reflection in the glass changes to an image of the specter, as she worries about how others perceive her age.

heroine Mima sees her own reflection, it often resembles her pop idol persona. Gardner writes, "This image of 'Mima' appearing in the mirror is a visualization of . . . the intersubjective construction of her own public performance together with the desires of the primarily male producers and fans who have created and consumed the Pop Idol Mima."[6] In *Millennium Actress*, the specter's mixed love and hate could represent the way Chiyoko fears she'll be seen (the scorn or adoration of a fickle public), and also the way that this changes her self-image (an old woman's tenderness and jealousy toward her younger self).

Chiyoko finally overcomes all this at the end of the film, which collapses past, present, and future in a way that reconciles the three and dispels her terror of old age and death. As she gazes at a framed painting of herself as a girl (the one left by the painter on the storeroom wall), she sees her own elegant seventy-five-year-old face reflected in the glass of the frame; then the specter's decrepit visage replaces her own, so that all three faces are momentarily superimposed. Simultaneously there is an earthquake, which connects this moment to her birth (during the Great Kantō Earthquake of 1923) and her middle age (the earthquake in the studio that interrupted her final film). With this collapse of time, Chiyoko collapses physically as well, her life complete. In a final coda on her hospital deathbed, she tells Tachibana that she is now ready to continue chasing the painter into death. The curse is thus lifted, her career concluded, her fears dispelled.

Pursuing this reading, we can see that the key also constitutes a shifting image of time that signifies first the future, then the midpoint of midlife, and finally the past. When the painter first shows it to her he talks about his hopes for the future, and when he asks her what she thinks it unlocks (what is "the most important thing in the world?"), she says: "Don't tell me. Give me until tomorrow to think about it." Through her adulthood she wears the key around her neck as a talisman to remind her of their past meeting and the hoped-for reunion. She loses it when she abandons her film career, but when Tachibana returns it to her thirty years later at the interview, she describes it as the thing that unlocks her past memories in a way that permits the resolutions above.

This interpretation identifies the specter as Chiyoko's spirit, associating it with a narrative of psychological development or becoming that ultimately does not have much to do with the medium of film. But the specter also clearly seems to represent film itself. The same figure appears in Kurosawa Akira's samurai classic *Throne of Blood* (*Kumonosujō*, 1957), one of several references to that film in *Millennium Actress* (Figure 37).[7] *Throne of Blood* is Kurosawa's period adaptation of Shakespeare's *Macbeth*, and it features an identical ghostly crone at a spinning wheel who appears to the samurai protagonist and prophesies that he will rule the kingdom. Like the witches' prophecy in *Macbeth*, this prediction drives him to murder his lord. This connection suggests that for Chiyoko, the specter represents a bargain with fame—immortality at the price of personal emptiness or destruction. And the intertextual reference to Kurosawa, as well as the resemblance critics have noted between Kurosawa's spinning wheel and a film projector, both suggest that the bargain Chiyoko makes is with the film audience or with the medium of film itself. The specter (like the Latin "spectrum," or "image") is film, but it is also a spectator. It is the medium and the public that love Chiyoko and promise her immortal fame, but that also judge her fading beauty and finally drive her into isolation.

So we have two different ways to interpret the specter (corresponding to anime's characteristic oscillation): in terms of the story, as an aspect of the heroine's psychology; or in terms of the film's formal structure, as a metatextual symbol for film as medium and industry. Kon cleverly brings those two alternatives together in the film's final line. Chiyoko, at peace in her hospital bed, reveals to Tachibana that she knows the painter has long since died and characterizes her own death as a continuation of her search for him. Tachibana says he's sure they will meet, but her reply surprises: "I wonder," she says. "But perhaps it does not matter. After all . . ." At this point we transition to a scene from her last film, in which a forty-year-old Chiyoko plays an astronaut blasting off in search of her lover. The astronaut continues the last line: "After all, the person I really love is myself chasing after him" (*Datte, ano hito o oikaketeiru watashi ga suki nan da mono*).

In some senses this line turns the plot of the film on its head: in this epic love story, Chiyoko was only ever in love with herself or her own image. She seems to know that the search for the painter was ultimately a fiction, no more real than her films, no more original than their repeated plots. That is why Chiyoko can transition so seamlessly between fictional film and fictional biography.

What of the key, then? It might be read as a crude phallic symbol, the key to Chiyoko's heart or body.[8] But with the film's final twist, the key seems to be transformed into the kind of Lacanian or forgetful phallus we saw in the previous chapter: a key with no lock and no owner, a figure for representation and representation's inability to capture the real. What Chiyoko eventually

FIGURE 37. The specter, which starts as a character in Chiyoko's film and then invades her reality, matches a similar figure in Kurosawa Akira's *Throne of Blood.* This is one of several references to the Kurosawa film in *Millennium Actress,* and one of countless intertextual references to twentieth-century Japanese cinema. *Throne of Blood* still from the Criterion Blu-ray disc (2015).

realizes is that *she* is the representation she has been searching for, that she is the key to everything. This realization could place her in the same category as the "phallic girls" we examined in the previous chapter. But while Saitō Tamaki discusses the phallic girl only in terms of her significance to the otaku, *Millennium Actress* looks at things from the "girl's" perspective: what does it mean to become conscious not just of the world and the other as texts but of the self as a text as well?

Below, we look to Judith Butler for some answers to this last question. But here let's ask more generally what it feels like to be a character in Kon's world. In works like *Perfect Blue, Paprika,* and *Paranoia Agent (Mōsō dairinin,* 2004), the mass media (television, film, and anime) act as a corrosive force eating away at the distinction between reality and fiction, and with it the characters' mental well-being. Kon's work can clearly be read as a critique of a postmodern world in which all the narratives we might use to shape our lives seem to be written or directed by someone else. But Chiyoko's final words give *Millennium Actress* an optimistic spin: if love always has to fit into a kind of story we tell ourselves (a story drawn from the fictions around us), and if every part of our lives is part of a role we take on in a constructed world, then we have to be aware of that and play these roles in a way that is meaningful to us. Each one of us has to be our own best audience.

Kon elaborated on this optimistic postmodernism in interviews, suggesting that there is nothing new or pathological about the ways in which our attention is divided between different times and experiences at any given moment. ("Even as we speak, for example, we might be thinking of the dinner to come one hour later.") Kon said that his nonlinear editing realistically captures this normal everyday experience. Furthermore, all of us inhabit multiple realities that inform one another. Kon says, "There's a 'main' reality, but then there's the Internet, TV, our own memories, these things we experience together. I think it isn't good to stress the divisions between them too much, because an important part of the human can be misplaced that way. . . . The unreal comes from the real and there's a dialectic between them."[9]

Other Kon heroines also manage to tame the uncertainty of their mediated lives and arrive at happy endings in which they recover a sense of self. In many ways this is an attractive vision for recovering agency in our media-saturated world. Compared with the films treated in previous chapters, Chiyoko does not have to suffer the violent posthuman transformations of the cyborg or the girl/demon in order to exist in the world, nor do Kon's worlds have to undergo the apocalyptic rebirth desired or required in *Akira.* For

Kon, the radical mixing and remixing of languages that we have been characterizing as postmodern is arguably a healthy aspect of everyday experience, growth, and self-actualization.

Running in Place? Chiyoko as Spectacle

I find Kon's optimistic postmodernism compelling in many ways, but *Millennium Actress*'s tidy conclusion does prompt some additional questions. First, where does the ending leave Tachibana, the loyal fan who has protected Chiyoko, and by extension where does it leave us fans (men and women alike)? If the actress is her own audience, the only important audience, is the spectator beside the point? And since questions of otaku spectatorship inevitably turn and return to questions of gender, we might ask: if Chiyoko is free to define herself, can she define her own gender roles? The fact that she does not seem to need a male romantic partner suggests a kind of independence, but there is also a sense that a life spent chasing an imaginary male love object is a depressingly static existence: in all these scenes of forward motion, has she only ever been running in place? And beyond these plot questions, what about our experience of the film as a whole? If we enjoy *Millennium Actress*, at least part of that enjoyment seems to stem not from the idea of Chiyoko's independence but the reverse: a conservative pleasure of recognition at the nostalgic parade of genre films, with Chiyoko transformed from one stock costume role to another.

In a review for Midnight Eye, Michael Arnold points out this conservatism, using Laura Mulvey's influential theory of the cinematic male gaze to link spectacle with sexual objectification:

> Throughout the 20th century male directors including Mizo-guchi, Naruse, Imamura, and many others, in everything from program pictures to pornos, energetically contributed to a modern mythology of the Japanese female, assigning her the spirit and character to resist the forces that bound her. Foreign viewers are sometimes too quick to simply label these films "feminist"; as others have noted the movies can objectify their heroines and create lustworthy spectacles out of their trials rather than suggest possibilities for change and empowerment. . . . Instead of critically addressing the spectacle [*Millennium Actress*] simply enjoys the

view. . . . rather than use that view to take a fresh look at "history" Kon delivers the standard tear-jerking melodrama. Chiyoko ends up like the empty vessel Laura Mulvey wrote about nearly 30 years ago, "still tied to her place as bearer of meaning, not maker of meaning," and in an otherwise "post-modern" story that is so explicitly about men who watch films on women the adoration of such a shallow character is very frustrating (especially with a unique and talented director like Kon at the helm).

In fact, in almost all of Kon's films, the fragmentation of the subject and its eventual reintegration are played out on women's bodies and in women's minds. It is up to women to suffer this violence and overcome it. It is relatively easy to read Kon's films as conflicted in the same way as *Ghost in the Shell* or anime horror: divided between a desperate desire to see the subject as a radically transformable (technological or supernatural) being and a more conservative attachment to stereotypically beautiful (female) bodies and stereotypically traditional (female) roles. In the last part of this chapter I would like to ask if a more careful consideration of *Millennium Actress* might still label the film "feminist." If so, what kind of feminism would that be?

To answer that question, I will compare Chiyoko's performances and genre crossing with Judith Butler's notion of performativity and gender crossing. And to highlight these questions of performance and performativity, I would like to compare *Millennium Actress* with live theater, specifically a dramatic version of *Millennium Actress* in which five actresses on a largely bare stage play all the film's parts in rotation. The stage version subtracts the anime's elaborate visual effects and grounds itself in the live bodies of the actresses, but it also involves the audience and multiplies the layers of the simulation in ways that bring these bodily performances and performativities to the fore.

Gender as Genre: Who Should Chiyoko Be?

Judith Butler's work is both a continuation and a counterpoint to the critical methodologies we've employed in earlier chapters—poststructuralism, posthumanism, phenomenology, and psychoanalysis. Chapter 3 argued that the ambivalence toward the body in *Ghost in the Shell* (both loved and scorned, to paraphrase Kon's specter) maps to a potential ambivalence toward the body in Haraway's posthuman or poststructuralist feminism, which dissolves human and bodily boundaries as an image of freedom from fixed categories and a move toward networked solidarity. In contrast, Vivian Sobchack's phenomenology of film spectatorship, discussed in chapter 2, seeks to reemphasize the importance of the concrete individual body (the spectator's body and the film's body) by turning from poststructuralism to phenomenology. Modern phenomenology focuses on the way subjects constitute themselves through acts of communication and perception they direct at one another, and Sobchack sees traditional film as an embodied subject in its own right, an act of vision that functions as a medial point of communication between embodied human subjects. In contrast to Haraway, Sobchack worries that digital media (particularly the fragmented, disembodied perception represented by digital media) might erode the coherence of the film's body and undermine film's role as that mediating subject. Judith Butler combines elements of Haraway and Sobchack, engaging phenomenology but from a resolutely poststructuralist perspective, committing to the body and the individual but categorically rejecting fixed categories of gender and subject.

Butler is associated with a complex feminist critique of an already complex body of feminist and psychoanalytical theory. To simplify things here, I would like to begin from Butler's links to phenomenology, which we can understand through a comparison with Sobchack. For the latter, Maurice Merleau-Ponty's phenomenology suggests a view of the subject that productively rejects the notion of a transcendental subject or perspective. Sobchack says any belief that we can escape our own subjectivity and grasp a universal subject from a transcendent position outside that subject is naive or dangerous. Merleau-Ponty's subject is not universal or transcendent but concrete and contingent—embodied and perceiving but also formed in dialogue with the way other subjects perceive it. As described in chapter 2, this applies both to human subjects and artistic ones, including film. Neither film nor the spectator are transcendent in a way that allows them to dominate or define the other: film challenges us to interpret and communicate with it, talking back to us and allowing us to talk back to it.

Butler shares some of the same phenomenological heritage, including a belief that we construct ourselves actively and intersubjectively in the process of interaction with one another. But Butler takes this rejection of the transcendental several steps further, to reject the clearly bounded subjects that Sobchack embraces. Butler's concern is above all to question the essentializing formations that trap the subject in what she regards as restrictive and heterosexist dichotomies like male/female and self/other. The result is that Butler's notion of performativity can be used to see Kon's fragmented subjects (the very thing Sobchack fears) as interesting and even liberatory.

Butler's early work constitutes a genealogy that begins with the phenomenology of Merleau-Ponty's contemporaries, Jean-Paul Sartre and Simone de Beauvoir.[10] Starting with Beauvoir and working up to structuralism, psychoanalysis, and a wide range of feminist theory, Butler's canonical book *Gender Trouble* investigates theories that posit gender as a social construction. In a series of subtle deconstructions, Butler argues that even in theories that seem to resist the notion of a transcendental subject, the progressive notion of a flexible gender is always anchored by conservative, essentializing notions of a stable individual subject (often with a stable sex) that exists prior to gender and wears it like a suit of clothing. For Butler, the model of a natural subject who chooses a gender is already too transcendental. So is a model where the subject's gender is defined by "society," if by society we mean something that the subject itself precedes and constitutes. Both of these models give insufficient attention to the ways in which so many other aspects of the subject are also arbitrary and socially constructed. Taking aim at feminist philosophies of gender that are unwilling or unable to discard some stable category "women," Butler counters that these underlying essentialisms inevitably reflect and promote inequality.

The question, then, is how to balance these convictions about the socially constructed subject (or suspicions about the well-delineated subject) with a politically productive vision of individual or collective agency. One answer comes in the form of Butler's theory of gender performativity. In contrast with the essentializing model of an actor (a preexisting subject) who chooses and then expresses a gender, performativity describes a process in which the gendered subject constructs itself and is constructed "through a *stylized repetition of acts.*" "My argument," writes Butler, "is that there need not be a 'doer behind the deed,' but that the 'doer' is variably constructed in and through the deed."[11] These acts or deeds are not free choices. Socially constructed, we are largely constrained to repeat the gender discourses or scripts that are given to us; but each repetition can (and inevitably does) generate incremental differences that create the possibility of diversity or gradual change.

> Hence, the sexuality that emerges within the matrix of power relations is not a simple replication or copy of the law itself, a uniform repetition of a masculinist economy of identity. The productions swerve from their original purposes and inadvertently mobilize possibilities of "subjects" that do not merely exceed the bounds of cultural intelligibility, but effectively expand the boundaries of what is, in fact, culturally intelligible.[12]

Gender Trouble focuses more on abstract arguments than concrete examples of performativity, but Butler does provide one example, in the form of parodic practices like cross-dressing and drag. Even these practices are productive only if they reject the imitation of a supposedly authentic object (e.g., a man trying to imitate an authentic woman) and instead parody gender norms themselves as arbitrary and constructed—if "the parody is *of* the very notion of an original." Analogously, drag confounds the inside/outside dichotomy that grounds the illusion of the preexisting subject who expresses a gender. Paraphrasing Butler's paraphrase of Esther Newton: there is a man inside the woman(s' clothing), but also a woman inside the man.[13]

Millennium Actress provides an evocative image of the processes Butler describes. At first it may seem an awkward combination of conservative story and imagery wrapped in a superficially experimental style: the editing blurs the outlines of the characters, but the plot portrays Chiyoko as a succession of female genre stereotypes, powerless to do anything except play out a series of roles that revolve inescapably around a man. But viewed in Butler's terms, this very repetition becomes a visible image and critique of gender expectations. The ceaseless parade of feminine arche-types constitutes a clever parodic double gesture: it portrays the social pressures of postwar Japan (the fact that for Chiyoko and other real women those roles are largely inescapable), while it si-multaneously exposes their arbitrariness and artificiality—like the game in which you repeat a word out loud over and over until it begins to sound counterintuitive, meaningless. Gender becomes just another genre. At the same time, the endless repetition in dif-ferent styles introduces the possibility of incremental change, the chance that Chiyoko may eventually gain some power to alter the script. The idea that the actress is "running in place" then becomes an apt, even guardedly optimistic figure for the situation Butler describes, where gender formation is constrained but where re-petitive motion contains the possibility of forward movement or change.

And what about the decorative pleasures of Kon's film? Initially they invite criticism that the film is about visual style or spectacle over political substance, but Butler suggests that style may in fact be the best figure or metaphor for the gendered subject, which is not an "abiding" substance or substantive but a series of altera-tions. Butler writes, "The effect of gender is produced through the stylization of the body and, hence, must be understood as the mundane way in which bodily gestures, movements, and styles of various kinds constitute the illusion of an abiding gendered self." Kon comments in curiously parallel language that "It isn't Chi-yoko's ego that's on display, it's . . . her style of life that's shown here." Kon's series of remediated costume dramas thus becomes a kind of drag show.[14]

Finally, Chiyoko's realization that she is both actor and audi-ence might be seen as another way of collapsing the dichotomies of inside and outside, self and other, viewer and viewed. This is exactly the gesture that sets Butler's discursive subjects apart from Sobchack's clearly delineated ones. Put another way, if the ghost is simultaneously spectator, specter, and film (simultane-ously Chiyoko, her audience, and her work) then this is perhaps a

Butler-like deconstruction or "queering" of earlier phenomenologies, whereby Sobchack's three subjects (self, interlocutor, mediator) collapse into one, or one human subject divides into three.

Millennium Actress on Stage: "Who Should Be Chiyoko?"

What else might it mean to call Chiyoko a drag performer, and how might it open our eyes not just to new things in the film but to new things in Butler's work? Here I would like to consider a live stage version of *Millennium Actress* in which all the parts, male and female, are acted by women. *Millennium Actress* is not the only anime to be adapted for the stage, but this live version, created and directed by Suematsu Ken'ichi and performed by the all-female company Take It Easy! in 2009 and 2011, is unique in that five actresses play all the roles in rotation.[15] For example, the actress playing Chiyoko in one scene may play a different character in the next. In the sense that the actresses play the male as well as the female roles, they are often "in drag." But it is not a costume drag, because there are no realistic costumes in this production. The actresses dress similarly in white, and to keep things straight, the one currently playing Tachibana wears a fedora, while others have their own characteristic props. Some characters are signified by posture or intonation, or just by context (Figure 38).

Similarly there are no sets or other props beyond a few chairs. The panorama of decorative settings and the kaleidoscopic editing that connects them in Kon's film are suggested in other ways. For example, in the climactic travel scene that takes Chiyoko from Tokyo to Hokkaido, the actress *runs in place* at center stage while lighting effects, sound effects, and the four actresses around her suggest her progress through different worlds. But while the visual language of the stage adaptation is completely different from the anime, the verbal language is the same: Suematsu's dialogue is taken almost verbatim from Kon's film.

I saw a performance of this production in Osaka in 2011, and it was a remarkable experience. The oscillation between intimacy and distance is if anything more pronounced in the live version. The acting is largely realistic, and when I interviewed Suematsu

FIGURE 38. In the stage version of *Millennium Actress* by Suematsu Ken'ichi and the all-female troupe Take It Easy! all the roles are played in rotation by five actresses. Here the other actresses move around Chiyoko in a series of shifting roles, to suggest one of Kon's complexly edited sequences. From the Lotus DVD of a 2009 performance.

and producer Mizuguchi Mika, both spoke about the desire to re-create a believable or identifiable psychology for Chiyoko. On the other hand, structurally or stylistically, the stage version is even more experimental than Kon's film, and it reminds the audience more insistently of its own devices. Suematsu described to me how the production uses a visual style borrowed from film and video, moving the actresses to recreate camera techniques like framing, panning, and slow motion. In this way, we could say the stage version adds to Kon's layered structure by positioning itself not as a live version of the story but as a live remediation of the anime. Suematsu also talked about his desire to recreate the intellectual experience of the original anime: instead of having to keep track of what character Chiyoko is playing at any moment, the audience now has to keep track of which actress is playing Chiyoko.[16]

At one point even the actresses pretend to become confused about who is playing what part, and the action degenerates into fragments of various earlier scenes, with some actresses switching randomly from one part to another and others trying vainly to restore order. Finally one calls time-out, they huddle, and agree to reset. They ask a member of the audience to straighten things out by reassigning roles—choosing who should play Chiyoko and each of the other characters going forward. This breaches the fourth wall in more ways than one: not only do the actresses break character, not only do they interact directly with the audience, but this moment calls attention to the virtuosic quality of the performance, as the confused audience realizes that the actresses are far from lost—that in fact they all know all the parts and can switch on the fly. It is analogous to the moment in the puppet theater where we are so taken with the technique that we momentarily forget the characters and their story, and applaud for the puppeteers.

This moment in the production comes at a point of peak romantic tension in the story, just before Chiyoko's director Ōtaki tries to seduce the actress. On a DVD version of the 2009 performance, this scene is played awkwardly for laughs, with Yamane Chika (the actress assigned to play Chiyoko by an audience member moments before), laughing uncomfortably in the face of Matsumura Satomi's enthusiastic advances. The sense of layeredness continues as we seem to be watching a shy Chiyoko resist Ōtaki at the same time we see a shy Yamane resist Nakamura.

But on the other hand, the five actresses (all beautiful, idol-like figures with powerful stage presence) have a palpable physical reality that the animated Chiyoko lacks, so that the interactions with the audience (in the middle of the performance, afterward signing autographs in the lobby) offer a kind of attraction and intimacy with the actresses that is at odds with the virtual quality of the performance itself.[17]

The layered quality of these representations pushes Kon's focus on representation even further. Watching these women play all the roles without props not only calls attention to the arbitrary quality of gender norms, as Butler hopes, but also the arbitrary quality of representation itself. In the theater it forces us to notice not only the artificial way reality is represented on stage but also the way that each character is a subject created and held in a dynamic tension between actor and audience.

For me these considerations fill a gap in *Gender Trouble*, which argues compellingly that the body is a signifying text, but which does not discuss how literary or media depictions of the body might introduce additional layers of signification over top of that, textual layers that have to be dealt with on their own terms. Butler later extended *Gender Trouble*'s discussion of drag with a reading of Jennie Livingston's 1990 drag documentary *Paris Is Burning*, but she proves puzzlingly unable to tease any meaning from the style and structure of the documentary itself. She critiques the objective ethnographic stance she says the film claims for itself, but shows no ability to see how the *style* of the film (Livingston's clever approach to titles, transitions, narration, and structure, for example) ironizes the notion of objectivity and calls attention to the arbitrary quality of documentary representation.[18]

Butler characterizes gender as a "crossroads" or "nexus" where different discourses intersect.[19] But the stage version of *Millennium Actress* reminds us that discourses do not just intersect in a single plane; they are stacked and layered three-dimensionally, remediating one another in complex ways. So Kon remediates postwar cinema to produce a kind of drag show that is in turn remediated by Suematsu and Take It Easy! The stage version calls our attention to the ways (that Kon calls our attention to the ways) that just as gender is reproduced endlessly and changed incrementally through performative repetition, literary or media representations of gender lengthen and destabilize that chain.

Queer Spectatorship

Earlier chapters treated particular critics as representative of larger critical movements—structuralism and poststructuralism, postmodernism, posthumanism, phenomenology, or psychoanalysis. Butler's work is frequently identified with the origins of queer theory, in the way it employs poststructuralist philosophy politically, to reject fixed sexual categories. "Queer" expresses the existing but nondelimited, nonconforming genders that Butler wants to make visible or "intelligible."

So is Chiyoko queer? Asking that question is not an attempt to explain the absence of men in Chiyoko's life by writing a lesbian backstory. Criticism is not fan fiction, and a queer reading must be about escaping reductive categories rather than reassigning them. But this question does connect back to a query we left hanging several pages ago: when Chiyoko finally claims to be her own most important audience, where does that leave her other audience, Tachibana? What does the film finally say about fandom? In fact, maybe the queerest thing about *Millennium Actress* is the mode of spectatorship it enables, a mode that allows our way of reading to shift freely between different registers. I close with two queer readings focused on spectatorship that return us to the figure of Hara Setsuko.

Above I noted the parallels between Chiyoko and Hara, who started acting in the 1930s at the age of fifteen and went on to become one of Japan's biggest stars, then quit suddenly in the 1960s and went into seclusion. Hara is known in Japan as "the eternal virgin" *(eien no shojo)*. It is a nickname that captures the innocent purity of her roles, particularly in three famous films directed by Ozu Yasujirō: *Late Spring (Banshun, 1949), Early Summer (Bakushu, 1951),* and *Tokyo Story (Tōkyō monogatari, 1953)*. In all three films she plays similar characters, all named Noriko and all conspicuously reluctant to marry. (Hara also never married.) For some spectators, Hara has attained the status of queer icon, like Audrey Hepburn or Marlene Dietrich, and there is a famous scene in *Early Summer* where her love of Hepburn movies and her lack of a husband prompt someone to ask jokingly(?) if she is a lesbian.

Nothing in Hara's life provides any definitive answers to questions we might ask about Chiyoko. But queer ways of reading Hara suggest some interesting ways to read *Millennium Actress*. For example, Kanno Yūka's inspired reading of Hara focuses on a mode of "queer spectatorship," where that term takes in the location of these several different subjects (the contemporary viewer, the character of Noriko, the actress Hara, and the intradiegetic actress Hepburn) as well as the relationships of identification and desire between them. Kanno's work combines characteristics of Sobchack and Butler, perhaps even Saitō: it has a sense of these discrete subjects but also of the layers of representation that link them, and it argues that queer fans can exercise agency by rereading these subjects and reconfiguring the relationship between them in radically new ways—effectively reauthoring their own subject positions vis-à-vis the character, actress, and film. But maybe the queer reading of Noriko or spectatorship that fits *Millennium Actress* best is an essay by film director Yoshida Kijū that focuses on the sexual tension between Noriko and her father (played by Chishu Ryū) in a famous bedroom scene from *Late Spring*. This film is consistently lauded for its touching depiction of the love between a father and daughter, so Yoshida's incestuous reading is deliberately blasphemous; but his point seems to be that even though (or more likely because) the film avoids any discussion of Noriko's sexuality, when we see the twenty-three-year-old actress Hara lying next to the forty-four-year-old actor Chishu, we inevitably perceive or imagine some sexual tension between them. Yoshida effectively links the incest prohibition to another, different prohibition: classical cinema's cardinal injunction to remain immersed in the diegesis, not to confuse the feelings of the characters with those of the actors. Yoshida suggests that it is a rule we inevitably and enjoyably break—with Ozu's encouragement— slipping out of *Late Spring's* story in the same way that *Millennium Actress* slips between its various layers.[20]

The idea behind this book is that many anime will become more interesting if we engage in this kind of active and creative spectatorship and interpretation. But Kon's work in particular demands this kind of initiative, for specific reasons. From 1997 to 2006, Kon directed four feature films and one short series, each of which seemed to raise the bar set by the one before. Then in 2010, even as audiences were eagerly anticipating his next trick, Kon died of liver cancer at the age of forty-six. One is forced to wonder what the director would have produced if he had not died so young. At his best, Kon was always revealing another layer, another story, another reality beyond the present one, and his death could be seen as bringing a tragic halt to that ongoing process of revelation.[21] Certainly previous chapters have shown how directors like Oshii Mamoru used sequels and later installments to revisit and rethink their earlier work, and we will examine this dynamic even more closely in the next chapter, which takes up several different anime in the decades-long *Blood* franchise. Kon was denied this kind of opportunity. But perhaps that just means that instead of waiting for Kon to reveal the next layer, we now have to write it ourselves. Reading and rereading these few rich works, we must make that repetition produce its own diversity, generating new films for ourselves, new selves for the films.

6

The Quick and the Undead

Blood: The Last Vampire and Television Anime

This chapter turns our attention to something uncanny—a shape-shifter that exerts a magnetic attraction on those who behold it. It is doubled or accompanied by its familiars: a single consciousness shared across different species that goes forth in different bodies and different guises to do its work. It passes effortlessly through physical barriers and across cultural and international borders, its origins uncertain. Exotic but somehow familiar, it is at home wherever it appears. And it crosses time, too, reborn in different forms and different decades, sleeping for years then waking to feed again.

The vampire is a perennial subject for anime, and this description could apply to any one of several vampire protagonists in different anime franchises. But this is also a good description of the franchise itself, the coven of related titles and products that trails each of these characters, spreading outward from the original manga or anime into countless other media: manga–anime crossovers and hybrids, novelizations, foreign adaptations, video games, live-action films, theatrical productions, soundtracks, model figures, character goods, and an array of homegrown media from fan fiction, fan art, and *dōjinshi* manga to anime music videos, costumes, and more.

Some critics refer to this larger complex of texts as the "media mix," to highlight this movement across media. Here I am using "franchise" to take in the spread of titles both within and between media, as well as across times and cultures. Whatever we call it, the effect of this spread is to extend the fascination of the original title over different markets and even different generations, giving the most successful series an immortal or undying quality as they are continually reinvented for new times and places. This chapter takes up one such constellation, the *Blood* franchise, which starts from a fifty-minute theatrical film released in 2000, *Blood: The Last Vampire*. Directed by Kitakubo Hiroyuki, the film was a collaborative project by a team of young creators working at Production I.G under the guidance of Oshii Mamoru (the studio and director introduced in chapters 2 and 3). The visuals and politics of the film bear Oshii's distinctive mark, but over the next decade *Blood: The Last Vampire* spun off dozens of very different texts by very different creators, across all the media described above.

As the title of this chapter suggests, my reading of *Blood* is concerned with speed and movement, and one sense of this is the energy and rapidity with which the film's vampire protagonist Saya moves from one medium and one series to another—the portability of these characters that can anchor so many different kinds of texts. The other sense is the way in which Saya's drawn image moves on screen, or how she is animated. Recent criticism has attempted to link these two things, asking which specific visual qualities of these characters allow them to move so fluidly between media. This allows us to sustain our focus on anime's form, but also extend our consideration to other kinds of texts.

The first half of this chapter considers the original film as a metaphor for postwar and Cold War U.S.–Japan relations, returning to some of the political issues examined in the context of *Akira* and *Patlabor 2* at the outset of the book. As a narrative, the vampire story is a pointed and powerful figure for the U.S.– Japan political relationship; but as always, we will go beyond plot to see how the anime's formal qualities also generate meaning. In this chapter, we turn to the work of Thomas Lamarre, whose writing on the anime image constitutes the most elaborate and sustained formal theory of this medium to date. Lamarre examines how movements and compositions specific to anime (especially portrayals of depth and motion) create a sense of freedom, possibility, and agency in the image itself. Applying Lamarre's ideas to *Blood: The Last Vampire* will suggest ways in which the movie's visuals might answer some of the political questions posed by its plot.

In the second part of this chapter, we will look beyond the original film to the broader franchise and consider some other recent theories of anime that supplement or even challenge the methodology of this book. These theories argue that anime studies should focus less on individual films and more on individual characters across multiple platforms, less on individual film directors and more on collaborative teams of media producers, not just on the interpretation of works but on the circumstances of their production and distribution. Can we reconcile these perspectives with this book's more interpretive approach? This latter part of the chapter looks at a few more pieces of the *Blood* franchise, including two television series produced in 2005–6 and 2011, and asks how this additional material might augment or change our interpretation of the original film.

Parasites, Plots, and Panty Shots: The Politics of *Blood: The Last Vampire*

Blood: The Last Vampire opens on a nearly deserted Tokyo subway train as it approaches its final stop of the night. The film was one of the first anime to make extensive use of photorealistic digital effects, and shots of the train highlight this from the outset, using digital image processing to create complex lighting effects and three-dimensional digital modeling to animate the moving train. Inside the subway car, a coldly attractive young girl stares at the only other passenger in the car, an exhausted office worker. Several complex perspective shots inside and outside the moving train alternate with close-ups of the more two-dimensional characters and the opening credits, building tension while showcasing the film's digital effects. Then suddenly the girl leaps from her seat, races toward her fellow passenger in a dramatic blur of action, and cuts him down with a samurai sword.

As the girl exits the train, she is met by two American agents of an unnamed secret organization, and we learn from their conversation that her victim belonged to a vampire-like race of monsters who can take human form. The monsters are called "chiropterans" (after the biological order that includes bats), and the girl, Saya, has been enlisted to hunt them down. This terse dialogue between Saya and the agents, David and Louis, is the only background the film provides, but it establishes that Saya is also a vampire herself.

The link and the distinction between her and the chiropterans is explained only with David's single cryptic comment that "she is the only remaining original." (The line is spoken in English, as is most of the dialogue in the film.)

The scene also sets up the mission that will occupy Saya for the rest of the fifty-minute film: the monsters have emerged from hibernation and infiltrated the United States Air Force base in Yokota, outside Tokyo, where they have already murdered several people. Saya poses as a student to visit the base high school where the last murder took place, in hopes of ferreting out the chiropterans who are passing as humans. She locates them on Halloween night and fights three of them in a running battle, climaxing with a dramatic fight in a burning hangar and a chase across the runways.

The monsters are killed, and the incident is hushed up. In the final scene some days later, the sole civilian witness (the school nurse) wonders what she has seen. All of the scenes up to now have been at night or in the fading light of the late afternoon, with beautiful lighting effects created and layered over cell animation using digital drawing software. But now in the brighter daylight, the monsters seem no more than a bad dream. At the same time a suspicion or a fear that has lain in the shadows for the whole film now comes into the light: it is clear right from the opening shot (of a rotary dial telephone) that the film is set in the near past, but aside from small details in the background of one or two scenes, there is no indication of the year. In the closing minutes, though, we see a prominent calendar marked 1966, and the final shot shows a B-52 bomber taking off into the clear blue sky while an English voiceover describes the bombing war in Vietnam. This places us near the beginning of the U.S. war in Vietnam, which would continue for a decade, claim more than a million American and Vietnamese lives, and become a focal point for 1960s political protest in America and Japan. The end credits allude to this history with dim, grainy (ghostly) news footage of the war.

Here we might consider some of the various critical tools and interpretive strategies we have covered in the preceding chapters, and ask which might shed light on this film. The time and place immediately recall the postwar political background we discussed in the context of *Akira* and *Patlabor 2*, and if we start with the plot of the film, vampirism is a clear metaphor for U.S.–Japan relations, though the vampire in this case could be either America or Japan. As discussed in chapters 1 and 2, the U.S. military bases that were established in Japan after World War II became staging areas for U.S. combat operations in Korea, Vietnam, and beyond. In the heated Japanese debates that center on these bases, one position has portrayed the United States as a foreign parasite that has exploited its Japanese host in order to prosecute its own wars; another accuses Japan of being the parasite—of enjoying the shelter of the U.S. military umbrella with minimal expenditure and risk.

This international dialectic of exploitation and dependence is reproduced in local communities around the bases. Large U.S. installations support local economies, but in Okinawa particularly, there have been a number of well-publicized rapes and murders committed by U.S. marines and base workers who were then allegedly shielded by the American military. This has created a nationwide image of the bases as Dracula's castles, harboring monsters who raid the populace and then escape back to the safety of the manor. And the deafening jet noise from Air Force bases like Yokota has become a charged symbol of U.S. indifference to the surrounding Japanese communities. In *Blood: The Last Vampire,* the military bars and brothels around Yokota are a hunting ground for the chiropterans. When the body of a murdered hostess is discovered early in the film, one character speculates that the woman's American boyfriend might be involved in her death, but the comment is all but drowned out by the noise of a passing plane.

As this scene suggests, the uncertainty about who plays the vampire in the U.S.–Japan political relationship is reflected in the difficulty of deciding whether the vampires and other monsters in this anime are American or Japanese. In fact, the vampire is a privileged figure for racial or cultural mixing in much popular culture, something we might unpack with the theories of the posthuman body discussed in chapter 3.[1] At least since Bram Stoker's turn-of-the-century novel *Dracula,* the vampire has been cast as familiar but also foreign. ("The impression I had was that we were leaving the West and entering the East," says Englishman Jonathan Harker as his train nears Transylvania in the first lines of the novel.) At the same time, the vampire's eroticism and the way it breaches blood and body boundaries suggest sexual communion but also perversion and pollution. All this leads Donna Haraway to make the vampire a central metaphor in her work on the construction of race in twentieth-century biology. In our reading of *Ghost in the Shell*, we discussed Haraway's posthumanism and her use of the cyborg to challenge the artificial dichotomies that define the modern gendered subject: male and female, mind and body, self and other. Haraway's vampire functions in the same way, as a corruption of the naturalized subject that makes us realize how constructed and unnatural that subject was to begin with.

> A figure that both promises and threatens racial and sexual mixing, the vampire feeds off the normalized human. . . . Deeply shaped by murderous ideologies since their modern popularization in European accounts in the late eighteenth century—especially racism, sexism and homophobia—stories of the undead also exceed and invert each of those systems of discrimination to show the violence infesting supposedly wholesome life and nature and the revivifying promise of what is supposed to be decadent and against nature.[2]

Extending this kind of reading to Japan, Kotani Mari argues that the vampire represents a similar kind of otherness in Japanese manga and prose fiction, but an otherness that is doubled because vampire stories enter Japanese literature as a foreign genre. Kotani writes that vampires have represented the threat and appeal of a Western Other since the first Japanese vampire fiction in the 1930s. But she also describes how later authors like Kasai Kiyoshi reversed this paradigm, casting the Japanese as a race of vampires themselves. The nationalist metaphor is transformed further by the hybrid human–vampire heroes of Kikuchi Hideyuki's *Vampire Hunter-D* novels (the basis of a popular anime franchise), as well as Ōhara Mariko's parasitic vampires that infest and manipulate their human hosts: both blur or erase the lines between native and foreign, or self and other, and show us "how we should speculate on the topic of 'hybridity' in a post-colonialist and post-creolian age, a topic that puts into jeopardy the very metaphysics of originality."[3]

Like Haraway's vampires or Kotani's, *Blood's* vampires symbolize racial or cultural difference, conflict, and hybridity—the way that one culture can regard another as monstrous, but also the need to come to terms with our own colonial histories and the realization that we are in some sense vampires ourselves.[4] This accounts for the liminality of the chiropterans (bat-like creatures who can masquerade as humans) and Saya (a creature suspended between us and them). As Kotani predicts, the ambiguity of Saya's vampire identity is matched by a cultural ambiguity. More than one character asks her uncertainly if she is Japanese, but she pointedly refuses to answer. Voiced by bilingual actress Kudō Yūki, she speaks Japanese and English with nearly equal fluency. And she seems to be passing for a Japanese visitor at the base school, although she is unfamiliar with Japanese customs: David has to explain to her that the sailor suit she has been given to wear is a Japanese school uniform.

Like Haraway's hybrids, Saya has a transgressive quality that is both threatening and alluring, but where Haraway hopes the vampire can expose and overturn an established order, it is hard to see Saya as progressive, or even serious. The schoolgirl uniform constitutes a sexual fetish in many anime, but it feels ironic on Saya, who has become jaded and perverted over the course of her unnaturally long life, even as she retains the body of a little girl. Saya is sexy in the vampire's liminal, transgressive way, but the vampire's eternal youth and seductive power have been translated into a series of exaggerated anime archetypes. Saya is both little girl and demon lover, a sword-wielding samurai in an up-skirt pose (Figure 39).

The events of the plot do not really resolve these cultural ambiguities. The climax comes on the night of the base Halloween party (a backdrop that further ironizes these horror stereotypes), when Saya shows up at the school infirmary just in time to save the school nurse from two chiropterans disguised as female students. The nurse is the film's emblematic victim, and she too seems alternately American and Japanese, with an apparently bicultural name (Makiko Caroline Asano), and many of the same ambiguous qualities as Saya (Figure 40). Saya kills one monster and wounds the other, but her sword is broken in the struggle. The creatures are immune to gunfire, and only a genuine warrior's blade is

AT YOKOTA AIR FORCE BASE
BEASTS LURK WITHIN
VICIOUS KILLERS WITH AN APPETITE FOR BLOOD
ONLY ONE WOMAN CAN ELIMINATE THEM

...THE LAST REMAINING ORIGINAL

FIGURE 39. Saya in *Blood: The Last Vampire*. This captures her portrayal as a kind of veteran and maiden—a violent, sexualized, child warrior. From a package insert in the Manga Entertainment DVD (2001).

strong enough to cut them, so Saya steals a replacement sword from the window of a nearby antique store and gives chase. When she strikes the chiropteran, however, the sword turns out to be a fake modern reproduction, and it bends in half. With the tables turned, the monster traps the weaponless Saya and the nurse in an airplane hangar, which catches fire. Finally in the scene's feverish climax, David arrives with a genuine sword that he flings desperately toward Saya. Framed dramatically against the flames, she screams for the sword and then catches, draws, and swings the blade in a blur of motion to cut the chiropteran in half.

This climax provides no simple answer to the question of who is the vampire and who is the prey in the U.S.–Japan relationship. Neither the heroine nor the central victim are definitively American or Japanese. Both are threatened by the chiropterans, but do these monsters represent America menacing Japan, or Japan taking its revenge on the American interloper? The tangled symbolism of the film stems at least in part from the tangled politics of

FIGURE 40. In *Blood: The Last Vampire,* Saya and the school nurse have features and behaviors that mark them as both American and Japanese. In the
second image, characters from the bars near the base show the caricatured
quality of the film's other human figures. The cross-dressing bar owner on the
left turns out to be a monster in disguise. All *Blood: The Last Vampire* stills are
from the Manga Entertainment Blu-ray disc (2009).

postwar Japan. As discussed in the opening chapters, the constitution imposed on Japan after World War II and the joint security
treaties that followed rested on the principle that Japan would receive protection from U.S. forces based there while renouncing the
right to wage war itself. The legacy of this policy was a Japanese
national identity that was split: a militarily noninterventionist
and constitutionally pacifist country on the one hand, but also

a key supporter of several U.S. wars. The paradox of Japan's position is seen in the fact that calls for a more militarily independent Japan have come from the right and left: from conservative nationalists who think Japan should assert itself militarily abroad, and from an alternative left that believes an independent Japanese foreign policy could exert moral and diplomatic pressure to stem U.S. aggression. But for many others the idea of a rearmed Japan represents an alarming echo of the 1930s and 1940s, when Imperial Japan invaded its Asian neighbors ostensibly to "protect" them from Western encroachment.

In this context, the chiropterans might be associated with violent militarism and war itself—both postwar U.S. interventions and the Japanese militarism of World War II. In that reading, the hibernating monster of Japanese militarism has lain dormant or disguised since the end of the war, but now threatens to reemerge. Only Saya can stop it. Clothed in a military-style school uniform and armed with a samurai sword, she might represent a truer, nobler, and more disciplined warrior spirit ("the only remaining original"), which could rein in violence. Saya is to rescue Japan from the loss of that warrior spirit, a crisis symbolized here by the sword that turns out to be fake. *Blood: The Last Vampire* can be read to suggest that if the country does not regain its martial and cultural identity it will fall into the animal violence of the chiropterans—supporting U.S. imperialism by proxy or resorting to military adventurism itself.

In other words, as much as Saya is a sexual fantasy cobbled together from fetishistic images, she is simultaneously a fantasy of national agency and identity. Japanese and not Japanese, she is the force that will cut through the knot of Japanese politics. By the time the repressed tension between David and Saya achieves violent release in the burning hangar, it is as much political as it is sexual: from David (the United States) she receives the sword she could not find. With it, she regains the warrior spirit Japan lost after World War II, and with this new blade she incarnates a new Japan, one on an independent equal footing with the West. With youth's innocent strength and age's sad wisdom, Saya can then rescue both countries (in the person of the nurse) from the militarism and imperialism of the past, a threat represented by the ravening chiropterans. With her sword reforged, she will conquer war itself and guard the peace.

Described at the level of the plot, this political metaphor of a sword-wielding vampire schoolgirl in a sailor suit seems ridiculous, a perfect parody. If sexy Saya fits the profile of Saitō Tamaki's "beautiful fighting girl" analyzed in chapter 4 and symbolizes the unattainable sexual desires of her otaku fans, then perhaps the pastiche of overlapping national fantasies conveys unconsummated yearnings of a more political kind: the intractability of these geopolitical issues, the contradictions that seem to inhere in every (im)possible solution.

And yet there remains something compelling about this anime, which is able to convey the danger, the seductive excitement, even the hopefulness of these fantasies while simultaneously critiquing them from within. Evocative, even provocative, *Blood: The Last Vampire* does not feel as silly as a plot summary makes it sound. That is because the real key to the film's dynamic tension between fantasy and reality is not in the story but elsewhere, in the experience of the film, and particularly the way the characters look and move on screen.

Trains, Planes, and Lamarre's "Anime Machine"

After Saya kills the monster inside the burning hangar, yet another chiropteran appears and perches dramatically on the hangar roof, then grows wings and glides out over the runways. As Saya and David pursue it in a jeep, they realize it is heading for a plane that is taxiing toward takeoff. For some reason they desperately need to stop it before it reaches the plane, but it is not exactly clear why. Will it attack and crash the aircraft? Perhaps it will cling to the wing and escape beyond their reach—though if it can fly by itself, why does it need to hitch a ride on the plane? And if the chiropteran only wants to get away, why did it come to the base in the first place? The plot of the film does not really provide any decisive answers, but we can solve the riddle of this scene and learn more about politics and representation in the film by asking how Saya and the planes move, and what their movements represent.

In *Akira* we encountered a political confusion similar to the confusion in *Blood,* centering on the political significance of characters and events that seemed to mix real-world political references with fantasy. *Akira's* visual features emphasized that confusion: the manga included deep perspective shots that oriented and located the characters and structured the narratives of search, navigation, and discovery that gave the manga its sense of development; but the anime had a flatness that made it difficult to map the postmodern space of the city, and it was correspondingly difficult to fix the characters' position in the physical and political landscape. This uncertainty was amplified by a light/dark dynamic that left the characters hurtling through space but unable to see where they were going or what lay ahead. However, we also considered more optimistic theories of the postmodern and their idea that a degree of uncertainty could be productive. Jean-François Lyotard suggests it might be healthy to overcome the modern tropes of omniscient rationality and progress, ideas we can see emblemized by universal linear perspective and expressed politically in conquest, colony, and empire. *Blood: The Last Vampire* allows us to revisit these issues and bring some new critical tools to bear. In particular, Thomas Lamarre's book *The Anime Machine* provides a media theory of anime that links movement with politics. And it begins, like *Blood: The Last Vampire,* with the image of a train.

The train exemplifies the third of three "machines" that structure Lamarre's analysis. The first machine is associated with the technology used to make anime: the tools and processes for drawing, coloring, sequencing, and photographing images on cels to produce a moving image. Particularly important for Lamarre is the way transparent cells with painted details are layered on top of one another to produce the composite image, and the way those layers are moved in relation to one another as they are photographed to produce frames of film. Lamarre's second "machine" is anime itself: not the apparatus used to produce it but the abstract systems through which anime generates meaning for the viewer. This is the link between the look of anime and its ability to connect with the politics of the real world. Finally, those real-world politics are the third machine, linked to physical technologies like the train that shape our lived reality and perceptions. Lamarre's goal is to chart how "animetic" motion can help us rethink our relationship to technology and politics. "My emphasis is . . . on how technologies affect thought," he says. "It is on the positive and productive constraints that a machine places on thought, producing a positive unconscious, so to speak."[5]

In contrast with anime, the train represents an ideal of "cinematistic" motion. Here Lamarre draws on a body of theory that links the railroad and the cinema as related technologies of viewing. He quotes Paul Virilio: "What happens in the train window, in the car windshield, in the television screen, is the same kind of cinematism." The urge to greater depth and greater speed is linked to the baleful influence of technology, what Virilio calls a "ballistic motion" associated with the logic of war: a sense of speed and penetration that is dangerously aggressive. "As speed introduces a sense of separation between the world and the subject," writes Lamarre, "the eye becomes a kine-eye, desirous of greater velocity and mobility, bent on its own destruction."[6]

The key feature of Lamarre's cinematism is movement into depth, and this is where anime differs. Anime cannot generate an illusion of depth in the same way that live-action cinema can: instead, it represents depth by means of layers that slide against one another. "While it too is a modern art of the engine grounded in a speed-riddled instrumentalized perception of the world," says Lamarre, "animetism is not about movement *into depth* but movement *on and between surfaces*."[7] Near and distant objects are painted on different transparent cells, which are composited. That is, they are layered and moved past one another at different rates as successive frames are photographed, generating a perspectival sense of foreground, middle ground, and background. (For example, if we are following alongside a running character, she may remain in the same place within the frame while the fence just behind her rushes by in a blur, but a tree in the middle distance will change position more slowly, and a mountain on the horizon will not move at all.) One might dismiss this as a limitation, a clunky approximation of full linear perspective in which everything would recede smoothly toward a single vanishing point. But Lamarre is interested precisely in the discontinuous gap between layers. Anime exposes this "animetic interval" and discovers in it a kind of energy and mobility that correspond to being released from the limits of linear perspective and gaining a different kind of freedom.

A related concept is so-called limited animation, anime's practice of reducing the number of illustrations that make up an animated sequence. Often traced to cost-cutting strategies associated with the beginning of televised series in the 1960s, limited animation has given rise to a number of specific effects that have now come to be regarded as positive parts of anime's aesthetic. In the example above, our running figure will be represented by a series of different cels showing her in different poses, photographed successively to give the illusion of smoothly pumping arms and striding legs. If we draw fewer intermediate stages of each arm and leg movement, the smooth motion will turn into a jerky energy. Finally if we replace the articulated figure with a static drawing of the figure painted on a single cell, and then slide that cell across a static background ("moving the drawing" instead of "drawing the movement"), the figure will appear to rush through space in a rigid pose, as if flying.

Limited animation and the animetic interval appear in different forms and combinations that correspond to different cases of Lamarre's argument; but, collapsing these, we might say that these new spatial relations allow characters to escape the constraints of rigid geometric perspective, where every point has its place in a mathematically defined hierarchy, and slip from our existing ballistic relationship with technology into a freer world of less predictable motion across multiple fields. "Now characters do not simply move gracefully across the image; they can literally jump into and out of the image along angular trajectories that follow one or more of multiple fields of action crisscrossing the image. The animetic interval directs the force of the moving image in a manner that allows for leaps from field to field."[8]

The animetic also transforms the character's and viewer's relation to the background or environment. In our reading of the *Akira* manga, images of the characters looking down on the city signified locatability and a reassuring but also sinister sense of control (Figure 6), creating (to borrow Lamarre's language) "the impression of a rational subject who stands over and above the world, somehow separate from it."[9] Lamarre's animetism offers an alternative in which the character, environment, and viewer occupy sliding planes that place them on equal terms with one another. Lamarre cites a scene in Miyazaki Hayao's *Castle in the Sky* (*Tenkū no shiro Rapyuta*, 1986), where the child protagonists reach the flying castle city of Laputa and look down from a tower at the rest of the marvelous structure while clouds slide across their view.

> Such a technique of sliding the planes makes the children's viewing position (and ours as well) feel less instrumental. This way of looking does not encourage us to seize this place instrumentally, that is, to poke into its every corner, to plunder its treasures, to dominate and exploit it (as the bad guys are prone to do). Rather this is a world that opens to us even as it remains apart from us. As it opens, you see depth, but these depths are not calculable by Cartesian geometry. This manner of viewing thus invites awe and reverence. We are witnesses not raiders.[10]

Blood: The Last Vampire introduces an interesting new wrinkle into Lamarre's scheme with its combination of two- and three-dimensional animation techniques. One of the anime's innovations was to include backgrounds and objects that were modeled in three dimensions on computers. Because the computer can calculate the appearance of three-dimensional elements and environments from any angle and generate as many intermediate frames as needed, it allows animators to produce sequences in which intricate forms rotate smoothly, or scenes in which the virtual camera traces a complex path through space—both cases that are difficult to animate by hand.

While many of the characters in the anime are two-dimensional caricatures, the airplanes in the background are rendered in three dimensions, in mechanically accurate detail, and the juxtaposition seems to associate the planes with a more profound reality (Figure 41). As they take off or return from a destination we can imagine to be Vietnam, these aircraft are the film's most prominent signifier for the real world of war and geopolitics outside of the vampire fantasy. But what is more interesting is the way that the film *juxtaposes* three-dimensional computer-rendered elements with the kind of limited animation Lamarre describes. When Saya races through the train car toward the disguised chiropteran in the opening scene, the train cars are rendered with an almost exaggerated linear perspective, while Saya remains a "moving drawing"—frozen in one static pose as she flies through the car toward her target. Faster than a locomotive, she is also free of its ponderous inertia. As she strikes down postwar political threats in the person of the chiropteran, Saya may even be quick enough to evade the ballistic logic of war. This fast freedom is the ultimate object of desire that Saya represents, but in the end it is probably unattainable: all around her, the ponderous shapes of other figures (the train, the planes) remind us of a weightier reality.[11]

These, then, are the film's links between political and visual dynamics, or political movements and physical motion. This is also one more version of anime's characteristic oscillation between realism or immersion and distance or abstraction. At the most intuitive level, the film lulls us into a fantasy world not only with its occult plot but with its flat visuals; yet, whenever a plane appears, it possesses a cinematic realism that calls us back to the reality of the Vietnam war. And as the film juxtaposes two-dimensional cartoonishness with three-dimensional realism, it also juxtaposes visions of fast, floating freedom with the lumbering weighty responsibilities imposed on postwar Japan.[12]

We can now revisit and reread the film's final chase. Why must David and Saya prevent the chiropteran from reaching the plane? The aircraft is not in danger. It is a Hercules transport, a hundred feet long and forty feet tall, and as we get closer it towers over Saya and the monster. The real worry is about what powers the monster will gain if it joins with this machine. If the chiropterans represent an awakening Japanese militarism, then the fear of renewed Japanese intervention abroad is figured as the threat that the monster will escape Japan's shores on America's back, and reach out as far as Vietnam—a move that suggests the escalation of U.S. involvement after 1966, as well as Japan's expansion into Southeast Asia in 1940, a prelude to the Pacific War.

More broadly, and more in line with the visual argument above, the fear in this scene is that latent Japanese militarism (which has been pushed back into the realm of fantasy up to now) will some-

FIGURE 41. Planes landing and taxiing in *Blood: The Last Vampire*. Computer modeling allows the planes or the camera to rotate realistically, exposing different sides of the aircraft. Lighting effects were also produced digitally, using imaging software.

how merge with the three-dimensional space of the aircraft and reassert itself in the real world. The fear that the chiropteran will reach the plane is the fear that Japan's imperialists will rise from the (un)dead, that the two-dimensional nightmare will somehow become a three-dimensional reality. This is the catastrophe Saya averts. When David pulls the speeding jeep alongside the plane, she slashes the monster just short of the plane's wing. As the aircraft turns away from her and wheels into the sky, Saya remains a flattened silhouette in the foreground. She has succeeded in keeping the creature in her own two-dimensional world, but she cannot enter the real world either. For now anyway, the rearmed peaceful Japan she symbolizes is just a pipe dream.

But even if Saya fails to transcend the two-dimensional world of fantasy to engage with the real world, she does go somewhere, traversing several other fantasy worlds and other media as the star of a rapidly expanding *Blood* franchise. That is the topic of this chapter's second half.

Character-Based Criticism and Theories of the Media Mix

Blood: The Last Vampire's conclusion notwithstanding, five years later Saya and the chiropterans both turn up in Vietnam, in the first episode of the 2005–6 anime television series *Blood+* (pronounced as written, "Blood plus"). *Blood+* opens with grainy footage of U.S. combat troops in a Vietnamese village, fighting a pitched battle with chiropterans. Saya appears (incongruously clothed in a hospital gown) and cuts down the chiropterans in a rage. Then, looking more and more like a monster herself, she slaughters the Vietnamese villagers and finally turns on the American troops before we fade to black.

This seems to be precisely the fear that lies at the heart of the original film, the fear that violence might be used to meet violence, but that once unleashed it will never be controlled. But does this scene rewrite or revise the end of the earlier film, which seemed to keep the violence from spreading beyond Japan? Is this scene real or just a nightmare, Saya herself or an evil twin? Does that grainy visual texture suggest a memory, a newsreel, an old war film, or something else? Does what we are watching even belong to the same logical universe as the film? Viewers with the patience to watch all fifty episodes of the series will get answers to some of these queries, but none that really address the political questions underneath. As we will see below, in *Blood+* Saya is far more two-dimensional than she is in *Blood: The Last Vampire,* and she remains trapped in a cartoon world right to the end.

Perhaps the larger question here is this: in order to construct a reading of the 2000 film, how much of the whole franchise should we be expected to take into account? The world of *Blood* now includes anime films, television series, a live-action movie, novels, manga, video games, a stage play, and a great deal more. In the same way, almost all of the films and OVAs discussed in the preceding chapters have their own sequels, series, manga, etcetera. By and large we have focused on one film and one media comparison at a time, in the interest of being able to say something specific about each work. But as we near the end of this book, perhaps we should consider the alternatives to that approach, and ask what we might learn by trying to digest a little more of the *Blood* megatext.

A number of recent writers have argued that anime criticism should give less attention to individual narratives and more attention to (1) larger franchises and (2) the character as the thing that links these different media products together. In his pivotal book *Tezuka Is Dead* (*Tezuka izu deddo*, 2005), manga critic Itō Gō critiques traditional modes of manga criticism that he says overemphasize story and fail to appreciate manga's formal characteristics, including character designs formed in dialogue with other media like anime and video games.

Pop culture critic and creator Ōtsuka Eiji's theory of "narrative consumption" argues that the plots of individual episodes, installments, or elements in these franchises mean little or nothing individually, but that what is really being sold and consumed is a larger fictional narrative (an overall story, history, or world) that consumers must reconstruct from these individual fragments— "the grand narrative or order (*chitsujo*) that they hold in partial form and as their background."[13] (One of Ōtsuka's examples is the anime and manga megafranchise *Gundam*, set in a sprawling world whose hyperdetailed technologies, histories, and politics unfold over countless individual works and series.) Ōtsuka emphasizes that the narrative fragments can be almost entirely character based: his central example is a series of stickers included in packages of Bikkuriman chocolates in the 1980s, each featuring an original character with a very brief description on the back. Together, the descriptions on all 772 cards added up to a larger narrative about the fictional world these characters inhabited, encouraging children to collect the whole set.

Finally Azuma Hiroki's theory of database culture (introduced in chapter 4) draws on Jean-François Lyotard's ideas about the postmodern decline of the grand narratives of national and human identity, and uses them to take Ōtsuka's ideas a step further. Azuma suggests that at some point Ōtsuka's grand fictional narratives (like *Gundam*) replaced the philosophical and civilizational narratives Lyotard identifies, but that now we have moved to a further stage of consumption where there is no narrative whatsoever—only a parade of characters popular for their visual design. (Azuma cites Di Gi Charat, the mascot of an anime retailer that spun off a series of related characters and garnered a huge fan following with no associated story at all.) For Azuma, Lyotard's grand historical narratives and Ōtsuka's grand fictional narratives have now been replaced by a "grand non-narrative," a database of elements that can be reassembled to construct these characters.[14]

With Ōtsuka and Azuma we see a shift in focus from *interpreting* narratives to tracking the circumstances of their production and consumption, a shift that takes us beyond literary studies alone and into new disciplines. For example, Marc Steinberg's book *Anime's Media Mix* draws on Ōtsuka to analyze anime from the perspective of media history. Where I refer to franchises, Steinberg uses the term "media mix" to focus attention on the spread of texts and characters from one medium to another. He traces this phenomenon to the beginnings of television anime, particularly a cross-promotion between Tezuka Osamu's *Astro Boy* TV series (*Tetsuwan Atomu*, 1963–66) and Meiji Marble chocolates. In *Astro Boy*, Tezuka used the kind of limited animation described above, reducing the number of drawn images to satisfy the time and cost constraints of television. Steinberg argues beautifully that it is the resulting combination of movement and stillness in the characters' visual design (the hero's rigid flying pose, for example) that allowed them to move so easily from Tezuka's manga to television animation, then to the character stickers included in packages of Meiji chocolate. "The anime series . . . developed an interplay between mobility and immobility that generated the synergy between media and commodity forms," Steinberg writes. "The graphically immobile Atomu image was what allowed media and commodity forms to establish connections and to communicate."[15]

If Steinberg's focus is media history, other approaches are more ethnographic. Anthropologist Anne Allison followed up her early influential work on manga with *Millennial Monsters*, a study of Japanese character toys and their associated media. Drawing on interviews with consumers and producers, Allison makes a connection between the ability of Japanese character goods to adapt to different audiences and the motifs of transformation that we see in the narratives themselves. Another ethnography that treats anime and the media mix is Ian Condry's book *The Soul of Anime: Collaborative Creativity and Japan's Media Success Story*, a study of anime production based on fieldwork at anime studios. For Condry the "soul" and "success" of anime both lie in the distinctive teamwork that produces it and the connections it generates between people.

Condry's emphasis on joint authorship certainly fits *Blood: The Last Vampire*, which famously grew out of Oshii Mamoru's class for young creators at Production I.G, and reportedly started from a general character concept for Saya.[16] The original staff came from a range of backgrounds and went on to have a variety of roles in later parts of the *Blood* franchise. (To cite just one example, Fujisaku Jun'ichi helped develop the original character concept for Saya, then went on to write several of the novels, pen scripts for virtually all of the anime that followed, direct a video game, and act as supervising director for the *Blood+* TV series.) Condry suggests that media crossovers are the natural result of this collaborative process: characters naturally spread to other projects and media as different creative teams cooperate with one another and as fans join in. "Anime characters and worlds, combined with the attachments that people feel toward them, become platforms on which others can innovate."[17]

With their ideas about the decline of individual narratives and individual auteurs, and/or the need to focus more broadly on characters, collaborations, franchises, and commercial contexts, the critics above position their work variously as a supplement, alternative, or replacement for the kind of interpretive close readings of individual anime and individual directors practiced in this book. My question is whether we can combine these two approaches to bring interpretation back into the mix. How would reading across a franchise or focusing on characters change the reading of *Blood's* politics in the first part of this chapter? Let's start by examining the broader world of *Blood*.

As of this writing, the *Blood* franchise has three different phases (listed in the chronology at the back of the book). *Blood: The Last Vampire* was accompanied in 2000 by a smattering of related works, equally idiosyncratic, including a political novel by Oshii, *Night of the Beasts,* and a pornographic but very political manga by Benkyō Tamaoki. The second phase, "*Blood+,*" includes a series of new works starting in 2005 that were aimed at a younger, broader audience. *Blood+* was a dramatic expansion, anchored in a year-long weekly television series and more than a dozen volumes of mainstream or young adult manga and prose fiction. Featuring a distinctly softer Saya, these texts traced a new millennial chapter in her story, with periodic flashbacks to earlier events in her 170-year life, including the Russian Revolution and the U.S. war in Vietnam. The third phase of the franchise, "*Blood-C,*" begins in 2011. The anime portion consists of a twelve-part television series and a new theatrical film that once again transformed Saya's characterization and appearance. *Blood-C* restored some of the franchise's experimental feel and once again brought the setting (and politics) up to the present day.[18]

With its English dialogue and a Canadian film festival premier, *Blood: The Last Vampire* was already positioned for an international audience. *Blood+* and *Blood-C* also gained popularity outside Japan, another way one could trace Saya's mobility. The year 2009 even saw a live-action Hollywood film, with Korean actress Ji-hyun Jun as Saya and French filmmaker Chris Nahon directing. And of course beyond these official works is another universe of fan-produced content: fan fiction, artwork, cosplay, anime music videos, and more.

A sense of these other texts might change our reading of Saya, but an analysis that takes in everything would be too general to say anything. Criticism always involves choices. Where, then, do we draw the line? Will the poseable Saya action figure reveal something new about her character? My box set of *Blood+* DVDs included a knit watch cap with a series logo. Do I have to wear the hat?

The most extensive elements of *Blood*'s media mix (and the most prominent candidates for comparison with the original film) would be the manga, the novels, and the television anime series. We have already compared manga to anime in chapter 1, and chapter 7 will devote its attention to prose fiction, so in the remainder of this chapter let us consider the *Blood* television series that anchored the second and third phases of the franchise.

Repetition and Doubling in *Blood+*

The *Blood+* television anime (supervising director Fujisaku Jun'ichi) was broadcast weekly from fall 2005 to fall 2006, in fifty half-hour episodes. A series like this is very different from a theatrical film or a short series released direct to video (like *3x3 Eyes* or *Read or Die*). We will not make much headway trying to summarize the whole plot, but if we consider the overall structure of the series (the rhythm with which it develops), we find a motif examined in the previous two chapters: repetition. The series endlessly doubles and repeats the same elements. The results resemble the database structure Azuma relates to video games, where each play-through or episode involves a kind of dissociative reset, and then a repetition or recombination of similar patterns and events.[19] This is sustained in the plot by a narrative of amnesia, like we encountered in chapter 4: characters (and perhaps viewers) are continually forgetting what has come before, allowing the narrative to repeat itself. All of this informs *Blood+*'s politics in decisive ways.

The pattern of amnesia and repetition is established in the first minutes of episode 1. Right after the bloody Vietnam scene described above, we go to the opening credits, and when we return from the commercial we realize it was all a flashback or a nightmare. We are in present-day Okinawa, and a transformed Saya is in a schoolyard practicing her high jump, eating lunch, chatting happily with a friend. She is not the growling, scowling killer of the original movie, but slighter, friendlier, short-haired, cute. The autumn evenings of the earlier film have given way to a summer day, and the burnt color palette has been replaced by bright blues, greens, and whites. As for Saya, she has no recollection of her identity or her past, except for the last year living on

Okinawa with an adopted family. When a huge plane with U.S. markings lumbers noisily overhead (repeating a similar shot from *Blood: The Last Vampire*), Saya's friend has to explain to her what it is, a bomber flying from one of the American airfields on the Japanese island (Figure 42). "My mom works at the base," the girl tells Saya. "She says bombers from Okinawa are all flying to wars somewhere. That's how it is, and that is how it's always been." The parallel shots and the dialogue call our attention to the repetition, but for Saya the plane stirs only a vague sense of déjà vu.

As suggested by this scene of warfare forgotten, the concerns developed over the course of this series are more personal than political. The theme of *Blood+* (and the meaning of the title) lie in the tension between two different things: the characters' familial or racial history and legacy, on the one hand, versus the things that go beyond blood, their freedom to select their own allies and chart their own futures. Saya can choose to remember her past and as-

FIGURE 42. The 2005–6 *Blood+* television series has a more lighthearted character design. Here in a scene set in Okinawa, Saya sees planes from an American base pass overhead, closely mirroring a shot from the original film (Figure 41). From the Sony DVDs (2001).

sume her place in an ancient vampire hierarchy, or she can choose to make a new life with a new family in the present. Most of the other characters face similar conflicts, and as their complex back-stories are revealed over the course of the series, the good ones learn to acknowledge their pasts without being wholly defined by them. Saya, for example, finally accepts her violent, inherited role as a warrior, but embraces it to defend the adopted family and friends she has chosen herself.

Given the themes of the earlier film, one is ready to see all this as a contemplation of nationalism and war memory: the need to recall, accept, and acknowledge our past history, including the tragedies of our own making, but also to learn and move beyond them. And superficially the series provides plenty of appropriate hooks, including a six-episode arc set in present-day Vietnam. (One subplot involves a Vietnamese girl Mui who has lost her brother and her leg to a leftover American bomb, and who supports her family by digging up other unexploded bombs to sell as scrap.) But in *Blood+* the political importance of remembering and learning are undercut by the repetitive structure that constantly returns us to square one.

This repetition occurs at all levels of *Blood+*: we learn that Saya's biology forces her to sleep for decades at a time then awake and start over. She turns up in Russia during the Russian Revolution, in Vietnam during the war, and (in one of the novels) in Shanghai on the eve of the 1932 Japanese invasion, suggesting a cyclicality of violence and forgetting that foils any sense of progress. The TV series not only repeats things from the original film, like the bomb-er's flyover, but constantly repeats *itself*: it is divided into four parts or seasons, and each begins the same way, with a family idyll in a place of refuge that is then invaded or interrupted. (For example in episode 14, which begins the second season, we find ourselves back in Okinawa at school months later and watch Saya repeat the high jump from episode 1.) This is also the structure of many individual episodes, where grisly combats are followed directly by domestic scenes in which the same characters play house. Finally many of the fight scenes have a sadistically repetitious quality all by them-selves, as the nearly indestructible characters battle inconclusively.

Characters, too, are repeated or duplicated so that the same stories can play out again and again. Saya's allies include David and Lewis, who have the same names and a passing resemblance to the agents in the original film, set forty years before. New David is the son of the original David, one of several characters following in their fathers' footsteps. Saya gets her own double, Diva, who is an evil twin born from the same mother 170 years ago. Diva's five immortal servants (her "chevalier") are opposed by Saya's chevalier, Haji. The heroes are led by the wheelchair-bound Joel Goldschmidt, latest in a line of Joel Goldschmidts that goes back to the time of Saya's birth; his evil double is Amshell Goldsmith, Diva's first chevalier and Joel's own distant relative.

It goes on: the chiropterans are doubled by a group of good vampires in the same bloodline, the "Schiff," and the Schiff are then redoubled by evil clones of themselves. As if to counter this repetition, the series regularly serves up plot twists that turn on genetic uniqueness: only Saya's blood can kill the chiropterans; only Diva's blood can extend the lives of the Schiff; only Haji can impregnate Diva; only Diva's blood can kill Haji. But after a while these narratives of uniqueness themselves become repetitive, variations on a theme. For this weary viewer, the series quickly started to resemble its undead subjects: eternal, unkillable, but hardly alive.

What *is* interesting (and more than a little discouraging) is how this repetition affects the politics of the series. Despite *Blood+*'s overt themes of an inherited history versus a chosen future, all this cyclicality, doubling, and repetition undermine any sense of individual or political responsibility or realization. The characters remember their pasts, but never really come to terms with them. The plot only ever flirts with real politics. Saya's rampage in Vietnam, the terrible image from the first episode that haunts her and us through much of the series, is revealed to be someone else's accident: she was awakened too early from hibernation by her desperate handlers, causing her to lose control. In the end, the chiropteran breeding project turns out to be financed by the United States as part of a plot for world domination, and with that the more complicated and realistic questions that made the original film interesting—about race, complicity, and war responsibility—are flattened into a cartoon.

In chapters 4 and 5, we saw the same structures of repetition, doubling, and memory or amnesia in *Millennium Actress, Vampire Princess Miyu,* and *3x3 Eyes.* The last featured an amnesiac demon who thinks she is a simple schoolgirl and gradually realizes her violent past. *3x3 Eyes* also had the same alternation between syrupy domestic scenes and repetitive, violent combat, supported by the schizophrenic quality of the heroine and all the characters, who pass easily from combat to domestic downtime and back again. The difference is that these earlier works foregrounded this obliviousness in ways that offered some perspective—for example through the puppet-like demons or mediatized specters in all three works, which trapped their otaku victims in catatonic fictional worlds. This provided an ironic or self-conscious quality, and the resulting dynamic between forgetful immersion and critical distance exposed the risk of becoming lost in these fantasies, even as we inhabited them. But in *Blood+* this repetition is so interwoven, so sustained and extended over the whole twenty-five hours of the series, that it is hard to see any kind of irony or self-awareness in it.

While Lyotard hoped that modernity's received grand narratives would give way to a more self-conscious (more critical) choice between the numberless little narratives of postmodernity, *Blood+* is arguably the worst of both worlds: the same trivial script replayed endlessly without any room for self-awareness or choice. This seems to be a risk inherent in serial television anime. Even as the extended time frame allows for more involved plots, the formulaic quality that often characterizes television can quickly undermine any sense of critical perspective. While it is hard to generalize about everything in this vast medium, long-running television anime series often turn on rigidly repeating formulas. There are numberless adventure series similar to *Blood+* where the protagonist undergoes the same transformation or apotheosis each week in order to come from behind and beat the bad guys— whether the transformation is magical, technological, athletic, or occult. In extreme cases these climactic transformations occur at the same minute of the episode and present themselves with the same recycled stock footage each time.[20] This is ultimately why I would identify television anime as a distinct medium, separate from shorter OVA series and anime films. This book has focused on the latter for their ability to do what repetitive television series cannot—move us between immersion and distance in a way that periodically lifts us outside the story and provides some critical purchase on the form of the text.

Of course there are exceptions. There are interesting television series (like Anno Hideaki's 1995–96 *Evangelion* series) that sustain a formula just long enough to lull the audience into complacency, then undermine it in ways that keep the viewers both emotionally *and* critically engaged. *Blood* fans hoping for such a move would have to wait for the third phase of the franchise, *Blood-C*. But before we get to that, there is one element of *Blood+* that hints at this broader perspective, the ability to step back and ask how different media depict or distort our lived political reality. It comes at the end of the series, and it begins with the music.

Blood+ features a top-shelf soundtrack composed by Mark Mancina and produced by cinema impresario Hans Zimmer. The plot revolves around music as well: Saya's chevalier Haji is a cellist whose playing unlocks her memories, and the Vietnamese girl Mui is a pianist whose music expresses her spirit. Most centrally, Saya's double Diva is a real diva, a singer whose vampire charms work through her voice. In the plot of the series, Diva's song is the trigger that causes people who have been infected with her blood to transform into chiropterans. After distributing contaminated food that spreads this latent infection secretly throughout the world, the bad guys arrange for Diva's debut in a performance of *Faust* at the Metropolitan Opera in New York City, at which point a worldwide simulcast will turn tens of thousands of people into monsters. Alerted to this plot, Saya and her allies converge on the opera house the night of the performance for a final showdown.

The one in charge of the performance is Diva's chevalier Nathan Mahler, a flamboyantly effeminate opera producer. But he cares little about whether the evil plan succeeds or who wins the final duel between Diva and Saya, as long as it results in a dramatic, tragic finish to the whole affair. The climax becomes distinctly metafictional: Nathan sets the performance on a stage that represents a location from previous seasons of the show, while Diva is costumed to resemble a combination of other characters from other parts in the series. So their final duel looks like a staged replay of earlier episodes of the anime itself, set to an ostentatiously operatic score. In this way, the Nathan character becomes a figure for the anime's creators, effectively pulling back the curtain to expose the program's dramatic logic.[21] This hint of self-awareness in the final episodes promptly sinks into its coffin and sleeps out the decade. But five years later it rises again—with a vengeance—in *Blood-C.*

Blood-C Catches Up with Politics (or Politics Catches Up with It)

The twelve episodes of the *Blood-C* television series aired from July to September 2011, with Mizushima Tsutomu as supervising director. The following summer a two-hour theatrical film picked up where the series left off and brought the story to a conclusion. The television series opens in what looks like the contemporary world, though it is missing overt cues about the decade. (There's no electronic technology in evidence anywhere, for example.) Initially the characters seem to have only a tenuous connection to the earlier series: Saya is now a high-school student living with her father, head priest of the Ukijima shrine. Like her mother before her, this Saya is a *miko* or shrine maiden, armed with a sacred sword and charged with the responsibility for hunting and killing a race of supernatural monsters called *furukimono* ("Elder Bairns" in the subtitles). Besides her new backstory, she looks very different: the *Blood-C* franchise is a collaboration between Production I.G and the legendary female manga collective CLAMP, so the character designs have CLAMP's characteristic look: great clothes, impossibly long slender limbs, and for Saya a cloud of black hair that spreads out like a character in its own right.

We seem to have left the world of *Blood+*, but structural similarities quickly emerge. Saya is a high school student by day and killer by night, and each episode divides, once again, into scenes of violent combat alternating with domestic (now comedic) scenes of high school life. The school scenes are particularly loopy, with a stock cast of characters, locations, and situations: the neighborhood cafe and its kind proprietor, the sexy female teacher Tsutsutori-sensei, the tough-girl classmate, the tough-guy love

FIGURE 43. CLAMP's character concepts for the 2010 *Blood-C* television series altered Saya yet again. Here she is with twins Nene and Nono in the background. Schoolyard scenes like this one alternate with scenes so gory that blood spatters even the simulated camera lens. From the Funimation Blu-ray discs (2013).

interest, the nice-guy love interest, etcetera. The doubling motif of *Blood+* is parodied by twin sisters, Nene and Nono, who are exact mirror images of one another, down to their synchronized (but reversed) hand gestures (Figure 43).

Juxtaposed with these goofy school scenes, the combat is particularly gruesome and creative. Each week's monster displays a new form, and several point self-referentially back at anime itself. One of the *furukimono* takes the shape of a familiar train that pulls up on a deserted section of track, lures its victim inside the car, then drops tentacles from the ceiling that rend him limb from limb. In another episode, a bird-like creature telepathically directs a pair of monster servants like puppets, and cryptically accuses Saya of being a puppet herself. One of the final monsters seems to parody CLAMP's pretty faces, thin bodies, and long tresses: it consists of a floating mask trailing a human spine, surrounded by a huge cloud of prehensile hair.

As *Blood-C* continues, the disjunction between the violent battles and the domesticity of the school or cafe scenes becomes more and more pronounced, emphasized by Satō Naoki's clever soundtrack, which slides between eerie minimalism and hokey musical doodling. Saya's (and our own) ability to switch between these two worlds, the alternation that is never really questioned in *Blood+*, becomes progressively harder to believe. The monsters start to kill residents horribly before Saya's eyes, but the silly love plot advances. Nene's head is bitten off by a centipede creature while Saya is trying to protect her, but a day later Saya shows up for school again. Nono's shadow comes alive and swallows a series of bystanders, then when Saya dives into the shadow to battle it from the inside, it explodes in a cloud of blood, leaving nothing of Nono but a severed foot lying in the roadway, still in the shoe. Saya takes a day off, then shows up again at the cafe for her morning coffee.

There are only twelve episodes (one secret of the series' success), and they are cleverly paced, so that these disjunctions become odd, then creepy, then ridiculous, and eventually unbearable. Finally, with its logic coming apart at the seams, the series reaches the final reveal. Nono and Nene reappear, alive and in one piece, and say: "Let's put an end to this farce, shall we?"

In what follows, Saya's companions break character one at a time and express their growing impatience with their stupid roles and the repetitive plot. It turns out that they are all actors, hired to simulate a normal high school life for Saya as part of a sadistic experiment filmed by cameras hidden throughout the village. The grainy quality of certain scenes in earlier episodes is now explained retroactively as surveillance footage. The characters also mock the series' other unrealistic details, like the improbably fashionable red and black school uniforms (though Nene and Nono observe that they'd be good for cosplay or fetish wear).

The mastermind behind the experiment is Nanahara Fumito, who has been playing the role of the proprietor at Saya's favorite cafe. Saya's history as a shrine maiden and her sacred mission are inventions: it is only Fumito's drugged coffee that has been keeping her in a state of obliviousness about where and what she really is. The *furukimono* are genuine, but they are under Fumito's control. The deaths of Saya's friends ("the main cast") have been supernaturally staged, and only the deaths of the townspeople ("the extras") are real. The motivation for the whole exercise is not compellingly described, but it references the themes of *Blood+*. Fumito has captured Saya and forced her into the experiment as part of a bet with her about nature versus nurture: can his staged environment change what she is, or will she remain true to her blood, to herself? Fumito's motivation for the elaborate bet is not satisfactorily explained, perhaps because by this point he is not functioning as a character so much as a figure for the anime's creators. (His surname Nanahara resembles the name of one of *Blood-C*'s writers, CLAMP leader Ōkawa Nanase.)

As the artificiality of the characters and story undermine our sense of involvement or immersion, the fascination or horror of this revelation takes on a metafictional quality, becoming a revelation of anime's own hollowed-out conventions. Ōkawa comments:

> When we finished all twelve episodes, I realized that this anime without any emotional connection between the characters was even creepier than I had imagined it would be. Anime's codes and conventions are infused with their own essences—that's how they are formed. . . . The girl with the sacred sword and her ongoing crusade, the kind father who supports her, the older brother who looks after her, the bad boy, the class leader, the older sister figure, the cute twins, the sexy teacher—they are just placed there and do nothing, feel nothing for Saya. There's no one who cares about her. That was even more disturbing than we had intended.[22]

Significantly, perhaps, the one who exposes all of this is the teacher, Tsutsutori-sensei, who turns out to be a figure for the critic: she is actually a researcher, impatient for the experiment (and the series) to end so she can publish something about it and climb the academic ladder. But when she and the other actors betray Fumito, he releases the *furukimono* to murder them and the rest of the town's population, and then retreats to the airport. Like *Blood: The Last Vampire*, the final sequence uses three-dimensionally rendered vehicles to signal the re-intrusion of the real world, but this time Saya is unable to prevent the monster (Fumito) from escaping on a conspicuously computer-rendered helicopter. However, she picks up his trail again in the movie, *Blood-C: The Last Dark*, which is set six months later in Tokyo.

The Last Dark, directed by Shiotani Noayoshi, is everything we now expect, with scenes, devices, and characters doubled or repeated from earlier texts: a train scene quoted from *Blood: The Last Vampire*, a mug of drugged coffee from the *Blood-C* TV series, a beneficent patron in a wheelchair and his evil brother/uncle/cousin, borrowed from *Blood+*. And of course there is a return to high school so Saya can once again don the uniform. But now, filtered through so many layers of repetition and the explicit plot about performance, it is all so self-conscious that it starts to make us think again. The climax comes in Saya's final showdown with Fumito, whom she finds in a giant room paneled entirely in video screens that show images of her and replay scenes from earlier in the film (Figure 44). A computer-modeled rotational shot spins the camera around Saya so that the screens whirr past: we are now seeing everything. We've reached the heart of the story, the editing room.

Blood-C has found its politics, which is not the politics of war or war memory. There's no mention of war, and the fantastic *furukimono* are pure fantasy. Nor is it the politics of nationality or race. Instead, it is the politics of media. Surveillance, staging, enforced amnesia—all of these are metaphors for the power of media, media manipulation, and thought control. Accordingly, the concrete political references in the film are to censorship and information control. We learn at the outset of the film that Fumito has the governor of Tokyo in his pocket, and that he has engineered the

FIGURE 44. In the climax of the film *Blood-C: The Last Dark,* Saya confronts her nemesis in a room paneled entirely in monitors that display images of herself and scenes from earlier in the film. From the Funimation Blu-ray disc (2013).

passing of a "Youth Protection Law" *(Seishōnen hogo jōrei),* with a curfew and a system of police patrols designed to limit the freedom of Tokyo's young people. One of the film's hacker heroines suggests that this is to restrict the flow of information, by controlling the younger generation that reads and posts information on the Internet.

This is clearly a reference to the real politics of 2010–11, when governor Ishihara Shintarō and the Tokyo metropolitan government revised existing antipornography legislation, "The Youth Healthy Development Law" *(Seishōnen no kenzen na ikusei ni kansuru jōrei)* to support Internet access restrictions for minors and place tighter limits on sexually explicit media. Key to the new law were restrictions on sexualized depictions not just of real children but of child characters in anime and manga, referred to in early drafts of the legislation as "nonexistent youth" *(hijutsuzai seishōnen).* Manga and anime creators reacted with alarm, sometimes responding with polemical or parodic works. *Blood-C: The Last Dark* is one example, and director Shiotani Naoyoshi would go on to create other anime with similar themes. Born in 1977, Shiotani is the youngest director we have considered, a member of the Internet generation rather than the protest generation. After

The Last Dark he directed *Psycho-Pass* (*Saikopasu*, 2012–15), a series
and film with a distinctly surveillance-based take on familiar issues of pacifism and justice. It is set in a dystopic future where the
Japanese government monitors the emotional state of all residents
and confines or kills anyone with violent thoughts.

So in 2012, *Blood* finally catches up with politics, or politics
catches up with it. Which raises the question of whether things
like *Blood* would, should, or could qualify for censorship. Saya is
clearly a fetish figure. (One has only to search fan art sites for her
image.) But is a 170-year-old vampire in the body of a high school
student a "youth," even a "nonexistent youth?" There is a long tradition of sexually explicit manga and anime with boys and girls
who look human, but who are technically aliens, demons, robots,
etcetera.[23] One could regard this as a cynical effort to skirt censure
or censorship on a technicality. On the other hand, we've seen that
while Saya is certainly a fantasy, she's a tangled one that combines
elements of sex and politics, youth and age, violence, nationalism,
and pacifism, belonging and freedom. In *Blood-C: The Last Dark*,
that freedom (or fetish) is finally about freedom of speech.[24]

The idea of the information society brings us back to Bram Stoker's 1897 *Dracula*, which is a novel curiously suspended between
Gothic Romance and twentieth-century information theory.
Count Dracula is incomparably old and incomparably foreign, an
Orientalist nightmare. But in the way of backward cultures (as the
novel imagines everything east of Budapest), Dracula is vulnerable to technology. When Jonathan Harker nears Transylvania and
says "we were leaving the West and entering the East," he follows
it soon after with this: "It seems to me that the further east you go
the more unpunctual the trains. What ought they to be in China?"
This is prophetic, as it is finally the trains and modern communication technologies (telegraph, phonograph, and typewriter) that
allow Harker and his friends to defeat Dracula, who must travel
by sea and communicate in dreams. The most potent of these
modern weapons is Mina Harker's typewriter, which is used to
produce a single typescript (the ostensible text of the novel) that
combines all the various diaries, documents, and case notes the
main characters produce in different media (telegram, shorthand,

wax cylinder) over the course of the story. The novel states explicitly that it is only this homogenization of different voices and media that enables the heroes to read one another's words, grasp the whole picture, and figure out how to defeat the vampire.

This is one approach to taming the monster—the mysterious creature that is Dracula, or the mystery of language's own variety and richness. But other novels are more adventurous about embracing the possibility of different voices and perspectives, and retaining or even highlighting the gaps between them. Chapter 7 considers prose fiction and its potential to achieve the same effect I have identified for anime: forcing us to think actively not just about the story but about how the story is told. At the same time, we will see that not every anime director pursues this oscillation. Some choose to disguise these seams and flatten these different voices, frames, or layers into one smooth, immersive experience, conveyed in a single, unified style. One such director is Miyazaki Hayao, the subject of the next chapter.

7

It's Art, but Is It Anime?

Howl's Moving Castle and the Novel

Miyazaki Hayao is Japan's most celebrated animation director, but he insists that he does not make anime. In this final chapter we turn to Miyazaki and ask what his aversion to the word "anime" has to say about the limits of that term. The preceding chapters have traced an alternation between immersion and distance in a wide range of anime films, suggesting that this is a signature, if not absolutely universal feature of this medium. But Miyazaki's films arguably seek to avoid that alternation and instead strive for a completely immersive experience. In that sense Miyazaki's work (no matter what term we use to name it) does seem to be different from the anime we've examined up to now.

Below we compare Miyazaki's film *Howl's Moving Castle* (*Hauru no ugoku shiro*, 2004) with the fantasy novel by Diana Wynne Jones the film is based on. Novelists have at their disposal a wide range of devices to immerse or distance the reader, and while fantasy and particularly young adult fantasy often veer away from distancing effects, Jones does not, constantly interrogating the limits and boundaries of her own genre and her own language with wordplay and other metafictional intrusions. Miyazaki flattens out these elements to create a more immersive experience, producing a very different effect.

Miyazaki's Art

Based on his combined reputation inside and outside of Japan, Miyazaki is almost certainly Japan's most famous living film-maker, in animation or live action. If we were to go back to 2013, when Miyazaki released what was billed as his final feature film, and look at the twenty films with the highest Japanese box office totals of all time, we would see that thirteen were Hollywood movies, but of the seven Japanese films, five were directed by Miyazaki. That included 2001's *Spirited Away (Sen to Chihiro no kamikakushi)*, which held the number one spot by a wide margin. For two decades, every film Miyazaki made was Japan's number one film of the year, while in the United States, he has had more commercial and critical success than any other Japanese director alive today. His work enjoyed a cult popularity in the West from the early days of the anime boom, even before his name became a household word in his own country. Then in 1996, with his popularity growing in Japan, Miyazaki's studio signed an international distribution deal with Disney that raised his global profile. *Spirited Away* won the Oscar in 2003 for best animated film and was shown in more than fifty countries, including a wide U.S. release following its Oscar win. The deal with Disney eventually led to high-end video releases of all his feature films in the United States, with voices dubbed by A-list Hollywood actors.[1]

Born in 1941, Miyazaki is of a different generation than the other directors we have discussed, just about all of whom were born in the 1950s or 1960s. (*Blood-C: The Last Dark* director Shiotani Naoyoshi was born in the 1970s.) Miyazaki spent his early career at a series of different studios, starting in 1956 with Tōei Dōga, the new animation division at one of Japan's newest and largest film studios. He started as an animator and worked his way up to his first directorial assignments, on TV series. In 1979 he directed his first feature film, the excellent *Lupin the Third: The Castle of Cagliostro (Rupan sansei: Kariosutoro no shiro)*, and in 1982 he left his studio position to make *Nausicaä of the Valley of the Wind (Kaze no tani no Naushika*, 1984). Based on a sweeping manga epic Miyazaki was drawing at the time, the film is set in a postapocalyptic world of deserts, poisonous forests, and huge, dangerous insects, where human states struggle against nature and one another. The titular heroine Nausicaä is a heroic pilot and princess from the Valley of the Wind, and she is the only one who can suspend the violence by restoring some balance and understanding between humans and the natural world. *Nausicaä*'s animation is not as sophisticated as Miyazaki's later high-budget films, but it already contains many of the visual and thematic elements that would become Miyazaki's signatures: a fantasy setting, an ecological theme, a strong but gentle heroine whose powers are expressed in exuberant flying scenes, and a message of empathy for nature and other people, combined with an acknowledgment of the world's frequent cruelty and indifference.

In 1985, building on the success of *Nausicaä*, Miyazaki and director Takahata Isao formed Studio Ghibli, named after a World War II–era Italian airplane. Studio Ghibli has produced several fine films by Takahata, and more recently a few titles by a small stable of other directors, but Miyazaki is unquestionably the central figure. He went on to direct nine films at Ghibli, concluding in 2013 with *The Wind Rises (Kaze tachinu)*, which he declared his last feature film.[2]

Miyazaki's popularity in Japan and abroad is not hard to fathom. The Ghibli brand, and Miyazaki's films in particular, are engineered for broad appeal. First and foremost, they are characterized by beautiful animation that is accessible rather than experimental, executed with an incredible attention to craft, color, and detail. Their stories and characters also resonate with a wide audience of children and grownups, and their happy endings are tinged with just the right amount of adult melancholy. In the tradition of cinematic auteurs or auteur criticism, these features of Miyazaki's films have all been closely associated with the director's own personality—his reputation as a workaholic and perfectionist, an old man disillusioned with the modern world but still capable of childlike wonder, a "positive pessimist."[3]

Some of Miyazaki's most famous comments on anime come in a 1988 article, "Thoughts on Japanese Animation" *(Nihon no animeeshon ni tsuite)*. At this point he was doing some of his best work, but on the state of animation in general, he wrote:

Compared with certain works of the 1950s that I have taken as my model, the animation we are making in the 1980s is like airline food. Mass production has changed things. The ideas and sincere emotions that should permeate our work have given way to bluster, nervousness, and pandering. What should be loving handmade work has slipped into a production system where we're simply paid by the image. I hate the shortened term "anime" because for me it just symbolizes this desolation.[4]

The essay goes on to identify two problems with anime, both of which start with a fall from the ambitious cinematic full animation of Tōei Animation's early work and the rise of animated television series and print manga. First, Japanese animation has become characterized by "exaggerated representation" (kajō hyō-gen): driven by the need to draw more frames in a shorter time for weekly TV series, animators have abandoned the effort to represent human gestures and expressions, simplifying the human figure to the point of manga-like caricature. Eventually even space and time are deformed, as the natural motion of full animation is replaced by melodramatic (and cost-saving) tricks that combine stillness and motion to reduce the number of drawn frames. Miyazaki scoffs at the idea that this "limited motion" can achieve interesting effects that full animation cannot, concluding, "Increasingly, what distinguishes Japanese anime is works in which utterly deformed characters, characters that convey no sense of reality, strike empty poses in garishly-colored, deformed worlds where time is distorted at whim."[5]

The second problem according to Miyazaki is the narrative counterpart to this lack of convincing expression: it is the characters' lack of convincing motivations, or more precisely the lack of independent motives grounded in real values. Here Miyazaki criticizes the two-dimensional notions of romantic love or good and evil that drive many anime plots. And yet, Miyazaki maintains that the value of animation still lies in fundamental, even simple human emotions, including real love and love of real justice—emotions that can be conveyed to a wide audience. Communicating these fundamental feelings without visual exaggeration or narrative oversimplification seems to be the balancing act animation must undertake. As Miyazaki says of his target audience: "Even if children no longer take encouragement from the superheroes (seigi no hiirō) that they depended on in the past, they still want to be taught how to be encouraged, how to perceive the world as something beautiful."[6]

Although this was written in 1988, Miyazaki has remained consistent on these points. More recently he gained attention for a related pronouncement that being able to draw animated figures depended on being able to observe and imagine real people. "Japan's animation is not grounded in observing human beings," he complained. "It's done by people who hate observing others. That's why it's become such a nest of otaku."[7] We might paraphrase Miyazaki as distinguishing between "anime" as an industry and the animated film as a form of art. Miyazaki refers here to one of anime's founding narratives: the development of limited animation techniques linked to the advent of animated television series in the 1960s, starting with Tezuka Osamu's studio Mushi Pro and their series *Astro Boy,* which had a tight schedule and budget that did not permit the large number of complex drawings required for full animation. In versions of this narrative (including Miyazaki's essay), television anime is contrasted with the theatrical animation of the Tōei studio, which is associated with a more polished, more cinematic style. This dovetails with Miyazaki's devotion to high-quality theatrical anime: after forming Ghibli he never directed a television series again.

Many historical accounts of anime's development dwell on the Tōei/Mushi Pro dichotomy—though several also complicate it in some way. Thomas Lamarre traces the importance of a Tōei style in Ghibli's films and in its own founding narrative, but Lamarre also blurs the distinction between "full" and "limited" animation, in Miyazaki's case by combining the analysis of motion with a consideration of depth, and by analyzing the movement of figures relative to the depth and motion of the world they inhabit. The result is a nuanced argument that Miyazaki's work combines elements of full and limited animation in rich and subtle ways.[8] My own approach regards the more immersively "realistic" (Miyazaki might say "true to life") full motion and the distancing abstractions of limited animation as two tendencies that anime oscillates between. *Howl's Moving Castle* might be an interesting work to analyze from Lamarre's perspective, not least of all because the moving castle functions as a kind of architectural character that exists somewhere between the backgrounds and the moving human beings. (It is even animated with a special "harmony process" that blends the painting style used for backgrounds with the cel-animation techniques used for the characters.) However, chapter 5 has already discussed the idea of limited motion and Lamarre's theories of character motion in the context of other films, so here I would like to use a comparison with prose fiction to focus on Miyazaki's second point about realism or immersion:

the importance of character motivations and values, and the goal of kindling a sincere emotional response in the audience.

In this book I have not wanted to draw narrow boundaries around the term "anime," defining it simply as drawn animation that originates in Japan. I would certainly characterize Miyazaki as an anime director, but I think he is right when he sets his own work apart in some way, because if other anime oscillate between immersion and distance, Miyazaki's films strive to immerse the viewer from start to finish, never breaking their own spell.

Praise for Miyazaki's films often focuses on his immersive worlds. Peter Docter, who directed the English adaptation of *Howl's Moving Castle* for Disney, describes his first viewing of the original film: "It felt like a dream. . . . There are things that later on I go, 'What? I didn't quite understand that.' But at the time you are just completely caught up in the dream, and it's so satisfying." Docter nicely captures the experience of these films, which are oneiric rather than realistic, which don't always make complete sense in terms of their plots, but which nevertheless have an all-encompassing quality that makes us suspend disbelief, unable or unwilling to leave Miyazaki's world. Here the dream that is indistinguishable from reality (the trope that was disturbing or unnerving in the work of Kon Satoshi and so many other directors) becomes comfortable, even reassuring. Only Miyazaki's partner at Ghibli, Takahata Isao, describes it with an edge: "With Miyazaki, you have to totally believe in the world of the film." "He is demanding that the audience enter the world he has created completely. The audience is being asked to surrender."[9]

This immersion is supported by a number of things common to nearly all of Miyazaki's films. The tone is carefully modulated, with the comedic bits never too silly and the drama never too intense. But foremost is the level of visual detail and the way those details fit together: his settings convey a sense of organic unity, suggesting a coherent (if quirky) history and culture behind them, even when this background is not explicitly described. "The viewer finds in each film a topography that is exotic," writes Susan Napier, "but at the same time so richly realized down to minute details that it seems at least potentially contiguous to our own world." Helping this along is a similarity between successive films: they are all set in different worlds with different characters, but they share visual and stylistic similarities that make each new one seem vaguely familiar to Miyazaki's fans. Napier refers to this unity (encompassing the films, the studio, and a fan base that is ardent even by anime standards) as a coherent world unto itself, what she terms "MiyazakiWorld."[10] This immersion and involvement are key elements in supporting the emotional investment that Miyazaki's essay names as the goal of his films. Below we consider more concretely how this works in *Howl's Moving Castle*, using the novel for comparison.

Two Versions of *Howl's Moving Castle*

Miyazaki's film and Jones's novel have identical setups, though eventually they tell very different stories. Both are set in a magical kingdom (named Ingary in the novel), where the teenage heroine Sophie works in the family hat shop. One day the feared Witch of the Waste visits the shop and places a spell on Sophie, a curse that ages her several decades. Embarrassed (or possibly liberated) by her elderly form, Sophie runs away from home and finds her way to the castle of the magician Howl.

Howl's is a moving castle, in more ways than one. From the inside, the front door can be set to open on any one of four locations, using a colored dial. At the start of the story, the red and blue settings open on towns in Ingary, towns where the castle door appears as the door of a normal house or shop front. Howl goes by a different name in each town. The green setting opens on a wilderness, where the castle appears in its magical form as a giant moving building. (In the anime it walks around on big chicken legs.) The door's fourth, black setting remains a mystery until further along in the story.

Howl is youthful and dashing, and particularly in the novel he seems to spend most of his time courting pretty young girls. (In the film he is voiced by perennial romantic lead Kimura Takuya.) Part of Sophie's curse is that she cannot tell Howl or anyone else what has happened to her, but the magician takes pity on this strange old woman, and she becomes a member of his odd household, along with his young servant Markl (*Marukuru*, or Michael in the novel), and his fire demon Calcifer. Howl and Calcifer are bound together by a magical contract or curse of their own, one Calcifer cannot describe in detail but which he begs Sophie to help him break. As the film and the novel progress, the castle accumulates more occupants, including an animated scarecrow with a turnip head (whose motives and origins remain a mystery because he cannot speak), and a series of other colorful characters that differ from novel to film. Meanwhile Sophie grows more and more attached to Howl and learns more about the magical shadow that haunts him, finally determining to save him from it. But the nature of this shadow is different in the two versions, and the difference takes them in distinct directions.

Obviously this setup turns heavily on transformed identities: all the characters are disguised as something else or harbor a past secret they cannot speak of. In Jones's novel, this is part of a shifting perspective that portrays the characters and their motivations in constantly changing ways. For some of the novel's characters, like Sophie, this transformation takes the form of a curse; but Sophie's sisters exchange fates and achieve their dreams by magically disguising themselves as each other. Just when Sophie thinks she understands Howl, Calcifer, or her family, they reveal new sides. Likewise there are things she only belatedly realizes about herself, like her feelings for Howl, or the fact that she is a powerful magician in her own right, who has been unwittingly spelling the things around her just by talking to them. This theme of shifting perspectives runs through everything in Jones's novel—not just its characters but the twists of its plot and even the wordplay of its prose.

Miyazaki takes the same motifs of disguise and transformation, and makes them tell a different story. This is less about shifting perspectives and discovering new sides to people than about discovering a singular true self, or being true to yourself. The characters in the film may cycle through different guises, but eventually these must be stripped away to reveal who they *really* are. In both the book and the film, Sophie's premature aging allows her to grow and change, turning her from a shy, reticent young girl to an assertive adult who feels she has little to prove and nothing to lose. But if the novel shows Sophie constantly discovering new aspects of herself, in the film she is simply coming into her final adult personality, even as her body remains trapped in a form that is not really her own. This is represented in the film by having her revert to her younger voice and appearance in unguarded moments, an effect supported by clever animation and some deft voice acting by seventy-year-old Baishō Chieko, one-time romantic lead and now a matron of Japanese cinema.

In the novel, magic is the means or metaphor for these productive shifts in perspective, but in the film, magic becomes something distorting or worse. The film's central example is Howl, whose body and mind are being slowly twisted by his most powerful spells, which the film associates with violence and war. War does not play any role in the novel, but it is central to the film. Miyazaki sets his story during wartime, with flying gunships firebombing vulnerable cities. In the film, the black door leads to the war: at night Howl passes through it and assumes the form of a giant bird creature to battle the warplanes. Howl does not fight for one side or the other; he only tries to defend the civilians by downing the bombers. But the longer he spends in this monstrous body, the harder it is to remember and return to human form. This is part of the film's clearly pacifist message: the more Howl fights, even as an old fashioned "superhero," the more he risks losing his essential humanity. Sophie struggles to rescue him by opposing any kind of violence, telling him "You mustn't fight" even when the bombers reach her own village. The Sophie of the film has no magic powers (except perhaps the generalized life-giving power of her love), and this is the emblem of her pacifism and her purity.

If Oshii Mamoru's 1993 *Patlabor 2* was prompted by the 1991 Gulf War against Iraq, Miyazaki describes *Howl's Moving Castle* as a reaction to the 2003 Iraq war, which followed the 9/11 terrorist attacks of 2001 and the war in Afghanistan that started later that same year. When Miyazaki started production on the film in early 2003, the Iraq war was just beginning. Three days after the start of the U.S.-led invasion, he boycotted the Academy Awards ceremony at which *Spirited Away* received an Oscar. "Actually, your country had just started the war against Iraq, and I had a great deal of rage about that," he told *Newsweek* in 2005. "So I felt some hesitation about the award. In fact, I had just started to make *Howl's Moving Castle*, so the film is profoundly affected by the war in Iraq."[11]

Several critics have analyzed *Howl's Moving Castle* as a war protest film. Lindsay Smith argues cleverly that:

> The mobility of the castle creates a new outlet for experiencing the immediacy of a war that seems to be happening everywhere all

at once; the ability to actually *go* to where the war is taking place removes the façade that the war is merely happening elsewhere, and instead brings the characters into direct conflict with reality. In invoking the Iraq War . . . the film performs a similar function for viewers, providing them with an account of war that [is] more accessible than the televised news reports on the fighting taking place in Iraq at the time.[12]

Miyazaki was a young child during World War II and has memories of the American firebombing and of watching his own hometown go up in flames. Oshii Mamoru and Ōtomo Katsuhiro, a decade younger than Miyazaki, did not experience the war; but they did come of age amid the postwar debates about Japan's security partnership with the United States, and we saw how films like *Akira* or *Patlabor 2* combine progressive political critique with elements of nationalism, anarchism, and militarism. *Blood: The Last Vampire* (by an even younger generation of creators working under Oshii) presents the fantasy of a warrior who can somehow battle war itself, a solution we might equate with Howl's efforts to fight against both sides. But Miyazaki's own politics are more resolutely pacifist. In recent years, as Japan's conservative political elements have worked toward revising Article 9 of the constitution and expanding the country's global military role, Miyazaki has emerged as an outspoken critic of those efforts.[13]

It is often said that Miyazaki avoids black-and-white distinctions between good and evil, that even his antagonists are complex, but his pacifism seems uncompromising. I think it would be most accurate to say that his films believe there is good in all people, which is why even his villains often turn out to have a sympathetic side. The Witch of the Waste curses Sophie at the beginning of the story, but she later earns Sophie's sympathy when she loses her powers and is reduced to a kindly but doddering old woman (another departure from the novel). This conviction that everyone is good at heart supports the film's message that violence can always be avoided.

And yet in the midst of all this, Miyazaki's films, like Oshii's, still capitalize on the excitement of violence. Miyazaki's producer Suzuki Toshio notes, "He's a pacifist but loves drawing weapons and gunships,"[14] and in many of Miyazaki's films the visual and narrative excitement turn on the thrill of these machines. In *Howl's Moving Castle*, magic and technology are the linked forces that power the weapons of war. They are destructive, but incomparably seductive, and Howl's dilemma becomes the viewer's dilemma as well: indulge in the violent, exciting transformation of combat, or heed Sophie's pleas to look away (Figure 45). Like other Miyazaki films, *Howl's Moving Castle* is divided in this way, but it is not a division that encourages us to step back from the film or our feelings, or to examine them critically; rather, the film's exciting

FIGURE 45. In *Howl's Moving Castle,* scenes of firebombing and Howl's monstrous form both convey the horrors of war, but they also have an undeniable excitement. Here Sophie covers Howl's eyes to arrest his aggressive transformation, but as spectators we inevitably want to see these images. All stills are from the Disney Blu-ray disc (2013).

violence and Sophie's hatred of violence are both part of the truth of the film's immersive, diegetic world.

As a compromise, Miyazaki's films limit these technologies, favoring wind-powered machines or unwieldy mechanical contraptions like the castle itself (which is bristling with cannon but also undeniably cute). These limited technologies also dovetail with the environmentalist message of his films and are reinforced by the handmade quality of the animation itself, which assiduously avoids or conceals the use of computer graphics.[15] In *Howl's Moving Castle*, Miyazaki represents the opposite pole through Madam Suliman, Howl's former teacher and the emblem of a magic and technology that are attractive and dangerously advanced. Suliman is the King's royal magician and a figure whose magic helps sustain the war, a darkly compelling character who seems concerned for Howl but also determined to bend him to her will. The magic she uses against him is represented with some of the film's most intrusive computer graphics, which generate some of its most frightening, and frighteningly beautiful special effects (Figure 46). At the end of the film, Suliman looks into her crystal ball (more digital effects) and sees Sophie save Howl. Sophie's kiss also lifts the curse from the scarecrow, who regains his true form as a prince of the neighboring kingdom and promises to return home to stop the war. Seeing this, Suliman sighs "Oh well" ("*Haa. Shō ga nai wa*

FIGURE 46. Madame Suliman's powerful and dangerous magic is expressed with some of the film's most obviously computer-generated effects. Both the film's story and its style associate magic and technology with dangerous power.

nee"), and says that she, too, will intervene with her government to end the hostilities; but the suddenness of the ending might suggest that it is she who has been orchestrating the conflict from the outset, perhaps even she who cursed the scarecrow prince.

Novel Perspectives: Diana Wynne Jones's Metafictional Worlds

In Diana Wynne Jones's novel, each character has their own kind of magic, and it is part of who they are. This is in keeping with the book's idea that we never know everything about anyone, that we can always discover new and different perspectives on any situation—something that contrasts perceptibly with the film's message that we are all alike, and pure at heart. (Jones praises the film but notes that "Howl and Sophie . . . are gentler and more noble than the characters in my books.")[16] The novel always emphasizes this multiplicity of meaning, particularly when meaning is represented in language, which is slippery. This is reflected not only in the shifting identities and disguises described above, but also in a continual play with words and genre conventions. Let's consider some of these elements, none of which appear in the film. The novel begins:

> In the land of Ingary, where such things as seven-league boots and cloaks of invisibility really exist, it is quite a misfortune to be born the eldest of three. Everyone knows you are the one who will fail first, and worst, if the three of you set out to seek your fortunes.
>   Sophie Hatter was the eldest of three sisters. She was not even the child of a poor woodcutter, which might have given her some chance of success! . . . She read a great deal, and very soon realized how little chance she had of an interesting future.[17]

A reader, Sophie is right about most fairy tales but wrong about her own book. And so from the opening, the novel foregrounds and questions the conventions of literary fantasy, and it goes on to repeat this pattern, sustaining the reader's immersion for a while, then pulling the rug out from under itself.

David Rudd cleverly catalogs these moments of metafiction, which he associates specifically with poststructuralist criticism and its tendency to overturn received meanings and narratives ("demonstrating how what we think of as solid ground is always prone to dissolution").[18] Besides narrative elements like the ones above, Rudd discusses wordplay, reversal of gender roles, and the magic topography of the castle itself, which turns things inside out in a way that questions the boundedness of the subjects who inhabit it. (Rudd cites Jacques Derrida, but we might relate this to Roland Barthes's poststructuralism, and the way he used the inside-out bodies of the bunraku puppets to question the bounded subject in chapter 3.)

The way the novel plays with language is among its most interesting features, starting with Sophie's magical ability to talk people and objects into doing what she wants. But the climax is a spell that she and Michael discover in Howl's study and labor to figure out. It begins:

> Go and catch a falling star,
> Get with child a mandrake root,
> Tell me where all past years are,
> or who cleft the Devil's foot.[19]

It goes on listing further impossibilities, causing Sophie to wonder how she or Michael could possibly follow its instructions, but the spell turns out to be a curse the Witch of the Waste has set on Howl, to take effect when all the conditions are fulfilled. And although they seem impossible, one by one they come true in various clever (sometimes metaphorical) ways. But readers who recognize the verse realize that there is a further joke here: this is one stanza from a poem by the English Renaissance poet John Donne, which escalates the novel's metafiction. When Howl sees the poem, he turns the door to the mysterious black setting and takes Sophie and Michael through, emerging not on a battlefield (as in the film) but in the reader's own world, in present-day Britain. There he visits his sister and determines that the spell is part of an English assignment given to his nephew. Howl's real name is "Howell," and it is actually our world that is the source of Ingary's magic: Howl explains to his nephew's English teacher that he "wrote a doctoral thesis on charms and spells," and he learns that the Witch of the Waste has smuggled the curse into his castle via the unexpected route of Donne's poetry.[20] (The schoolteacher turns out to be the central villain; the homework assignment should have made Howl suspicious, but in the novel's shifting maze of identities and realities, he is often as baffled as we are.)

In other words, the novel disrupts this immersion in a different world by popping us back into our own: the world of John Donne, English classes, and PhDs. But as Jones breaks one spell she weaves another, helping us see magic in our own lives. Our technology appears miraculous to Sophie, Donne's poetry has palpable power, and those PhDs are magicians of a sort. In fact, Howl's description of casting a spell sounds a bit like literary analysis:

> Always read it right through, carefully, first. The shape of it should tell you a lot, whether it's self-fulfilling, or self-discovering, or simple incantation, or mixed action and speech. When you've decided that, go through again and decide which bits mean what they say and which bits are put as a puzzle. . . . You'll find every spell of power has at least one deliberate mistake or mystery in it. . . . You have to spot those.[21]

In contrast with Jones, when Miyazaki's films point outside themselves it is only to his other films, giving us the sense that we are still in Miyazaki's world (or Napier's "MiyazakiWorld"). In *Howl's Moving Castle* we can find references to many of Miyazaki's earlier films: the pastiched European setting echoes *Kiki's Delivery Service* (*Majo no takkyūbin*, 1986); the theme of a cursed hero(ine) deformed or disguised by magic appears in *Porco Rosso* (*Kurenai buta*, 1992) and *Princess Mononoke* (*Mononoke-hime*, 1997); the Witch of the Waste's character design resembles Zenibaba, another frightening but eventually lovable sorceress from *Spirited Away*; and the dragonfly airplanes and Sophie's magic ring both borrow visual motifs from *Castle in the Sky* (*Tenkū no shiro Rapyuta*, 1986) (Figure 47).

Miyazaki's Immersive Message

At this point it will be apparent that the powers I am associating with the novel correspond to the powers I have associated with anime throughout this book: an ability to move us in and out of the story in a way that makes us critically consider how language,

FIGURE 47. Sophie's ring visually quotes Sheeta's pendant, from *Castle in the Sky*. Just as these talismans point the heroines unerringly toward home, references in Miyazaki's films always seem to point back to other Miyazaki films. *Castle in the Sky* still from the Disney Blu-ray disc (2012).

fiction, and media shape our experience of the world. As Rudd says: "Jones shows us how easy it is to become enslaved by the narrative conventions these tales represent, and to interpret our lived experience accordingly."[22]

Miyazaki's films are ideologically persuasive because, for better or worse, they trade away this hedging critical perspective for moral or ethical certainty. The films' immersiveness powerfully conveys their worldview, which is in many ways very progressive (environmentalist, pacifist) and in some ways quite conservative (emphasizing conventional gender roles, avoiding sexuality). I don't believe it is an accident that the sources of Miyazaki's popularity I identified at the outset of this chapter (consistency, accessibility, idealism) build on and reinforce this sense of moral certainty. I have suggested throughout this book that directors like Ōtomo, Oshii, and Kon are politically productive because they make us ask where our politics come from, often by starting from issues of media, language, and representation. The risk they run is a fall into cynicism, relativism, or just confusion. Miyazaki's films run the opposite risk, the risk of certainty, the loss of critical distance.

There is a sequence in *Howl's Moving Castle* where Sophie and Markl see a badly damaged warship limping into port, its sailors jumping overboard to escape their burning, sinking vessel. Markl wants a closer look, but Sophie looks faint and says, "No. I can't handle this. Let's go home." A moment later an enemy plane flies overhead and drops propaganda leaflets, which police forbid people from reading, and shortly afterward we see town officials scattering propaganda flyers of their own, but we see or hear only snatches of what is on these leaflets. Lindsay Smith cites the unread leaflets as a failure of dialogue, arguing that in the film "senseless conflicts can only be avoided, and resolved, through open communication."[23] But to me even the idea of "communication" suggests a discursive engagement across the vagaries of language, while I think what Miyazaki's films really yearn for is an almost prelinguistic kind of mutual understanding—like the wordless communion between children and fantastic creatures in *My Neighbor Totoro* (*Tonari no Totoro*, 1988) or *Ponyo* (*Gake no ue no Ponyo*, 2008). In this scene, the film is just following its own lead, refusing to digress into other stories (the story of the battleship), other texts (the leaflets), or any point of view but Sophie's. You don't need to hear that, Miyazaki is telling us: you know what to believe.

If there is any quality in Miyazaki's films that does threaten to break the frame and bring us out of the story and back to ourselves, I think it would be the breathtaking beauty of the animation itself. There are always moments in Miyazaki's films where (as in the puppet theater) we are forced to acknowledge the creators.

In Miyazaki's later films, this feeling often reaches a peak near the end, with a visual climax that seems to leave the plot behind. In *Howl's Moving Castle*, this happens when an air raid threatens one of the towns on the other side of the castle's magic door (Sophie's home town, in fact). This climax is completely different from the novel's. Howl flies to defend the castle and its occupants, but Sophie undoes the castle's magic, apparently to sever the door's connections to the town so that Howl can stop defending the town and retreat. This sets off a chain of events that disintegrates the castle, leaving Sophie in the wilderness surrounded by the building's wreckage. But among the bits and pieces, Sophie finds the castle door leaning against a rock, and when she steps through it, it transports her back in time, to Howl's childhood.

The events described above are confusing the first time through: one reviewer said, "the narrative of *Howl's Moving Castle* is rather like the castle itself—a constantly evolving structure made out of a jumble of diverse fragments."[24] But the results are undeniably beautiful. Transported to the past, Sophie sees Howl in a meadow surrounded by shooting stars that are falling to earth, and as she watches, he catches one and unites it with his own heart to produce Calcifer. This trade—giving up his heart to harness the demon—is the source of Howl's power and also his incompleteness. Seeing and understanding, Sophie calls to him, "Wait for me in the future!" before the spell is broken and she is returned to the present. There she separates the heart from Calcifer and puts it back into Howl, finally restoring his humanity.

The meadow scene is a visual triumph, with a glorious nighttime setting and falling stars that land and skitter along the ground before sizzling out. The moment where Howl grasps his own burning heart recalls a similar scene from *Akira* (Figures 9 and 48), but this image of sincerity (a true heart, a heart light) is more convincing in Miyazaki's sincere film than it was in Ōtomo's more complexly ironic work. At this moment even the consummate animation does not seem to lift us out of the action but only immerse us more deeply in Miyazaki's world.

This sequence does not advance the plot very much. (The riddle of Howl's missing heart is actually revealed in the scene that precedes this one.) But it conveys visually that Sophie has witnessed

FIGURE 48. Transported to the past, Sophie witnesses Howl catch a shooting star and unite it with his own heart to form Calcifer. Compare this with the similar image in *Akira* (Figure 9).

something beautiful, and with it a pure, innocent version of Howl that somehow opens her eyes to goodness.

As an academic critic, I confess to feeling at this moment that I, like Sophie, have been taken back in time. Leaving aside poststructuralism and postmodernism, the transparent equation of beauty with goodness seems to belong to a Romanticism right out of the nineteenth century. (And "Romantic" is in fact the word Miyazaki himself chooses to describe the film.)[25] In the logic of Miyazaki's world or worldview, it does indeed seem to be beauty that grounds the film's optimistic, ecological, pacifist ethics. Borrowing the director's own words, Sophie learns "how to be encouraged" precisely by learning "how to perceive the world as something beautiful."[26]

This is the final way in which Miyazaki's films harken to an earlier time: not just in their pre-industrial settings, their valorization of childhood, or their minimization of computer graphics, but in their idealized image of art itself—though the beauty of technology and the excitement of violence are there as well, like a worm in the apple or an apple in the garden, in tension with the film's dominant message.

This brings us to the inevitable final question for a chapter on Miyazaki: what comes after Miyazaki, particularly for Studio Ghibli, which has built such a following based on this director's work? Miyazaki, now in his late seventies, has announced his retirement from feature filmmaking, and his partner at Ghibli, Takahata Isao, is in his eighties. Younger (or slightly younger) directors at other studios (at least the ones examined in preceding chapters) don't seem to share Miyazaki's interest in innocent beauty, political certainty, and transparent communication, focusing instead on the ambiguities and aporias of representation, politics, and language. Is there a new generation of directors willing and able to sustain, or possibly update, Miyazaki's nostalgic message and style?

So far Studio Ghibli has not found an auteur to replace Miyazaki and Takahata, though recently the studio has produced a few films by other directors who have stretched the Ghibli vision in interesting new directions. Miyazaki's son Gorō made his directorial debut in 2006 with *Tales from Earthsea (Gedo senki)*, a film Miyazaki criticized.[27] Based on the fantasy series by Ursula K. Le Guin, the film gives an interesting Oedipal spin to Le Guin's world and Ghibli's internal politics by centering the story on the son of a great king who murders his father for reasons even he does not really understand. Gorō's second film, *From Up on Poppy Hill (Kokuriko-zaka kara*, 2011), also dealt with absent fathers in a way that might move the viewer's attention back and forth between the world of the film and the world of Ghibli itself. Yonebayashi Hiromasa has directed two Ghibli films, including 2014's *When Marnie Was There (Maanii no omoide)*, an adolescent ghost story with an intriguingly queer subtext.

But the best candidate for Miyazaki's spiritual successor may not be a Ghibli director at all, but a filmmaker who left Ghibli over disagreements about *Howl's Moving Castle*. Hosoda Mamoru later went on to make a series of successful films including *Summer Wars (Samaa wōzu*, 2009), which took Miyazaki's touchstone themes and aesthetic and transformed them into something completely and compellingly new. Hosoda's film serves as a final case study for the conclusion of this book.

Conclusion

Summer Wars

Chapter 7's discussion of Miyazaki Hayao and *Howl's Moving Castle* could prompt us to wonder how a different director might have adapted Diana Wynne Jones's novel. Would another director have retained or even magnified the self-conscious, layered structure that characterizes the novel and so much other anime? In fact, Studio Ghibli originally recruited an outsider, Hosoda Mamoru, to direct the film. Miyazaki had announced his intent to retire (one of several such announcements made at different points in his career), and *Howl's Moving Castle* was to be the first Ghibli feature film developed from the ground up by someone new. But Hosoda parted ways with Ghibli after he and the studio failed to agree on a concept for the film, and at that point Miyazaki took over the project.[1] Hosoda went on to success at the studio Madhouse where he made several compelling films. One of those was *Summer Wars* (*Samaa wōzu*, 2009), which takes up Miyazaki's themes of community and connection, but combines them with a more ironic or critical exploration of language and communication. This makes *Summer Wars* an interesting postscript to our discussion of Miyazaki, but also a final striking example of anime's characteristic oscillation between immediacy and distance.

In *Summer Wars* this oscillation is explicit, as the film moves between two distinct worlds. Part of the action takes place in rural Nagano, where four generations of the Jinnouchi family have gathered to celebrate the matriarch's ninetieth birthday. (We see the family through the eyes of seventeen-year-old Kenji, a guest who is overwhelmed by the imposing manor house, the Jinnouchi's samurai lineage, and the clan's large and colorful cast of characters.) But other parts of the film take place online, in the world of "OZ"—a three-dimensional virtual reality where the Jinnouchis and billions of other users conduct daily business and interact with one another as avatars. The control systems of the world's companies and governments all depend on the OZ network, so when a piece of intelligent malware called "Love Machine" gets loose there, it spawns financial, political, and physical chaos in the outside world as well. As the malware grows more powerful and dangerous, the family members join forces to fight it, each bringing their own quirky talents and resources to bear.

The film remains nicely balanced between this farfetched but exciting adventure plot and more serious domestic drama, including the matriarch's death midway through the film and the transformation of the birthday celebration into a wake. The themes of the film revolve decisively around family, friendship, and teamwork, as the protagonists mobilize a network of relatives, companions, and strangers to stop Love Machine.

I interviewed the film's charismatic producer Satō Yūichirō at the studio Madhouse in May 2011, and much of what he said recalled Miyazaki's comments on the state of Japanese animation. Satō also distinguished between the mass of commercial material he associated with the word "anime" and what he referred to as "filmmaking that harnesses animation as an expressive language." Retracing the canonical distinction between the golden age of Tōei Animation and the TV animation of Mushi Pro, he spoke about Hosoda's interest in a specifically theatrical experience, one he identified with sociality and family time. Television animation, Satō said, is driven by an escalation that seeks only to titillate or stimulate its viewer, at the same time becoming directed at an increasingly narrow, "superdomestic" audience of otaku fans. The hope with *Summer Wars*, he said, was to make a film about intimate, personal concerns like family, in a way that would give the film a global relevance (a hope that Hosoda himself echoed at the film's international premier).[2] Rather than engage in social criticism, Satō said, Hosoda's goal is to entertain audiences with an optimistic vision of these universal themes, to make films that are "deep" (*fukai*) rather than "difficult" (*nankai*).

All of this parallels Miyazaki's "Thoughts on Japanese Animation," the essay discussed in the previous chapter, and suggests some strong parallels between Miyazaki and Hosoda, particularly their concern with themes of mutual understanding and their distinction between commercial anime and animation as a higher art. But *Summer Wars* has its own interesting take on communication and its own unique relation to fine art, both of which set it apart from Miyazaki's work. The interest of *Summer Wars* lies in the way it portrays sociality across its two worlds: at one moment we are in OZ, watching the characters (or rather their avatars) gather allies from the global community of OZ users; in another scene we see the ninety-year-old great grandmother using the house's rotary telephone and her formidable social connections to mobilize a legion of volunteers. (The latter scene is accompanied by a clever montage of analog media representing *her* network: her paper address book, generations of black-and-white family photographs, and piles of cards and letters.)

This alternation between digital and physical networks is also expressed in the look of the film, which is a visual tour de force: it uses cel-style animation for the traditional world of the family estate, but animates the OZ scenes using computer graphics inspired by Murakami Takashi's Superflat art, with three-dimensional multicolored forms moving against flat backgrounds that suggest an endless, depthless space (Figure 49).

Murakami was one of our starting points in chapter 1, for his suggestion that *Akira* represented both an origin and a loss of origin. Now he becomes our endpoint as well, but not without some irony. Superflat and its analogous elements in *Akira* stood for the loss of geometric perspective, the loss of political perspective, and the radical destabilization that many associate with the crises of postmodernism. That Hosoda could take that symbolism and synthesize it with a Miyazaki-like realism to produce a film about family and community is an unexpected reversal, to say the least.

But even as *Summer Wars* challenges Superflat's brand of postmodernism, it deconstructs Miyazaki's immersive nostalgia as well. Some critics see the film's emphasis on group unity as a conservative message, and find the story of an ancient samurai household defending Japanese community values nationalistic. But while the story's feel-good theme of group solidarity does seem to be grounded in a certain conservatism, the sheer number

FIGURE 49. In Hosoda Mamoru's *Summer Wars,* a hand-drawn rural setting that recalls Miyazaki Hayao is mated with a computer generated virtual world inspired by Superflat artist Murakami Takashi. Here we see members of the Jinnouchi family and their avatars, icons that provide additional perspective on the personalities of the film's many distinct characters. From the Funimation Blu-ray disc (2013).

of characters in the Jinnouchi family, together with their various personalities and histories (married, unmarried, widowed, divorced), all combine to give some sense of diversity to the film's notion of family and belonging.[3] Hosoda preserves this sense of different perspectives and different values with a series of parallel plots: while some struggle against the malware in OZ, another group is preoccupied with preparations for the reunion (then the funeral), and a third is glued to the television for the high school baseball semifinals where one of the younger Jinnouchis is pitching. By moving back and forth between different plots and their associated visual registers (the traditional house, Superflat OZ, the remediated television), the anime emphasizes these shifts in perspective and makes us consider how these different priorities are constructed to begin with.

Hosoda makes this strategy work by ensuring that all of these different registers feel equally real to the viewer. What happens in OZ or on the television seems just as genuine and important as anything else, and not just because these simulations are connected to an outside reality, but because they have an internal weight or reality of their own. Where does this conviction come from in the film, and politically where does it lead? One could relate *Summer Wars* to the postmodern worlds of *Patlabor 2* or *Innocence* or *Millennium Actress* or the otaku—worlds in which experience is so mediated that it becomes difficult to see where simulation begins or ends. Yet, the message of *Summer Wars* is not Oshii's media and political critique, or the otaku's realization that all relationships could be described as virtual, that a fictional friendship can be as healthy as any other. Nor is it quite the guarded optimism of Kon Satoshi, whose characters get mixed up with their fictional avatars but eventually harness their own fictionality to rewrite the script of their own lives. In *Summer Wars* the parity of the physical and the virtual comes from an optimistic belief in the importance of communication and connection, whether those connections are physical or mediated, local or global, analog or electronic. The film sustains this optimism with a hopeful faith in language, a sense that no matter how language is accelerated or altered by technology (and no matter what changes that imposes on our world or our subjectivities), language joins us productively to one another.

That returns us to Satō and Hosoda's hope that watching anime could constitute a social experience, a hope that I share. For me the reason to talk, write, or teach about anime (or any literary text, for that matter) is to forge an encounter with other people across the language of that text—to touch and change and learn about each other. The more texts we have available to us and the more we have to say about them, the richer, the more nuanced, and the more creative those encounters will be. In that sense I believe that despite the challenges identified with the postmodern multiplication of languages, media, and interpretations, that multiplication is ultimately a resource and an opportunity for us.

This book is optimistically organized around just such a multiplication of texts and perspectives—a series of shifts or comparisons that I hope can yield broader perspectives or deeper insights. The most important of these shifts is the oscillation I have argued for in anime, the way it can feel immersive and even realistic at one moment, then ironic, virtual, and contingent in the next. At its best, this creates a unique combination of engagement and critical distance, letting us step back and think about representation at the very same moment these representations are pulling us in. The result can be a sharper sensitivity to the way language works and a more sophisticated understanding of the interaction between representation and what we regard as reality.

Another shift is between methods. Each chapter has introduced different critical tools, and certain readers may have a preference for certain theories, but my real hope is that moving from one theory to another has revealed powers and pitfalls in all of them. Structuralism and poststructuralism, excoriations and celebrations of postmodernism, phenomenology, psychoanalysis, posthumanism, queer theory, and media theory each provide their own crucial insights. None has a monopoly on truth (just as my own interpretations inevitably have their own particular blind spots). Finally, the critical perspective of each individual director reveals something different and worthwhile: Ōtomo's apocalyptic politics, Hosoda's faith in communication, Kon's optimistically fragmented subjectivity, Oshii's dire political and technological critique, and even Miyazaki's stubborn Romanticism each have their role to play, and each sheds light on the others.

The final shift is between different media. This begins with my decision to write about anime in the first place (and your decision to read about it), driven by curiosity about what this relatively new medium might teach us. Comparisons between anime and other media invite us to consider what each of these media can and cannot do, what it can and cannot represent. I cannot escape the limits language imposes upon me, any more than I can look into my own blind spot, stand apart from my own body, or speak outside my own voice; but by comparing different forms of language, we can at least begin to think about what those limits might be. With each new text and each new comparison, we are invited to consider more carefully what we are reading or watching. This includes anime's own risks and opportunities, its pleasures and frustrations, its reality and unreality—ultimately anime's role in our world of language and its place in the language of our world.

Chronology

Acknowledgments

The world of anime is populated by outsized characters with fantastic powers. But my real life has been graced by people just as incredible. Over the years that this book and the field it inhabits have taken shape, I have been privileged to work with some genuine superheroes.

I will always remain grateful to my first mentors, Makoto Ueda, Tom Hare, Susan Matisoff, and Nakagawa Shigemi, for an intellectual generosity that encouraged my interest in comparative literature. Susan Napier and Sharalyn Orbaugh also inspired and supported me early on, as they fearlessly blazed paths that anime scholarship would follow.

Two professional partnerships were turning points for me. The first was an editorial collaboration with Istvan Csicsery-Ronay Jr. and Tatsumi Takayuki. Istvan helped form my image of what an editor and critic should be: generous and rigorous, patient and engaged. Tatsumi-sensei showed me that this work can be an adventure, and took me along on several of his own academic exploits. The second turning point was a transformative friendship with Frenchy Lunning, the superhuman producer and mad scientist who conceived the *Mechademia* book series. I coedited ten volumes of *Mechademia* alongside Frenchy, Wendy Goldberg, Tom Lamarre, and the rest of the editorial team, and I feel lucky and proud to have been a member of this scholarly ninja band.

Many generous colleagues provided opportunities to present or publish earlier versions of this work, including Bruce Baird, David Bialock, Gunhild Borggreen, Will Bridges, Joseph Chen, Rebecca Copeland, Hikari Hori, Christer Johansson, Michele Mason, Jay McRoy, Jay Rubin, Atsuko Sakaki, Vyjayanthi Selinger, and especially Teri Silvio. Livia Monnet and Vivian Sobchack provided pivotal encouragement. Mimi Long and Miri Nakamura were key co-conspirators. Doug Easton prepared the index. And Rebecca Suter and Michael Foster gave careful and crucial feedback on the full manuscript; I feel privileged to have received input from two colleagues whose writing I admire so much.

A number of Japanese critics and creators kindly made time to discuss their work: Azuma Hiroki, Kotani Mari, Matsumoto Nobuyuki, Mizoguchi Mika, Saitō Tamaki, Satō Dai, and Suematsu Ken'ichi. Many thanks also to Satō Yūichirō, and to Ian Condry for introducing the two of us.

I have learned from many superlative students at Williams College and the University of California, Riverside (too many to name, but I remember you all). And I have drawn regular inspiration from the creative cast of Frenchy Lunning's annual Schoolgirls and Mobile Suits conference, among them Crispin Freeman, Barbara Guttman, Mark Hairston, Andrea Horbinski, Heather Luca, Megan Maude, Eron Rauch, Samantha Rei, Brian Ruh, Kaylene Ruwart, and Rio Saitō.

Jason Weidemann and the University of Minnesota Press looked into the future and provided early and sustained support for the study of Japanese popular culture. Jason's confidence and encouragement were both tremendously important for completing this book.

The Oakley Center for the Humanities and Social Sciences at Williams College provided financial support for this project as well as intellectual community and critical feedback. And some fantastic colleagues at Williams and beyond—especially Jørgen Bruhn, Gail Newman, Christopher Nugent, Paul Park, Leyla Rouhi, Ben Rubin, and Eiko Siniawer—supplied friendship and much more.

To my mom and dad, my brother, my daughters, and especially my wife: I have no words to thank you for your boundless love and patience. You are miraculous.

Notes

Introduction

1. This work is in dialogue with other texts in a large *R.O.D* franchise created by Kurata Hideyuki, including a long series of light novels by Kurata starting in 2000; two manga series (Kurata and Yamada Shutarō's *R.O.D: Read or Die* in 2000–2002, and Kurata and Ayanaga Ran's *R.O.D: Read or Dream* in 2003–5); and a twenty-six-episode *Read or Die* TV series (2003–4), also directed by Masunari Kōji and scripted by Kurata.

2. For example, see Berndt, "Considering Manga Discourse"; Berndt, ed., *Comics Worlds*, 5–14; and Berndt and Richter, eds., *Reading Manga*, 7–17, 107–23.

3. Marie-Laure Ryan compares immersion and interactivity in prose and virtual-reality media, and makes a start at theorizing immersion, even as she identifies "its resistance to theorization" (*Narrative as Virtual Reality*, 10). Her "poetics of immersion" focuses on fictional worlds and the spatial and temporal metaphors we use to describe navigating them. While I think this is a good starting point, the case studies in the following chapters associate immersion with the wider range of viewer responses I have described here, from visual recognition and emotional empathy, through political resonance, to visceral physical response.

4. Bolter and Grusin, *Remediation*. Among Bolter and Grusin's most interesting conclusions is the idea that in the quest for both "immediacy" and "hypermediacy," new media visually mimic earlier media. Some of the media comparisons in the chapters that follow do fall into this category of what they call "remediation," where anime seems to be simulating another medium like live-action film. But my approach is somewhat broader: other chapters treat cases of adaptation (where anime and another medium both take up the same content in entirely different ways) or less evident comparisons inspired by specific critical theory (comparisons between anime and drag performance, for example). Bolter and Grusin also focus heavily on the idea of perceived visual realism (and its putative origins in Renaissance painting or later photography),

which is a limiting assumption when dealing with stylized media like animation. This is another reason I am interested in the broader sense of immersion described above.

5. Coleridge, *Biographia Literaria*, 2:2; Brecht, "Alienation Effects in Chinese Theater"; Barthes, "Myth Today," 110; Jameson, *Postmodernism*, 1–54. This is perhaps an optimistic version of Jameson's ideas, which are discussed in more detail in chapter 1.

6. *R.O.D Official Archive*, 53.

7. For example, see the detailed entry on Nancy in the *Read or Die* Wiki, http://readordie.wikia.com.

8. To interpret *Read or Die* in geopolitical terms, one might start with its conspicuously international cast of villains and its apparently bicultural Japanese heroine fighting for Britain. Its setting is also ambiguously suspended between present-day Tokyo, nineteenth-century London, and the former British colonies of America, India, and (in the sequels) Hong Kong. This cosmopolitan quality is interesting in light of Japan's complex relationship to Western colonialism: largely closed to the West for more than 250 years, it was "opened" in the nineteenth century by England, France, and the United States. It learned the lessons of conquest only too well, establishing its own colonies and a far-reaching empire before defeat in World War II forced it to cede these holdings and repudiate its colonial past. This age of empire seems distinctly romanticized in the pastiche of *Read or Die*, even more so when the evil Nancy tries to conquer the world then has her mind changed, conveniently forgetting all her past sins.

9. On anime's history, see Clements, *Anime: A History*, and Patten, *Watching Anime, Reading Manga*. On anime fandom across times and cultures, see Annett, *Anime Fan Communities*, and Napier, *From Impressionism to Anime*. On the process and culture of anime production, see Condry, *The Soul of Anime*.

10. Related to this argument about anime's origin and definition is the question of whether anime is a separate *medium* or rather a segment of the medium of animation. If medium is primarily the materiality of the text, then anime has a specific materiality that overlaps partially but not completely with other "different" kinds of animation, like Hollywood animation, digitally rendered 3D animation, or stop-motion animation. Yet, anime also has important contextual and stylistic features (its Japanese origins or its character designs, for example) that we might associate with other categories, like "a literature" or "a genre." Anime (like most of the other media treated in this book) is a category that bridges these imprecise English terms, so here I refer to all as media in an expanded sense, one that begins from a text's materiality but also includes elements of its form and context. For similar approaches to medium, see Clements, *Anime*, 3; and Sobchack, *Carnal Thoughts*, 139–40.

1. From Origin to Oblivion

1. Armstrong, "Animated *Akira* a Hallucinogenic Masterwork."
2. Many U.S. reviews cited these technical achievements. See the reviews by Harrington, Baker, Armstrong, and Griffin, for example. For details of the film's production, see the documentary "Akira Production Report" on the special edition U.S. DVD. For a description of the anime production process at several different studios today, see Condry, *Soul of Anime*, 135–60.
3. Streamline had distributed two other anime in North America before *Akira*, Miyazaki Hayao's *Castle in the Sky (Tenkū no shiro Rapyuta*, 1986) and Yoshida Hiroaki's *Twilight of the Cockroaches (Gokiburitachi no tasogare*, 1987), but Beck and Fred Patten (who also worked for Streamline at the time) both confirmed to me that *Akira* was distributed on a much wider scale (personal communication, 2015). To locate *Akira* within the context of anime and manga's earlier history in North America, see, Patten, *Watching Anime, Reading Manga*, 50–73, 122–26, 128–29.
4. Richmond, *Rough Guide to Anime*, 36.
5. Kehr, "Japanese Cartoon *Akira* Isn't One for the Kids."
6. This move forward and backward is even clearer in the chronology of the *Akira* manga: there, World War III breaks out in December 1982, thirty-seven years after the end of World War II, and the main action takes place in 2019, thirty-seven years after World War III. December 1982 is also the same month and year the manga began serialization. The anime version and the English-language manga each altered the dates to associate the initial explosion with the audience's own present and locate the main action a generation later. Steven Brown points out that December 6, the date of the explosion in the manga, is also one day before the anniversary of the Japanese attack on Pearl Harbor. But Isolde Standish suggests that these references may not be firm anchors to actual history so much as simulacra refracted through other layers of media: she notes that the colonel resembles General Anami, Japan's War Minister in 1945, but filtered through Mifune Toshirō's portrayal of Anami in the 1967 film *Japan's Longest Day*. Brown, *Tokyo Cyberpunk*, 2; Standish, "*Akira*, Postmodernism and Resistance," 56–74.
7. Yonezawa, "Manga kara no ekusodasu," 149–50.
8. Murakami, *Little Boy*, 204–5, 109.
9. The extensive coverage of the "Little Boy" show in *The New York Times* and elsewhere largely repeated Murakami's arguments about Japanese art and history. Even negative reviews of the show treated the underlying ideas credulously. For example, see Smith, "From a Mushroom Cloud," and Gurewitsch, "Perpetual Adolescence."
10. Johnson, "Japan Crisis Evokes Comparisons." Within this article, Reed Johnson's reductionist opening was balanced by some nuanced

comments from two scholars of Japanese literature and visual culture, Akira Lippit and Thomas Lamarre.

11. For a more rigorous development of this argument, see Bolton, "Bunretsu aruiwa ryūnyū."

12. Derrida, *Writing and Difference*, 280.

13. Ibid.

14. Even looking beyond Japanese studies journals, there are only a couple of academic articles in English that reference anime before Napier. Koulikov, "The Origins of English-Language Anime Studies."

15. Jameson, *Postmodernism*, 27; Baudrillard, *Simulacra and Simulation*, 87.

16. Freiberg, "*Akira* and the Postnuclear Sublime," 95. See also Standish: "*Akira* is, above all else, concerned with the esthetics of movement and destruction, subordinating any sense of narrative sequence to images of the spectacular" ("*Akira*, Postmodernism, and Resistance," 64).

17. In a review of *Akira's* 2001 DVD release, Peter Nichols of *The New York Times* summed up these notions of origin, confusion, and oblivion: "Animation has gone in various directions, of course, but the film, which alludes to the destruction of Hiroshima and Nagasaki during World War II, helped popularize anime in the United States and remains fresh and startling despite its confused and repetitive plotline."

18. Napier, "Panic Sites," 248. Napier's early characterization of *Akira* as postmodern emphasized this destabilization of the bodily subject, as well as the film's open-ended narrative and its paranoid anxiety about capitalist society. After Napier, Freiberg and Standish characterized the film as postmodern particularly for its fast-paced pastiche of disconnected images. Writing in 2001, Napier summarizes all these ideas: "*Akira's* postmodern aspects include four major elements: the film's rapid narrative pace (reinforced by its soundtrack); its fascination with fluctuating identity, as evidenced in Tetsuo's metamorphoses; its use of pastiche both in relation to Japanese history and cinematic styles; and its ambivalent attitude toward history" (*Anime: From "Akira" to "Howl's Moving Castle,"* 260).

19. Saitō and Naitō, "*Patlabor the Movie*" Archives, 113. This is a somewhat one-sided history—it ignores liberal or progressive political victories in local politics, and in areas outside foreign policy, for example. But it is a narrative that seems to have captured the pessimistic imagination of many artists in Ōtomo and Oshii's generation.

20. For a brief but nuanced discussion of Japanese postmodernism that is roughly contemporary with *Akira*, see Ivy "Critical Texts, Mass Artifacts."

21. In the wake of the March 2011 earthquake in Japan and the subsequent disaster at the Fukushima nuclear power plants, some critics have sought to locate Fukushima as a new origin, one that brings to light Japan's fraught postwar relationship with U.S. nuclear weapons and nuclear power, and at the same time marks a turning point or endpoint in

postwar Japanese history, possibly attended by a new era of progressive grassroots antinuclear activism. This gesture seems to be a more optimistic or progressive version of Murakami Takashi's thesis: it has an undeniable narrative power, but it seems to me to risk the same kind of reductionism inherent in any search for historical origins.

22. Many early reviews warned audiences unfamiliar with anime that *Akira* was animation intended for adults. See the reviews by Armstrong, Harrington, and Kehr, the last titled "Japanese Cartoon *Akira* Isn't One for the Kids." But John Griffin notes that *Akira* does not feel entirely adult either: "The film's visual anarchy demands a snarling attitude that never manifests itself in the kids—they are the Sex Pistols as played by the Care Bears." Griffin's media references seem to reflect the gap discussed here, between 1960s- or 1970s-style activism and 1980s media culture.

23. Azuma, *Otaku*; Ōtsuka, "World and Variation" and *Monogatari shōhiron kai*, 3-23. See also Miyoshi and Harootunian, eds., *Postmodernism and Japan*. In *Apocalypse in Contemporary Japanese Science Fiction*, Tanaka Motoko develops the idea of "spiral time" in order to synthesize the linear time of modernity, the cyclical time of apocalyptic renewal, and the timelessness of the postmodern. For Tanaka, spiral time suggests a process of repetition or reproduction that nevertheless allows for incremental progress or change (146).

24. See Lyotard's *Postmodern Condition*, 41, and "What Is Postmodernism?" 80-81.

25. On pacing, see Forbes, "He's the Kubrick of Anime." On publication formats, see Goodwin, "Editor's Note." For detailed publication history, see the timeline in Ōtomo, *Akira Club*, n.p.

26. If Standish traces the postmodern fragmentation of the anime partly to the episodic quality of the manga, Steven Brown argues that the *Akira* manga is postmodern even in comparison with other manga, its multiple competing themes recalling Lyotard's little narratives as well as the laterally ramified "rhizomatic" structures described by postmodern philosophers Gilles Deleuze and Félix Guattari. Standish, "*Akira*, Postmodernism and Resistance," 64; Brown, *Tokyo Cyberpunk*, 3-10.

27. Ōtomo relates how, while drawing *Akira*, he collected photographic books with scenes of rubble. Ōtomo, *Akira Club*, n.p.

28. Susan Napier associates the film's darkness with its moral atmosphere ("Panic Sites," 245). Marc Steinberg's essay "The Trajectory of Apocalypse" equates light in *Akira* with weaponry, and notes that as spectators we repeatedly have this light directed at us before we somehow reverse our position and become its bearer, usually by climbing into the vehicles that have these lights mounted. Steinberg cleverly relates this to the mixture of threat and euphoria that we find in classical notions of the sublime, allowing us to link his work with theories of the postmodern sublime like Jameson's.

29. Even when it tries, the manga is not very good at portraying light and

darkness. The first volume depicts the night with dark backgrounds, but it is not as successful as the anime, and the bright lights cannot be duplicated on the page. A color version of *Akira* produced by Marvel Comics is only a little more successful in this respect. The history of this color version also shows the complexity of locating a single origin for the *Akira* franchise: it was republished in Japan as *Full Color Akira*, with sound effects in roman characters and pages mirrored to read right to left as in the U.S. comic, and with Ōtomo's original Japanese text now replaced by a Japanese reverse-translation of the English translation that had appeared in the U.S. version.

30. Lamarre, *Anime Machine*, 123.

31. Manga author and critic Natsume Fusanosuke also suggests that the manga responds to a loss of meaning and political agency characteristic of 1980s Japan, a situation he describes in vocabulary associated with the postmodern. But Natsume does not find in the manga any visual solution to this dilemma. Contrasting Ōtomo's detailed ruins with the way he draws human bodies, Natsume argues that, "In the numberless explosions, these ruins recapitulate themselves as if immortal. But despite this apparent excitement, the image of ruins penetrates the individual and becomes internalized." This effect is focused in Tetsuo's body, whose outline shifts and shivers to express the "unease of a body saturated with technology and media images, a body society has invaded" (*Manga to sensō*, 130–31).

32. The serial version's final image appears in reworked form on page 6:399 of the English and Japanese collected editions. For the original image see Ōtomo, *Akira Club*, n.p. Part of the manga's look probably traces to the limited contrast possible in the cheaply printed newsprint magazine where *Akira* was originally serialized. I compared a 1989 issue of *Young Magazine* with the corresponding pages in the *Akira* collected volume, and the magazine version shows even less contrast.

33. Murakami Takashi reads this final image as ironic, a pastiche of Tezuka Osamu's utopian city images through which Ōtomo succeeded at "using manga to critique manga. Instead of defining a closed narrative circle, he strove to devise a 'meta-manga' " (*Little Boy*, 110–11). However, it seems to me that this reading neglects the way perspective has functioned in the manga up until this point.

34. Thomas Lamarre sees some optimism in the fact that the kingdom in this final scene is the Empire of *Tokyo*, representing a collapse of empire into something more local ("at once a city and national empire, and neither") and with it a "collapse of the national imaginary." Lamarre sees this as finally breaking a dichotomy that parallels the oscillation I have traced, a dichotomy between destruction and reconstruction that supports perpetual conflict ("Born of Trauma," 151).

35. Jameson, *Postmodernism*, 54, 51.

2. The Mecha's Blind Spot

1. Napier, *Anime: From "Akira" to "Howl's Moving Castle,"* 88.
2. On earlier robot series, see Schodt, *Inside the Robot Kingdom*, 73–90.
3. For biographical information on Oshii, see Oshii, "Profile." For a helpful English overview of Oshii's career and films, see Ruh, *Stray Dog*.
4. On the formation of Headgear and Oshii's role in the franchise, see Ruh, *Stray Dog*, 77–124, and Tom, "Never Forget," 94. On the evolution of the franchise under Oshii, see several interviews with Oshii and the commentary by Hikawa Ryūsuke in two volumes by Saitō and Naitō, *"Patlabor The Movie" Archives*, 112, 134–40 and *"Patlabor 2 The Movie" Archives*, 17–18, 116–18.
5. For details see Ruh, *Stray Dog*, 80; Saitō and Naitō, *"Patlabor The Movie" Archives*, 135; Saitō and Naitō, *"Patlabor 2 The Movie" Archives*, 15.
6. In a discussion with Oshii, rival anime director Miyazaki Hayao criticized the film's divided instincts: "Basically this is what Oshii wants. He wants to blow up bridges and rain down missiles (*laughs*). But these are things you shouldn't do, right? So there's another Oshii that appears to say 'Don't do that.' . . . I think the ideas Oshii had when he was active in the student movement in the 1970s are still swirling around inside him, and he still wants to stir things up or blow things up and expose the world for what it is—whether it's with missiles or Molotov cocktails or the laws against antisubversive elements [the weapons wielded by the military, the protestors, or the state itself]. In the way Oshii put the story together, I still feel an element of that. So he brings the Self Defense Forces into Tokyo and points out that they are an army. But where is Oshii in all this? He is on the side of the soldiers manning the tanks. So it's a film with sympathy for the common soldier (*laughs*), but none at all for the citizens living around them." One might make similar criticisms of Miyazaki's films (see chapter 7). But Oshii responded by questioning Miyazaki's effort to find a transparent political message in the film, saying, "It may appear realistic, but it's all a movie." Oshii and Miyazaki, "Jidai no keri," 83, 86 (my translation).
7. Sobchack, "Democratic Franchise," 731–32, and "Teenage Mutant Ninja Hackers," 577–79. Sobchack's critique came around the same time as *Patlabor 2*, at a time when euphoric rhetoric around virtual reality peaked in the United States, driven by the early expansion of the World Wide Web, the growth of postmodern theory and cyberpunk literature, and the first dot-com bubble. Sobchack's work could be seen as a reaction against the more ecstatically optimistic theories of the postmodern and posthuman described in chapters 1 and 3. But while some of her specific examples are now dated, Sobchack's overall argument seems as relevant now as it was then. For a later update, see her essay "A Leg to Stand On: Prosthetics, Metaphor, and Materiality" (*Carnal Thoughts*, 105–25).

8. Sobchack, *Screening Space*, 256–57.
9. Oshii and Miyazaki, "Jidai no keri," 83. This effect is most pronounced in the original version of the film. When the soundtrack was remastered in 1998, the new sound designer Shiba Shigeharu added an unfortunate musical element to the combat scene that undermines the sense of silence and isolation. For details, see Saitō and Naitō, "*Patlabor 2 The Movie*" *Archives*, 26–27. The 1999 Manga Entertainment DVD contains the original soundtrack; the 2006 limited collector's edition DVD from Honneamise contains the new one.
10. Saitō and Naitō, "*Patlabor The Movie*" *Archives*, 111.
11. Ihiroi, "Mieru mono, mienai mono," 165; Fisch, "Nation, War, and Japan's Future," 49–68.
12. Noda, *Zenryaku Oshii Mamoru-sama*, 77; see also 76–89.
13. Ruh, *Stray Dog*, 116.
14. Oshii, "Profile."
15. From a 1994 interview with Ueno Toshiya on the *Patlabor 2* collector's edition DVD. I've made some small changes to the translation given in the subtitles.
16. Oshii comments on the parallels with the subway gas attack in a 1996 interview with Carl Gustav Horn.
17. Anderson, "Terror, Theatricality, and Exceptions," 82. Anderson's article is helpful for understanding the Japanese political background in greater depth, including more recent debates around Article 9.
18. Ueno, *Kurenai no metaru sūtsu*, 38.
19. Ibid., 41–45, 50–57.
20. Ibid., 44.
21. Ueno writes: "One may have reservations about an artist like Oshii, who has not forgotten the mass demonstrations and student movement, making the police and Self Defense Forces his theme, as if coopted. But this is the rear-guard action he has chosen. What do these 'wild dogs' do, bound by the manacles of their organizations, orders, and rules, discarded by every ideology and philosophy? What do they decide? How do they choose? In this sense, one could certainly call Oshii's works 'political.' " Ibid., 63–64.
22. Noda, *Zenryaku Oshii Mamoru-sama*, 88–89, 100–101.
23. This parallel is highlighted in Saitō and Naitō, "*Patlabor 2 The Movie*" *Archives*, 120, 125.
24. Ueno, *Kurenai no metaru sūtsu*, 44.
25. Sobchack, *Carnal Thoughts*, 149. Sobchack published earlier versions of this essay in 1990 and 1994, around the same time as her essays on virtual reality discussed above.
26. Ibid., 153, 158.
27. Sobchack, *Address of the Eye*, 51.
28. Ibid., 299.
29. The effort to extrapolate film's body from its vision is important to Sob-

chack because it is related to the (inverse) process of seeing another person and imagining their internal perceptual world—the phenomenological dynamic that grounds communication. But Sobchack's full argument identifies cinema with a complex combination of the embodied and the hermeneutic. For more on phenomenology and communication, see chapter 5.

30. Baudrillard, *Simulacra and Simulation*, 51.
31. Sobchack, *Screening Space*, 255–62.
32. Today, these effects are rarely seen outside of documentary films, because computer animation is now routinely used to avoid screen flicker by drawing in the screens later, rather than filming them directly with a camera.
33. Oshii, interview by Horn, 136.
34. Jameson, *Postmodernism*, 418.
35. Saitō and Naitō, "*Patlabor The Movie*" Archives, 146–47.
36. Saitō and Naitō, "*Patlabor 2 The Movie*" Archives, 105–6. This is from a 1993 interview.
37. Baudrillard, *Simulacra and Simulation*, 1.

3. Puppet Voices, Cyborg Souls

1. My translation, from Ueno Toshiya's interview with Oshii on the *Patlabor 2* limited collector's edition DVDs (Honneamise, 2001).
2. Among other changes, *Ghost in the Shell 2.0* replaces the opening and a few other scenes with three-dimensional, computer-generated animation in a way that emphasizes the body: now the names of the film's creators are (as in *Read or Die*) superimposed over close-up images of the major's bare skin.
3. The 2017 live-action version of *Ghost in the Shell* directed by Rupert Sanders lovingly recreates many shots from the anime but is compelled to tone down the violence of the ending. For more on anime's live-action adaptations, see chapter 2.
4. Claudel, *L'oiseau noir*, 196. All translations from Claudel are my own. For an alternative English translation of the sections quoted in this chapter, see Claudel, *On the Theater*, 48–52.
5. Haraway, *Simians, Cyborgs, and Women*, 149–81. The quote is on page 149.
6. Ibid., 174.
7. Ibid., 151; Haraway, "Cyborgs at Large," 11–12.
8. Oshii, *Alles* interview (my translation).
9. Shirō, *Ghost in the Shell*, 1st English ed., 350–57.
10. Orbaugh, "Sex and the Single Cyborg," 183; Silvio, "Refiguring the Radical Cyborg," 72 (abstract); Napier, *Anime from "Akira" to "Princess Mononoke,"* 114. See also Bolton, "Wooden Cyborgs." These essays and their related conference presentations date from around 1999 and 2000, making them some of the earliest English scholarship on *Ghost in the*

Shell. For a more recent discussion of transcendence in Oshii's work, see Gardner, "Cyber Sublime," 44–53.

11. Haraway, "Cyborgs at Large," 20.

12. Besides "A Cyborg Manifesto," see "The Biopolitics of Postmodern Bodies: Constitutions of Self in Immune System Discourse," in Haraway, *Simians, Cyborgs, and Women*, 203–30.

13. Tatsumi, "Hitotsu de wa nai saibōgu no sei" [The cyborg sex which is not one] and "M. batafurai, aruiwa" [M. Butterfly, or perhaps . . .], in Tatsumi and Kotani, *Saibōgu feminizumu*, 8–22, 214–241.

14. Suan, *Anime Paradox*, 9–10, 171–228. Suan draws in part from a much earlier version of the present chapter (Bolton, "Wooden Cyborgs").

15. Hozumi Ikan, *Naniwa miyage*, in Chikamatsu, *Jōrurishū*, 2:356–59, translated in Keene, *Anthology*, 386–90. Quote on pages 2:356 and 386.

16. Chikamatsu, *Four Major Plays*, 5–6. The full play appears in the same volume.

17. Yūda, *Jōrurishi ronkō*, 151–71.

18. Chikamatsu, *Four Major Plays*, 203, 207.

19. The scene of the two bodies matches shots of lovers' bodies that open and conclude Shinoda Masahiro's live-action film *Double Suicide* (*Shinjū ten no Amijima*, 1969), one of the most famous cinematic adaptations of Chikamatsu. Shinoda's film uses live actors but recreates many elements of the puppet theater, including the black-clad manipulators in the background who seem to represent the lovers' artificiality and their fates. There are also walls painted with an enlarged text of the play, re-creating the sense that the characters and their world are forged from Chikamatsu's language. A full treatment of this rich film is beyond my scope here, but the ways in which Shinoda's work bridges the artificial world of the puppets and the live-action world of film speak to many of the issues raised in this chapter.

20. Chikamatsu, *Jōrurishū*, 2:356, translated in Keene, *Anthology*, 386–87. Keene's translation has "inanimate tree."

21. See *Karakuri Ningyō*, and Law, *Puppets of Nostalgia*, 30–59. See also Teri Silvio's "Pop-Culture Icons," a striking ethnographic study of the links between religious icons, theatrical puppets, and character toys in contemporary Taiwan.

22. Chikamatsu, *Jōrurishū*, 2:357–59, translated in Keene, *Anthology*, 388–90. The first translation (beginning "It is because") is my own.

23. Kittler, "Romanticism—Psychoanalysis—Film," 99.

24. Chikamatsu, *Jōrurishū*, 2:358, translated in Keene, *Anthology*, 389.

25. Barthes, *Empire of Signs*, 54–55.

26. See the making-of documentary "Ghost in the Shell Production Report," on the 2005 special edition DVD. In an updated version of the film, *Ghost in the Shell 2.0*, the puppet master has a female voice supplied by the actress who voices "Haraway" in the film's sequel (see below).

27. Oshii, *Alles* interview (my translation).

28. Barthes, *Empire of Signs*, 60. I have altered Howard's translation slightly.

29. Likewise Chikamatsu, while emphasizing the pathos of the puppets, also says "I take pathos to be entirely a matter of restraint," and another contemporary treatise advises that in the tragic style of chanting, "all the previous sentiments must be forgotten, only a lingering touch of love should remain." Chikamatsu, *Jōrurishū*, 2:358, translated in Keene, *Anthology*, 388; Uji, Preface to *Takenokoshū*, 403, translated in Gerstle, *Circles of Fantasy*, 184.

30. Operators are all male in the Osaka-based national troupe that dominates the medium, though there are female participants in other contexts, like the older amateur tradition based on Awaji Island. The impression conveyed by a female chanter is quite different. For women's role in the Awaji tradition, see Law, *Puppets of Nostalgia*.

31. Barrault, *Souvenirs pour demain*, 291, translated as *Memories for Tomorrow*, 247–48; Claudel, *L'oiseau noir*, 193–95. Both critics are cited by Barthes in "A Lesson in Writing."

32. Sontag, "Note on Bunraku," 16.

33. Sakai, *Voices of the Past*, 140–76. One more link in the chain between these different theories is Heinrich von Kleist's famous Romantic dialogue "On Puppet-Shows" ("Über das Marionettentheater," 1810), in which marionettes are said to possess a "symmetry, freedom of movement, lightness" that human beings lack, because their movements are free of the "disorder consciousness introduced into the natural grace of human beings" (143–44). While Barthes sees the puppet's grace as undermining Romantic belief in an essential soul, Kleist's speaker seems to see it as a Romantic attack on rational thought. The poststructuralist critic Paul de Man bridges the two positions, perceiving a powerful sense of irony in Kleist's essay. In *The Rhetoric of Romanticism*, de Man argues that underneath the ease and "grace" is a clear violence expressed by the puppet's artificial body and Kleist's other odd examples, which include a cyborg-like amputee dancing on artificial legs. That violence in turn is an expression of the violence of aesthetic interpretation or theory itself—the violence of a critic who must impose meaning on the text or "the trap of an aesthetic education which inevitably confuses dismemberment of language by the power of the letter with the gracefulness of a dance" (290). De Man's argument connects with Sakai's very similar idea that the bunraku puppets define themselves against a violent limit that corresponds to narration or description.

34. Barthes, *Empire of Signs*, 3.

35. Karatani, *Origins of Modern Japanese Literature*. For a preliminary discussion of continuities and discontinuities between premodern and contemporary Japanese visual culture, see Berndt, "Considering Manga Discourse," 305–9.

36. Sontag, "Note on Bunraku," 16.

37. Napier, *Anime: From "Akira" to "Howl's Moving Castle,"* 111–12; see also Silvio, "Refiguring the Radical Cyborg," 67–69.

38. Chikamatsu, *Four Major Plays*, 170–208.

39. Gunji, *Kabuki no bigaku*, 131–53.
40. Keene, *Four Major Plays*, 5; Tanizaki, "Recollections," 11. Other descriptions are based on a performance by the Awaji Ningyōza I saw at the Kyoto Geijutsu Gekijō in winter 2011, and performances at the National Bunraku Theater in Osaka I attended in winter 2011 and summer 2016.
41. Tanizaki, "Recollections," 12.
42. Tanizaki, *Some Prefer Nettles*, 23; Tanizaki, "Recollections," 11; Sontag, "Note on Bunraku," 16. See also Claudel, who argues that the floating quality of the puppets (lifted up by the manipulators as they move about the stage) contributes to the process of decentering the subject and distributing it among the participants (*L'oiseau noir*, 195–96).
43. Saitō and Naitō, "*Patlabor 2 The Movie*" *Archives*, 106.
44. Oshii, "Last Commentary," n.p.
45. Haraway, "Cyborgs at Large," 20.
46. Barthes, *Empire of Signs*, 60; Barrault, *Memories for Tomorrow*, 247.
47. Yūda, "Formation of Early Modern Jōruri," 35–37; Gerstle, *Circles of Fantasy*, 120–23; Gunji, *Kabuki no bigaku*, 145.
48. Chikamatsu, *Jōrurishū*, 1:87. This detail is cited in Gerstle, *Circles of Fantasy*, 121–22.
49. Suan, *Anime Paradox*, 6–63. Suan also argues that, in anime as in classical dramatic theory, the jo–ha–kyū structure is present at all levels: not only in the parts of an individual scene but in the way scenes are arranged in an episode, and episodes in a series. This fractal (Suan says "mosaic") structure suggests to me the way in which the oscillation between immersion and distance inheres in anime's every level: from *Akira*'s plot development, to the shifting visual styles we see in the opening scenes of *Ghost in the Shell* or *Patlabor 2*, down to the divided way we feel about a single image or movement of the major's body.
50. In Shirō's *Ghost in the Shell* manga, the Puppet Master's speech is illustrated with a dramatic montage of images unlike anything else in the text, a stylistic flourish faithful to the idea of the michiyuki (1st English ed., 335–44).
51. I first watched *Innocence* with a group of my students just a few days after it came out on DVD. None of us knew exactly what to expect, but the day before, one student had insisted to the class that he thought my analysis of the first film in terms of cyborg feminism was reading far too much into the text—that the director never intended these kinds of things. Needless to say, sitting next to him in the screening room and hearing this character introduce herself as "Haraway" was a gotcha moment I've never managed to surpass in the classroom. But as I described in the Introduction, I think what matters is not what a director deliberately put into a film but whether a critic can extract an interesting and convincing interpretation that will then resonate for other viewers. For those who are fixated on authorial intent, though, I think it would be risky to underestimate anime creators like Oshii and the thought that goes into their work. *Ghost in the Shell: Stand Alone Complex* (2002–3), a television anime series

directed by Kamiyama Kenji, also contains explicit references to post-structuralist philosophy—including a cameo in book form by postmodern philosophers Gilles Deleuze and Félix Guattari. *Ergo Proxy* (2006), a series with similar themes, features self-aware robots named "Lacan," "Derrida," and "Husserl." In a fall 2012 conversation with Satō Dai, one of the scriptwriters for both series, I asked if these were throwaway jokes or if he and the other creators were really interested in these philosophers. He told me there are limits to what you can do in a television series, but that he and the scriptwriting team were avid readers of critical theory. I confess that I thought he might be exaggerating, until he began to unfold for me a detailed and compelling interpretation of *Stand Alone Complex* that turned on critical theories of the postmodern. I asked him excitedly if he would be willing to publish this interpretation, but he just put a finger to his lips and paraphrased Roland Barthes: it is not the place of the author to explain the meaning of the text.

52. Orbaugh, "Emotional Infectivity," 165.
53. In contrast, in *Patlabor 2* the creators were careful to make the computer-animated portions look hand drawn so they would blend with the rest of the film. See the making-of documentary on the *Patlabor 2* limited collector's edition DVDs (Honneamise, 2001).
54. From a March 2004 interview on Yahoo Japan's Yahoo Books website, quoted in Caien, "*Inosensu* kanren jōhō matome." Caien's meticulous web page also tracks down many of the quotes used in the film.
55. Brown, *Tokyo Cyberpunk*, 28–29. Brown links the anime's dismembered and reassembled puppet bodies back to the intertextual body with a striking quote from the surrealist photographer Hans Bellmer: "The body resembles a sentence that seems to invite us to dismantle it into its component letters, so that its true meanings may be revealed ever anew through an endless stream of anagrams" (quoted 39). Brown's chapter on *Innocence* gives an extended account of the anime's doll and puppet motifs, many of which are borrowed explicitly from Bellmer's work (13–53).

4. The Forgetful Phallus and the Otaku's Third Eye

1. This description is based on a performance of *Hidakagawa iriaizakura* I saw at the National Bunraku Theater in Osaka in April 1991. For more on the different versions of the Dōjōji story, see Susan Klein, "Woman as Serpent."
2. Napier, *Anime: From "Akira" to "Howl's Moving Castle,"* 71.
3. Pointon, "Transcultural Orgasm," 49; Newitz, "Magical Girls," 2–15. Napier herself takes issue with these critics in an appendix that appears in the first edition of her anime book, *Anime: From "Akira" to "Princess Mononoke,"* 241–42.
4. Willemen, "The Fourth Look," 99–110; Napier, *Anime: From "Akira" to "Princess Mononoke,"* 242. In her book on Japanese fan culture, *From*

Impressionism to Anime, Napier again argues that contemporary Western anime fans have a sophisticated awareness of the gap between reality and Japan fantasies (166).

5. I am also departing from Willemen in my effort to bypass a mainstream psychoanalytical approach to film studies anchored in Lacan's theory of the gaze, in favor of different applications of Lacan described below. Creed does something similar in *The Monstrous Feminine,* replacing the gaze with alternative psychoanalytical frameworks like Julia Kristeva's theory of abjection and Creed's own rereadings of Freud.

6. Newitz, "Magical Girls," 5; Pointon, "Transcultural Orgasm," 55.

7. Two of the key Freudian texts here are "The Dissolution of the Oedipus Complex" and *The Interpretation of Dreams* (200–205).

8. Freud says that cutting off the hand can also be a figure for castration, which is framed as a punishment for masturbation ("Dissolution," 316–17). If anything, the image in *3x3 Eyes* of cutting off the hand *as it grips the sword* seems even more literal than Freud.

9. On the origins of the term "otaku," see Okada, *Otakugaku nyūmon,* 10–13. For an excellent overview of changes in the otaku's image over time, see Lamarre, *Anime Machine,* 144–54. While almost every discussion of otaku mentions the Miyazaki incident, one of the best critical discussions is in Treat, "Yoshimoto Banana Writes Home," 354–56. Two fine studies of anime fandom from a historical and transcultural perspective are Napier, *From Impressionism to Anime,* and Annett, *Anime Fan Communities.* On female fandom, see Annett, 173–80, as well as Kotani, "Introduction" and "Otakuiin."

10. Okada, *Otakugaku nyūmon,* 14, 116–32. Okada also divides otaku by generation. Anime otaku occupy roughly the second generation: those born between 1965–75, influenced by anime magazines and an early VCR culture that allowed some saving and rewatching, but on a limited scale that encouraged memorization and close analysis. Okada grew critical of later generations of otaku that followed his 1996 book and eventually abdicated the title of Ota-King as colorfully as he had assumed it. See Alt, "Speaker for the Dead."

11. In the 1996 book, Okada characterized otaku as savvy consumers whose eventual calling is to become pop culture's tastemakers, teaching the broader public what is worth their time and attention. In this, they are all too well adapted to contemporary consumer society, where "power is held not by producers or creators but distributors" (63). So while they may know how anime is produced, that does not give them the wider critical perspective on society, politics, or language that we have been seeking in anime so far.

12. Saitō, *Sentō bishōjo,* 44. J. Keith Vincent and Dawn Lawson word this somewhat differently in their excellent translation, *Beautiful Fighting Girl* (24–25).

13. Saitō, "Otaku Sexuality," 227.

14. Ibid. I have slightly altered my original published translation based on a suggestion from J. Keith Vincent (in "Making It Real," xv). See also Saitō, *Beautiful Fighting Girl*, 21–26, where Saitō invokes Okada.
15. Saitō, *Beautiful Fighting Girl*, 171.
16. Ibid., 22.
17. Ibid.; Vincent, "Making It Real," xxiii. Saitō notes that this is a first approximation of Lacan, whose subject is not really a bounded entity with an inside and an outside. In that sense, we could say that the interior of another is inaccessible to me because such an interior is illusory to begin with. We might explain this structure by tracing Lacan's connections to the phenomenological model introduced in chapter 2 and elaborated in chapter 5. In that model, subjects perceive themselves only in or through the eyes of another, and define themselves not as independent, self-sufficient entities but differentially in relation to others. On Lacan's relation to phenomenology, see Homer, *Jacques Lacan*, 19–21.
18. Saitō, *Beautiful Fighting Girl*, 129.
19. Different critics' summaries of Lacan can sound very different, so for the most part I have restricted myself to describing the way Saitō characterizes Lacan. But the reader will have to go outside Saitō to find some of these details on the Lacanian phallus and castration. For an introduction, see Homer, *Jacques Lacan*, 51–65 and Lacan, "Signification of the Phallus."
20. Saitō, *Beautiful Fighting Girl*, 161.
21. Ibid., 29. Otaku often refer to this attraction for fictional characters as *"moe,"* a created slang word whose orthography and pronunciation ("mo-ay") associate it with budding or burning in Japanese. Critics like Saitō and Azuma Hiroki (discussed below) have borrowed the term to highlight the ways otaku attraction differs from conventional desire. Saitō discusses the term in this passage and emphasizes its use by otaku themselves—the way this neologism ironizes the attraction or places it in quotation marks.
22. For a related but distinct perspective see Sandra Annett's *Anime Fan Communities*. Annett argues that this tendency of fans to see themselves in a work and critically consider their own identities is a feature not just of contemporary anime and its fans but of animation and animation audiences across different times and cultures. Citing a wide range of social media theory, Annett seeks a middle ground between extreme views of fans as either mindless media pawns or ecstatically liberated, self-fashioned subjects. She reads the portrayal of the audience in the text as an opportunity for fans to negotiate their identities with the text and with each other.
23. Saitō, *Beautiful Fighting Girl*, 144.
24. Saitō, *Sentō bishōjo*, 273. See also *Beautiful Fighting Girl* (167), where Vincent and Lawson translate this as "she identifies with the phallus."
25. Okada elevated the first generation of otaku by characterizing them as

human databanks, able to memorize and catalog visual information even before the advent of personal computers and video technology. But Azuma says that in the current generation, otaku do not drive the database but are driven by it. Here and elsewhere I am collapsing Azuma's distinctions between intervening generations of otaku in order to focus on this broad shift.

26. Azuma, *Otaku*, 84.

27. Ibid., 112. See also 110–13.

28. Azuma, "Super Flat Speculation," 138–51. Drawing on a discussion by Lacan of the links between perspective and symbolic castration, Azuma suggests that Murakami's eyes represent an "*uncastrated gaze*" (143), a way of viewing the world that is not limited by the conventions of the Symbolic. For a critique of Azuma's reading, see Lamarre, who resists this idea of radical flattening and argues that even the flattened plane of anime contains tensions and differences we should attend to. (We will take up Lamarre's ideas about perspective in chapter 6.) In his own theorization of the otaku, Lamarre stakes out a position between Saitō's Lacanian ideas about gender and Azuma's postmodern ideas about representation, while trying to theorize a female subject that is something more than an effect produced by the male one (*Anime Machine*, 242–76).

29. In Hindu mythology, Parvati is married to the three-eyed god Siva, and the anime riffs on this mythology elsewhere: Pai/Sanjiyan/Parvati's nemesis is Kai Yang Wang, the only other surviving member of her race. Three hundred years ago Kai Yang Wang was called Siva, and Sanjiyan/Parvati was his fiancée. Besides the trope of having multiple identities coexist in a single body, the characters are also repeatedly doubled by other characters in this way. This allows the same plots to repeat over and over with different people, and contributes to a postmodern sense that there is no original subject, only copies of copies of copies. We will explore this duplication and repetition further in chapter 6.

30. A manga series by Kakinouchi Narumi began serialization concurrently, and the franchise later grew to include a twenty-five-episode television series and other manga spinoffs.

31. Napier, "Vampires, Psychic Girls," 94–98; Saitō, *Beautiful Fighting Girl*, 129.

32. For example, Saitō suggests that it is in the nature of anime to portray progressively more transgressive sexualities. In this way it tempts the viewer, whose perceptions are confined to the psychological realm of his own Imaginary, to believe that the text is bringing him something new and unfamiliar from outside his own experience. This assumes a gap between fantasy sexuality and actual sexual practice, which is why, Saitō says, otaku do not act out the transgressive fantasies they consume (*Beautiful Fighting Girl*, 157–58). While Lamarre characterizes this scheme as a reactionary effort to place limits on fantasy and diversity (*Anime Machine*, 256), Vincent defends it as a progressive effort to

"decouple sexual desire from social identities and naturalized bodies" ("Making It Real," xx).

33. Saitō, *Beautiful Fighting Girl*, 20.

5. Anime in Drag

1. On Kon's biography and his work with Ōtomo and Oshii, see Osmond, *Satoshi Kon*, 7–24.

2. See "Making *Tokyo Godfathers*" on the *Tokyo Godfathers* DVD.

3. Osmond, *Satoshi Kon*, 18; Zhou, "Editing Space and Time." Zhou's superb video essay is an excellent introduction to Kon's style.

4. Writing on *Millennium Actress* that catalogs these references includes Arnold's review; Ortabasi, "Indexing the Past," 283–86; and Osmond, *Satoshi Kon*, 46–52.

5. Alternatively, we could figure these concerns in the broader terms of chapter 1: a desire to know Japan's "real history," competing with a postmodern sense that what we regard as cultural and historical origins are a mirage. As an example of the former, Paul Wells focuses on the film's realistic portrayal of Japanese history and psychology. In spite of their formal fragmentation, Wells sees Kon's films as searching for "an intrinsically Japanese sensibility," "a more authentic Japanese spirit," "the underpinning emotional terrain of Japanese culture" ("Playing the Kon Trick," 4–5). Melek Ortabasi emphasizes the opposite extreme, arguing that *Millennium Actress* seeks to reconfigure our very notion of history from a chronological narrative to a collection (Azuma might say a database) of visual images. Because it can remediate other visual media, anime then becomes the privileged language of record in Kon's postmodern world, "the rightful heir to that tradition of recording and (re)creating cultural and national history." Otaku like Tachibana (consummate collectors) become our new historians ("National History as Otaku Fantasy," 292).

6. Gardner, "Cyber Sublime and the Virtual Mirror," 57.

7. Other references to *Throne of Blood* include the title of the fictional film in which the specter appears (Kurosawa's literal title "Spider-web castle" becomes "Specter castle") and a scene in which Tachibana's cameraman is pinned down by a hail of arrows, duplicating the iconic final scene of Kurosawa's film.

8. On the key as phallic symbol and Kon's comments on psychoanalysis, see Osmond, *Satoshi Kon*, 23, 58. This book collects comments from several interviews Osmond conducted with the director.

9. Ibid., 18, 22.

10. Genealogy here is understood in Michel Foucault's terms: it "investigates the political stakes in designating as an *origin* and *cause* those identity categories that are in fact the *effects* of institutions, practices, discourses with multiple and diffuse points of origin." Butler, *Gender Trouble*, viii–ix. On Beauvoir, see also Butler's "Sex and Gender."

11. Butler, *Gender Trouble*, 140, 142. Butler also says: "*gender* is not a noun . . . gender is always a doing, though not a doing by a subject who might be said to preexist the deed. . . . There is no gender identity behind the expressions of gender; that identity is performatively constituted by the very 'expressions' that are said to be its results" (24–25).
12. Ibid., 29.
13. Ibid., 137–38.
14. Ibid., 140; Osmond, *Satoshi Kon*, 54.
15. For example, in 2009 Oshii Mamoru directed a stage drama based on the manga and anime series *Gigantor* (*Tetsujin 28-gō*). And the *Blood* franchise, discussed in the following chapter, spawned a 2015 stage production directed by Oku Shūtarō, *Blood-C: The Last Mind*.
16. Suematsu Ken'ichi and Mizuguchi Mika, interview by the author at Osaka HEP Hall in January 2011.
17. Some of these dynamics are familiar from the most famous of Japan's all-female revues, Takarazuka. In the Takarazuka troupes, certain actresses specialize in playing male roles in a stylized way that captures an ideal of beauty that is conventionalized but not conventionally male or female, and they attract legions of adoring female fans. This aesthetic is clearly linked to manga: Tezuka Osamu was a devotee of Takarazuka, and its repertoire includes a number of productions based on manga by Tezuka and others. In my experience, viewing a Takarazuka performance inevitably involves seeing these layers (manga, character, star) overlap on stage, but there is a serious and conservative atmosphere that does more to collapse these different layers into one subject than to tease them apart. While it can certainly be viewed ironically, I find Takarazuka itself has a limited sense of humor and does not embrace irony or metafiction in the way that Take It Easy! does.
18. Butler, *Bodies that Matter*, 81-97. "I would have liked to have seen the question of Livingston's cinematic desire reflexively thematized in the film itself," says Butler (94). But for a careful viewer, clues about the film's subject position are scattered everywhere.
19. Ibid., 84. Butler borrows "crossroads" from Gloria Anzaldúa.
20. The incest prohibition plays a key role not only in psychoanalysis but in structuralist anthropology. Butler identifies the prohibition (or its theorization) with the formation of marriage rules and the delineation of kinship groups and sees "structuralis[t], psychoanalytic and feminist accounts of the incest taboo as the mechanism that tries to enforce discrete and internally coherent gender identities within a heterosexual frame" (*Gender Trouble*, ix–x).
21. The pat final scenes in *Perfect Blue* and *Paprika* can feel like a letdown, in the way they put an end to uncertainty and mediation in favor of concrete resolutions. However, one can recover an interesting if unsettling sense of openness if one considers that these happy endings might be further simulations or delusions that enfold the protagonists.

6. The Quick and the Undead

1. For a connection to feminist theories of horror discussed in chapter 4, see Creed, *Monstrous-Feminine*, 59–72.
2. Haraway, *Modest_Witness*, 214–15.
3. Kotani, "Techno-Gothic Japan," 194.
4. This tendency to regard other races and cultures as monstrous is highlighted (and perhaps critiqued) by the exaggerated character designs. At one point a woman fleeing from a chiropteran runs into a black airman drawn as a caricature. She looks into his face and screams for several seconds before realizing that he is not a monster himself. The scene drives home these racial tensions by lynching this character a few frames later: a chiropteran lurking in a tree grabs him from above and pulls his head into the branches, then kills him as his legs dangle below.
5. Lamarre, *Anime Machine*, xxxiv. Properly speaking, Lamarre's "machines" are the abstract structures that underlie each of these concrete phenomena. "The machine is not an apparatus," he writes. "The challenge is to find the machine on which the apparatus depends" (xxvi).
6. Ibid., 5.
7. Ibid., 7.
8. Ibid., 196. I should emphasize that Lamarre rarely identifies a simple or straightforward link between a character's freedom of movement and their freedom in the context of an anime's plot or politics. His readings are inevitably more subtle or abstract, reflecting his idea that the structures and strictures of modernity and postmodernity are not easily escaped and often must be critiqued from within.
9. Ibid., 5.
10. Ibid., 38–39.
11. While *The Anime Machine* focuses primarily on cel-based animation, Lamarre argues elsewhere (in "First Time as Farce") that a deliberate gap between cel and digital animation can push us to abandon these very assumptions about cinema's nearness to reality, as well as broader notions about the historical indexicality of (visual) language, to suggest new ways of thinking about history itself. While I identify Saya's two-dimensional movements as representing an attractive freedom that is ultimately unrealistic, Lamarre sees a more radical and more sustainable freedom in the heroine of Rintarō's *Metropolis* (*Metoroporisu*, 2001), a cyborg who combines two- and three-dimensional attributes in a single character.
12. Here I am omitting a further complication, namely that while the planes can seem real and weighty, visually they also have a ghostly quality of their own, a suggestion of the dead returned to life. The fighter taxiing away from the camera in figure 41, for example, floats lightly into the air behind a shimmering veil of heat. Livia Monnet suggests that computer-animated versions of human bodies have an uncanny or

undead quality generated by the many layers of simulation that separate them from the humans whose data feeds into them, that these "virtual actors perform as undead, digital vampires or zombies" ("Invasion of the Women Snatchers," 197). If Freud's theory of the uncanny identifies it with the return of repressed ideas or beliefs, Monnet relates this to the haunting return of the human (specifically female) agency that is suppressed in computer animation. Applying this to the ghostly, uncanny planes of *Blood: The Last Vampire*, we might speculate that the planes represent the perceived loss of Japan's political or military agency after World War II, as well as the fear of reclaiming that agency and risking a return to prewar aggression. In this reading, what has been repressed is thoughtful consideration of Japan's and the United States' joint wartime responsibilities and history, and it is the F-4 Phantoms and other planes that are the film's true ghosts. For an expansion of this argument, see Bolton "The Quick and the Undead: Visual and Political Dynamics in *Blood: The Last Vampire*," 138–39.

13. Ōtsuka, "World and Variation," 107.
14. Azuma, *Otaku*, 25–58. Ōtsuka advanced the idea of narrative consumption in the 1980s, but his more recent reconsideration of the theory brings him closer to Azuma. Ōtsuka writes in 2012 that with the advent of the Internet, consumers of popular culture are now constructing their own narrative responses across different media and are no longer limited to a single grand fictional narrative marketed to them in fragments by content providers. On the other hand, this activity is not free. Narratively, it follows certain established channels; and politically, the Internet spreads certain narratives and mobilizes popular activity without requiring creativity, responsibility, or real political subjectivity on the part of users. The result is a kind of "dictatorless fascism" that contrasts with Lyotard's more optimistic hopes for little narrative. Ōtsuka, *Monogatari shōhiron kai*, 7–22.
15. Steinberg, *Anime's Media Mix*, 77. Lamarre makes a related argument in *The Anime Machine* (185–86, 202–6).
16. Kitakubo, interview, 37. For more on the role of different collaborators, see "The Making of *Blood*" on the DVD extras. For different, sometimes conflicting interpretations of the film by its different creators, see Ruh, *Stray Dog*, 163–74.
17. Condry, *Soul of Anime*, 214.
18. The most comprehensive resource for keeping track of all the different texts in this and other anime franchises is Wikipedia. In the way it catalogues the different works in a property, tracks the contributions of different creators, and describes the characters as a way of tying everything together, fan-authored critical activity like this is in tune with some of the academic critical ideas discussed above.
19. Azuma, *Otaku*, 84–86, 104–13.
20. Rebecca Suter called my attention to the range of these repetitions,

from theme songs and "the recurrent transformation scenes in . . . robot anime like those of Nagai Gō and magical anime such as *Creamy Mami* to the ubiquitous running scenes in sports anime such as *Captain Tsubasa,* to the combat scenes in series like *Fist of the North Star* and *Saint Seiya* that take an extremely stylized and ritual form in more recent anime such as *Revolutionary Girl Utena.*"

21. Nathan Mahler plays a role like Beethoven's in *Read or Die,* discussed in the Introduction. The character is apparently named for the Austrian Romantic composer Gustav Mahler (1860–1911), who also directed the Metropolitan Opera. There is even a passing resemblance. Fan criticism like Wikipedia has pulled clues from the series and elsewhere to argue that Nathan belongs to an earlier generation than the other characters, that he served the original chiropteran that gave birth to Diva and Saya. All these connections to frames and worlds outside the immediate story emphasize the idea of a metaperspective that the character might represent.

22. Enomoto, Kajii, and Satō, "*Blood-C*" *Official Complete Book,* 71.

23. For example, see the discussion of the *shota* genre in Saitō, "Otaku Sexuality," 236–37, 244–47. I know of at least a couple of U.S. anime scholars who have been asked to testify in pornography trials, in the hope of shedding light on the question of what is actually being depicted in manga and anime like these.

24. While almost nothing in the official *Blood* franchise seems sexually explicit enough to provoke a ban, apparently it remains dangerous. In April 2015, the Chinese government threatened sanctions against Chinese online services hosting anime clips with adult themes, and they singled out the violence of *Blood-C* in particular (Kelion "China Cracks Down"). In 2009 I was asked by a Japanese consulate in the United States to give a presentation at a regional anime convention. They suggested *Blood: The Last Vampire* as a possible topic, but when I sent them samples of my published work on the politics of the film, the invitation was withdrawn.

7. It's Art, but Is It Anime?

1. Some more specific landmarks tracing Miyazaki's popularity: *Castle in the Sky* (1986) was the first anime film Streamline Pictures distributed in the United States, even before *Akira* (Patten, "Streamline Pictures—Part 1"). *Kiki's Delivery Service* (1989) and *Porco Rosso* (1992) were both the top Japanese-language films of the year in Japan, earning 2–3 billion yen each. In 1997, *Princess Mononoke* was the top film period, earning more than 10 billion yen, but it received only a limited U.S. theatrical release (just over a hundred screens at its peak). At one point after the Oscars, *Spirited Away* was showing on more than seven hundred screens in the United States. More anecdotally, to view *Princess Mononoke* in 1999 I had

to seek out a Japanese VHS tape in LA's Japantown; four years later I could watch *Spirited Away* at the Disney Theater in Hollywood. In the summer of 2013, I took my daughters to see *The Wind Rises* at Tōhō's flagship theater in downtown Osaka, and the 700-seat theater was packed on a weekday afternoon. Box office figures from Wikipedia and the Motion Picture Producers Association of Japan website (http://www.eiren.org). Release data from the Internet Movie Database (http://imdb.com).

2. Miyazaki has announced his retirement several times, so whether *The Wind Rises* will in fact be his final feature film remains to be seen. For biographical information, see McCarthy, *Hayao Miyazaki*, 26–48, and Miyazaki, "Biographical Chronology."

3. This was the title of a *Newsweek* interview in which Miyazaki said, "My thoughts are very pessimistic, yes, but my general state of being is very positive" (62).

4. Miyazaki, "Nihon no animeeshon," 148. This and the translations that follow are my own, but I have benefited from consulting the translation by Beth Cary and Fredrick Schodt in Miyazaki, *Starting Point*, 70–85.

5. Ibid., 152.

6. Ibid., 156.

7. These comments are recorded in Arakawa Kaku's twelve-hour documentary *Ponyo wa kōshite umareta* (How Ponyo was born, 2009), in the section "October 23, 2007." They were taken up in 2014 when subtitled screenshots from the documentary propagated virally on the Web, leading to a popular Internet meme that featured images of Miyazaki with a false but vaguely plausible troll quote, "Anime was a mistake."

8. Lamarre, *Anime Machine*, chapters 5, 6, and 15. For example, Lamarre argues that "Where Miyazaki's open compositing makes for a sense of an underlying and abiding depth (reinforced with painterly backgrounds), the tendency of limited animation to flatten the relation between planes of the image makes for depth spread across a surface" (306). For other accounts of Tōei Animation and Mushi Pro, see Condry, who also points out the mutual borrowing between the two (*Soul of Anime*, 85–111); Steinberg, who sees this as one phase of an older split between cinema and the itinerant street narratives of *kamishibai* (*Anime's Media Mix*, 1–36); and finally Clements, who carefully traces the different economic pressures and production strategies at these and other contemporary studios (*Anime: A History*, 93–132).

9. Talbot, "Auteur of Anime," 73.

10. Napier, *Anime: From "Akira" to "Howl's Moving Castle,"* 152–53; Napier, *From Impressionism to Anime*, 192–93. Miyazaki's worlds are so fully realized that it is easy for viewers outside Japan to mistake the "history" of *Princess Mononoke* for real Japanese history, or the fantastic creatures of *Spirited Away* for elements of real Japanese folklore. In fact, these are pastiches drawn largely from Miyazaki's own imagination, just like the

fantastic Europeanized settings of films like *Howl's Moving Castle*. Peter Bradshaw's review of the latter describes the setting as "sort of Bath crossed with Bruges, with a hint of Vulgaria, the city-state in *Chitty Chitty Bang Bang*" (9, also quoted in Cavallaro, *Late Works*, 47). See also Michael Foster's "The Folkloresque Circle," which discusses "fuzzy allusion" in *Spirited Away*.

11. Miyazaki, "Positive Pessimist," 62.

12. Smith, "War, Wizards, and Words," n.p. Compare Smith's interpretation with the reading of *Patlabor 2* in chapter 2.

13. Miyazaki, "Kenpō o kaeru," 4. For an English summary of this essay see Penney, "Miyazaki Hayao and the Asia-Pacific War."

14. Condry, *Soul of Anime*, 150. Miyazaki's last film, *The Wind Rises*, is a fictionalized biography of Horikoshi Jirō, the aircraft engineer who designed the zero fighter. Here the paradox (or hypocrisy) of loving warplanes while hating war is taken up in the story itself.

15. On the film's blending of computer graphics and cell animation, see Studio Ghibli, *Art of "Howl's Moving Castle,"* 123, 188. Lamarre's Heideggerian reading of Miyazaki in *The Anime Machine* centers on even subtler ways that his work "minimizes technology" in order to point the way toward a new relationship with it (45–100).

16. See the interview with Jones included with the novel (5).

17. Jones, *Howl's Moving Castle*, 1–2.

18. Rudd, "Building Castles," 257.

19. Jones, *Howl's Moving Castle*, 176.

20. Ibid., 218.

21. Ibid., 105.

22. Rudd, "Building Castles," 257.

23. Smith, "War, Wizards, and Words," n.p.

24. Bye, "Connecting the Pieces," 116.

25. Talbot, "Auteur of Anime," 74. Miyazaki may be referring here to romantic love, but one might think of Romanticism à la Wordsworth: the idea that "Poetry is the image of man and nature," that "it is an acknowledgement of the beauty of the universe," that "its object is truth . . . carried alive into the heart by passion" and pleasure. Wordsworth, preface, 105.

26. There is also a more libidinal interpretation of this scene, based on the return of the thing that is repressed in all of Miyazaki's narratives: sexual attraction. In this reading, the fire demon represents that desire, which consumes Howl's innocent heart in adolescence. Sophie witnesses this primal scene or original sin, and sees the way it transforms Howl into a beast; but she forgives, accepts, and redeems him by separating heart from demon, sentiment from arousal. "It's so warm," Sophie says in the Disney subtitles as she holds his "fluttering" heart, but Calcifer reassures her: "It's still just the heart of a child."

27. See the "June 28, 2006" section of Arakawa, *Ponyo wa kōshite umareta*.

Conclusion

1. See Mark Schilling's reporting in *Screen International*: "Studio Ghibli's New Film to Be Directed by Rival" (September 2, 2001) and "New Hayao Miyazaki Film Heads Toho Line-Up" (December 17, 2002). LexisNexis Academic.

2. See the director's interview included on the *Summer Wars* DVD.

3. Hosoda noted that the film has close to thirty protagonists (Ibid.). Ian Condry's *Soul of Anime* devotes a chapter to Hosoda, and *Summer Wars* receives special attention because its overt themes dovetail so nicely with Condry's emphasis on anime production as a cooperative enterprise (35–53). For a more skeptical view of community in the film, see the review by Jonathan Abel.

Moving Image Sources

Sources are anime unless otherwise noted. I have omitted titles discussed only in passing, but nearly all of the anime mentioned in this book are available on DVD or Blu-ray disc.

Arakawa Kaku, script, filming, and narration. *Ponyo wa kōshite umareta: Miyazaki Hayao no shikō katei* [How Ponyo was born: The thought process of Miyazaki Hayao]. Produced by Hoshino Kōji, directed by Ariyoshi Nobuto. Live-action documentary. 5 DVDs. Ghibli / Disney, 2008.

Fujisaku Jun'ichi, dir. *Blood+*. TV series. 2 Parts. 50 episodes. 2005–6; translated as *Blood+: Part 1* and *Blood+: Part 2*. 10 DVDs. Sony, 2007.

Hirano Toshiki [as Hirano Toshihiro], dir. *Vanpaia Miyu*. Music by Kawai Kenji. OVA. 4 episodes. 1988–89; translated as *Vampire Princess Miyu: Vols. 1–2*. 2 DVDs. Animeigo, 2001.

Hosoda Mamoru, dir. *Samaa wōzu*. 2009; translated as *Summer Wars*. 2 DVDs + Blu-Ray disc. NTV / Funimation, 2013.

Kawajiri Yoshiaki, dir. *Yōjū toshi*. 1987; translated as *Wicked City*. Special ed. DVD. Urban Vision, 2000.

Kawamoto Kihachiro, dir. "Dōjōji." Stop-motion animated short. 1975. In *Kawamoto Kihachirō sakuhinshū* [Kawamoto Kihachirō film works]. DVD. Pioneer, 2002.

Kitakubo Hiroyuki, dir. *Blood The Last Vampire*. 2000; translated as *Blood: The Last Vampire*. DVD. Manga Entertainment, 2001.

Kon Satoshi, dir. *Paafekuto burū*. 1997; translated as *Perfect Blue*. DVD. Manga Entertainment, 2000.

———, dir. *Papurika*. 2006; translated as *Paprika*. DVD. Sony, 2007.

———, dir. *Sennen joyū*. 2001; translated as *Millennium Actress*. DVD. Dreamworks, 2003.

———, dir. *Tōkyō Goddofaazaazu*. 2003; translated as *Tokyo Godfathers*. DVD. Sony, 2004.

Kurosawa Akira, dir. *Kumonosujō*. Live-action film. 1959. Translated as *Throne of Blood*. Blu-ray disc. Criterion, 2015.

Masunari Kōji, dir. *R.O.D Read or Die*. Script by Kurata Hideyuki. Music by Iwasaki Taku. OVA. 3 episodes. 2001–2; translated as *R.O.D: Read or Die*. DVD. Manga Entertainment, 2003.

Miyazaki Hayao, dir. *Hauru no ugogku shiro*, 2004; translated as *Howl's Moving Castle*. DVD + Blu-Ray disc. Disney, 2013.

———, dir. *Kaze no tani no Naushika*, 1984; translated as *Nausicaä of the Valley of the Wind*. 2 DVDs. Disney, 2005.

———, dir. *Tenkū no shiro Rapyuta*, 1986; translated as *Castle in the Sky*. DVD + Blu-Ray disc. Disney, 2012.

Mizushima Tsutomu, dir. *Blood-C*. Supervising writer Ōkawa Nanase. Character concepts by CLAMP. TV series. 12 episodes. 2011; translated as *Blood-C: The Complete Series*. 2 DVDs + 2 Blu-ray discs. Production I.G / Funimation, 2013.

Morimoto Kōji, dir. *Kanojo no omoide / Magnetic Rose*. Screenplay by Kon Satoshi. Based on a manga by Ōtomo Katsuhiro. Episode 1 of *Memoriizu*. 1995; translated as *Memories*. DVD. Columbia, 2004.

Nishio Daisuke, dir. *3x3 Eyes*. OVA. 4 episodes. 1991–92; Translated as *3x3 Eyes: Immortals*. Disc 1 of *3x3 Eyes*. Collector's ed. DVD. Pioneer, 2000.

Oshii Mamoru, dir. *Inosensu*. 2004. Translated as *Ghost in the Shell 2: Innocence*. DVD + Blu-Ray disc. Funimation, 2017.

———, dir. *Kidō keisatsu patoreibaa 2 The Movie*. Music by Kawai Kenji. Sound director Asari Naoko. 1993; translated as *Patlabor 2: The Movie*. DVD. Manga Entertainment, 1999.

———, dir. *Kidō keisatsu patoreibaa 2 The Movie*. Music by Kawai Kenji. Sound director Shiba Shigeharu. Remastered audio ed. 1998; translated as *Patlabor 2: The Movie*. Limited collector's ed. 2 DVDs. Honneamise, 2006.

———, dir. *Kōkaku kidōtai / Ghost in the Shell*. Music by Kawai Kenji. 1995; translated as *Ghost in the Shell*. Special ed. 2 DVDs. Manga Entertainment, 2005.

———, dir. *Kōkaku kidōtai / Ghost in the Shell 2.0*. Music by Kawai Kenji. 2008; translated as *Ghost in the Shell 2.0*. Blu-ray disc. Manga Entertainment, 2009.

———, dir. *The Next Generation Patlabor Shuto kessen / Gray Ghost*. Live-action film. 2015. Director's cut special ed. 3 Blu-ray discs. Happinet, 2015.

Ōtomo Katsuhiro, dir. *Akira*. Music by Yamashiro Shōji. 1988; translated as *Akira*. Special ed. 2 DVDs. Pioneer, 2001.

Shinoda Masahiro. *Shinjū ten no Amijima*. Live-action film. 1969. Translated as *Double Suicide*. DVD. Criterion, 2000.

Shiotani Naoyoshi, dir. *Blood-C The Last Dark*. 2012; translated as *Blood-C: The Last Dark*. DVD + Blu-ray disc. Production I.G / Funimation, 2013.

Suematsu Ken'ichi, dir. *Butaiban Sennen joyū* [Millennium actress stage version]. Produced by Mizoguchi Mika. Performed by Shimizu Kaori, Nakamura Maria, Maebuchi Sanae, Yamane Chika, and Matsumura Satomi. January 17–18, 2009. Stage drama. DVD. Lotus, n.d.

Takenouchi Kazuhisa, dir. *3x3 Eyes: Seima densetsu*. Screenplay by Takenouchi Kazuhisa and Takada Yūzō. Additional direction Sayama Kiyoko. OVA. 3 episodes. 1995–96; translated as *3x3 Eyes: Legend of the Divine Demon*. Disc 2 of *3x3 Eyes*. Collectors ed. 2 DVDs. Pioneer, 2000.

Zhou, Tony. "Satoshi Kon: Editing Time and Space." Video essay. Every Frame a Painting. YouTube. July 24, 2014. https://www.youtube.com/watch?v=oz49vQwSoTE.

Bibliography

Abel, Jonathan E. Review of *Summer Wars*, by Hosoda Mamoru. *Mechademia Reviews*. Archived at http://web.archive.org/web/20120113104615/ http://mechademia.org/reviews/jonathan-e-abel-review-of-summer -wars-by-hosoda-mamoru/.

Allison, Anne. *Millennial Monsters: Japanese Toys and the Global Imagination.* Berkeley: University of California Press, 2006.

Alt, Matt. "Speaker for the Dead." Review of *Otaku wa sude ni shindeiru* [Otaku, you're dead men], by Okada Toshio. *Alt Japan* (blog), July 10, 2008. http://altjapan.typepad.com/my_weblog/2008/07/already-dead .html.

Anderson, Mark. "Terror, Theatricality, and Exceptions That Prove the Rule," *Mechademia* 4 (2009): 75–109.

Annett, Sandra. *Anime Fan Communities: Transcultural Flows and Frictions.* New York: Palgrave, 2014.

Armstrong, John. "Animated *Akira* a Hallucinogenic Masterwork." Review of *Akira*. *Vancouver Sun*, March 28, 1991. ProQuest.

Arnold, Michael. Review of *Millennium Actress*. *Midnight Eye*. August 26, 2002. http://www.midnighteye.com/reviews/millennium-actress.

Azuma Hiroki. *Dōbutsukasuru posutomodan: Otaku kara mita Nihon shakai.* Tokyo: Kōdansha, 2001; translated by Jonathan E. Abel and Shion Kono as *Otaku: Japan's Database Animals.* Minneapolis: University of Minnesota Press, 2009.

———. "Sūpaafuratto de shibensuru." Translated as "Super Flat Speculation." Both in *Super Flat*, edited by Murakami Takashi, 138–51. Tokyo: Madra, 2000.

Baker, Martha. "Brilliant Animation Can't Keep Japanese Action Tale on Track." Review of *Akira*. *St. Louis Post-Dispatch Everyday Magazine*, February 16, 1990. LexisNexis.

Barrault, Jean-Louis. *Souvenirs pour demain.* Paris: Editions de Seuil, 1972; translated by Jonathan Griffin as *Memories for Tomorrow.* London: Thames and Hudson, 1974.

Barthes, Roland. "Leçon d'écriture." *Tel Quel* 34 (Summer 1968): 28–33;

translated by Stephen Heath as "Lesson in Writing." In *Image-Music-Text*, 170–78. New York: Hill and Wang, 1977.

———. *L'Empire des signes*. Geneva: Editions d'Art Albert Skira, 1970; translated by Richard Howard as *The Empire of Signs*. London: Jonathan Cape, 1983.

———. "Myth Today." Translated by Annette Lavers. In *A Barthes Reader*, edited by Susan Sontag, 93–149. New York: Hill and Wang, 1982.

Baudrillard, Jean. *Simulacra and Simulation*. Translated by Sheila Faria Glaser. Ann Arbor: Michigan University Press, 1994.

Benkyō Tamaoki. *Blood The Last Vampire 2000*. Manga. Adapted by Carl Gustav Horn and translated by Yuji Oniki as *Blood: The Last Vampire 2002*. San Francisco: VIZ, 2002.

Berndt, Jaqueline. "Considering Manga Discourse: Location, Ambiguity, Historicity." In *Japanese Visual Culture: Explorations in the World of Manga and Anime*, edited by Mark W. MacWilliams, 274–94. Armonk, N.Y.: M.E. Sharpe, 2008.

———, ed. *Comics Worlds and the World of Comics*. Kyoto: International Manga Research Center / Kyoto Seika University, 2010.

Berndt, Jaqueline, and Steffi Richter, eds. *Reading Manga: Local and Global Perceptions of Japanese Comics*. Leipzig: Leipziger Universitätsverlag, 2006.

Bolter, Jay David, and Richard Grusin. *Remediation: Understanding New Media*. Cambridge, Mass.: MIT Press, 1999.

Bolton, Christopher. "Bunretsu aruiwa ryūnyū to shite no gengo: 3.11 go no Abe Kōbō ron" [Language as fission or flow: Reading Abe Kōbō after 3.11]. Translated into Japanese by Masuda Mamoru. In *3.11 no mirai: Nihon, SF, sōzōryoku* [The future after 3/11: Japan, science fiction, creativity], edited by Kasai Kiyoshi, Tatsumi Takayuki, Ebihara Yutaka, and Fujita Naoya, 284–99. Tokyo: Sakuhinsha, 2011.

———. "From Wooden Cyborgs to Celluloid Souls: Mechanical Bodies in Anime and Japanese Puppet Theater." *positions: east asia cultures critique* 10, no. 3 (Winter 2002): 729–71.

———. "The Quick and the Undead: Visual and Political Dynamics in *Blood: The Last Vampire*." *Mechademia* 2 (2007): 125–42.

Bolton, Christopher, Istvan Csicsery-Ronay Jr., and Takayuki Tatsumi, eds. *Robot Ghosts and Wired Dreams: Japanese Science Fiction from Origins to Anime*. Minneapolis: University of Minnesota Press, 2007.

Bradshaw, Peter. Review of *Howl's Moving Castle*. *The Guardian*, September 23, 2005, 9. ProQuest.

Brecht, Bertolt. "Alienation Effects in Chinese Acting." In *Brecht on Theatre: The Development of an Aesthetic*, edited and translated by John Willett, 91–99. New York: Hill and Wang, 1964.

Brown, Steven. *Tokyo Cyberpunk: Posthumanism in Japanese Visual Culture*. New York: Palgrave Macmillan, 2010.

Butler, Judith. *Bodies That Matter: On the Discursive Limits of "Sex."* 1993. London: Routledge, 2011. Ebook Library.

———. *Gender Trouble.* New York: Routledge, 1990.

———. "Sex and Gender in Simone de Beauvoir's *Second Sex.*" In *Simone de Beauvoir: A Critical Reader,* edited by Elizabeth Fallaize, 29–42. London: Routledge, 1998.

Bye, Susan. "Connecting the Pieces in *Howl's Moving Castle.*" *Screen Education* 74 (2014): 112–17. ProQuest.

Caien. "*Ghost in the Shell 2: Inosensu* kanren jōhō matome" [summary of references]. inner universe #GUARDIANS web page. Archived at http://web.archive.org/web/20160303171105/http://freett.com/iu/innocence/quote.html.

Cavallaro, Dani. *The Late Works of Hayao Miyazaki: A Critical Study, 2004–2013.* Jefferson, N.C.: McFarland, 2014. ProQuest Ebrary.

Chikamatsu Monzaemon. *Chikamatsu jōrurishū* [Chikamatsu's jōruri]. Vols. 49–50 of *Nihon koten bungaku taikei.* Tokyo: Iwanami Shoten, 1959.

———. *Four Major Plays of Chikamatsu.* Translated by Donald Keene. New York: Columbia University Press, 1961.

Claudel, Paul. *Claudel on the Theater.* Edited by Jacques Petit and Jean-Pierre Kempf. Translated by Christine Trollope. Coral Gables, Fla.: University of Miami Press, 1972.

———. "*Connaissance de l'Est*" suivi de "*L'oiseau noir dans le soleil levant*" ["Knowing the east" and "Black bird in the rising sun"]. Paris: Gallimard, 1974.

Clements, Jonathan. *Anime: A History.* London: BFI / Palgrave, 2013.

Coleridge, S[amuel] T[aylor]. *Biographia Literaria, or, Biographical Sketches of My Literary Life and Opinions.* 2 vols. London: Rest Fenner, 1817.

Condry, Ian. *The Soul of Anime: Collaborative Creativity and Japan's Media Success Story.* Durham, N.C.: Duke University Press, 2013.

Creed, Barbara. *The Monstrous-Feminine: Film, Feminism, Psychoanalysis.* New York: Routledge, 1993.

de Man, Paul. *The Rhetoric of Romanticism.* New York: Columbia University Press, 1984.

Derrida, Jacques. *Writing and Difference.* Translated by Alan Bass. Chicago: University of Chicago Press, 1978.

Enomoto Ikuko, Kajii Hitoshi, and Satō Fumiko, eds. "*Blood-C*" *Official Complete Book: Taidō* [quickening]. Tokyo: Kadokawa Shoten, 2011.

Fisch, Michael. "Nation, War, and Japan's Future in the Science Fiction Anime Film *Patlabor 2.*" *Science Fiction Studies* 27, no. 1 (2000): 49–68.

Forbes, Jake. "He's the Kubrick of Anime; Katsuhiro Otomo's feature *Steamboy* Was a Decade in the Making. And It's Not *Akira 2.*" Review of *Steamboy. Los Angeles Times,* March 17, 2005. ProQuest.

Foster, Michael Dylan. "The Folkloresque Circle: Toward a Theory of Fuzzy Allusion." In *The Folkloresque: Reframing Folklore in a Popular Culture*

World, edited by Michael Dylan Foster and Jeffrey A. Tolbert, 41–63. Logan: Utah State University Press, 2016.

Freiberg, Freda. "*Akira* and the Postnuclear Sublime." In *Hibakusha Cinema: Hiroshima, Nagasaki, and the Nuclear Image in Japanese Film*, edited by Mick Broderick, 92–102. London: Kegan Paul, 1996.

Freud, Sigmund. "The Dissolution of the Oedipus Complex." In *On Sexuality: Three Essays on the Theory of Sexuality and Other Works*, 313–22. Translated by James Strachey. Edited by Angela Richards. Penguin Freud Library 7. New York, Penguin, 1977.

———. *The Interpretation of Dreams*. Translated by Joyce Crick. Oxford: Oxford University Press, 1999.

———. "The 'Uncanny.'" In *The Standard Edition of the Complete Psychological Works of Sigmund Freud*, edited and translated by James Strachey, 17:218–52. London: Hogarth Press, 1955.

Gardner, William O. "The Cyber Sublime and the Virtual Mirror: Information and Media in the Works of Oshii Mamoru and Kon Satoshi." *Canadian Journal of Film Studies* 18, no. 1 (Spring 2009): 44–70.

Gerstle, Andrew. *Circles of Fantasy: Convention in the Plays of Chikamatsu*. Cambridge, Mass.: Harvard Council on East Asian Studies, 1986.

Goodwin, Archie. Editor's Note to *Akira*, by Ōtomo Katsuhiro. No. 1, n.p. New York: Epic Comics, 1988.

Griffin, John. Review of *Akira*. *The Gazette* (Montreal), January 26, 1991. ProQuest.

Gunji Masakatsu. *Kabuki no bigaku* [The aesthetics of kabuki]. Tokyo: Engeki, 1963.

Gurewitsch, Matthew. "Perpetual Adolescence as a Counterweight to History." Review of "Little Boy: The Arts of Japan's Exploding Subculture." *Wall Street Journal*, April 7, 2005, Eastern edition. ProQuest.

Haraway, Donna. "Cyborgs at Large." Interview by Constance Penley and Andrew Ross. *Social Text* 25/26 (1990): 8–23. JStor.

———. *Modest_Witness@Second_Millennium.FemaleMan©_Meets_ OncoMouse™: Feminism and Technoscience*. New York: Routledge, 1977.

———. *Simians, Cyborgs, and Women: The Reinvention of Nature*. New York: Routledge, 1991.

Harrington, Richard. Review of *Akira*. *Washington Post*, December 25, 1989. http://www.washingtonpost.com/wp-srv/style/longterm/movies/ videos/akira.htm.

Homer, Sean. *Jacques Lacan*. Routledge Critical Thinkers. New York: Routledge, 2005.

Ihiroi Tadashi. "Mieru mono, mienai mono: Eiga *Kidō keisatsu patoreebaa 2 o megutte*." [Visible and invisible: *Patlabor 2*]. In Noda, *Zenryaku Oshii Mamoru-sama*, 161–80.

Itō Gō. *Tezuka izu deddo: Hirakareta manga hyōgenron e* [Tezuka is dead: Postmodernist and modernist approaches to Japanese manga]. Tokyo: NTT, 2005; partially translated by Miri Nakamura as "Tezuka Is Dead:

Manga in Transformation and Its Dysfunctional Discourse," *Mechademia* 6 (2011): 69–82; and by Tetsuro Shimauchi as "Manga History Viewed through Proto-Characteristics," in *Tezuka: The Marvel of Manga*, edited by Philip Brophy, 106–13. Melbourne: National Gallery of Victoria, [2007]. Exhibition catalog.

Ivy, Marilyn. "Critical Texts, Mass Artifacts: The Consumption of Knowledge in Postmodern Japan." In Miyoshi and Harootunian, *Postmodernism and Japan*, 21–46.

Jameson, Fredric. *Postmodernism, or, The Cultural Logic of Late Capitalism.* Durham, N.C.: Duke University Press, 1991.

Jentsch, Ernst. "On the Psychology of the Uncanny." Translated by Roy Sellars. *Angelaki* 2, no. 1 (April 1995): 7–16.

Johnson, Reed. "Japan Crisis Evokes Comparisons to Its Pop Culture Disaster Narratives, Historic Events." *Los Angeles Times*, March 28, 2011. http://articles.latimes.com/2011/mar/28/entertainment/la-et-japan-apocalypse-20110328.

Jones, Diana Wynne. *Howl's Moving Castle.* 1986. New York: EOS, 2008.

Kakinouchi Narumi. "Ehon ni nemuru shōjotachi." Manga. 1988. In *Vanpaia Miyu*, vol. 1, 33–60. Tokyo: Akita Shoten, 2002; translated by Duane Johnson as "The Sleeping Girls in the Picture Book." In *Vampire Princess Miyu*, vol. 1, *Origins*, 33–60. Fredericksburg, Va.: I.C. Entertainment, 2001.

Kanno Yūka. "Implicational Spectatorship: Hara Setsuko and the Queer Joke." *Mechademia* 6 (2011): 287–99.

Karakuri Ningyō: An Exhibition of Ancient Festival Robots from Japan. London: Barbican Art Gallery, 1985. Exhibition catalog.

Karatani Kōjin. *The Origins of Modern Japanese Literature.* Translation ed. Brett de Bary. Durham, N.C.: Duke University Press, 1993.

Keene, Donald. *Anthology of Japanese Literature: From The Earliest Era to the Mid-Nineteenth Century.* New York: Grove Press, 1955.

Kehr, Dave. "Japanese Cartoon *Akira* Isn't One for the Kids." Review of *Akira*. *Chicago Tribune*, March 30, 1990. ProQuest.

Kelion, Leo. "China Cracks Down on Violent Anime Online Cartoons." BBC. com, April 1, 2015. http://www.bbc.com/news/technology-32149754.

Kitakubo Hiroyuki. Interview. *Animerica*, December 2001, 37.

Kittler, Friedrich. "Romanticism—Psychoanalysis—Film: A History of the Double." Translated by Stefanie Harris. In *Literature Media Information Systems*, edited by John Johnston, 85–100. Amsterdam: G+B Arts International, 1997.

Klein, Susan. "Woman as Serpent: The Demonic Feminine in the Noh Play *Dōjōji.*" In *Religious Reflections on the Human Body*, edited by Jane Marie Law, 100–136. Bloomington: Indiana University Press, 1995.

Kleist, Heinrich von. "On Puppet-Shows." Translated by David Paisey. *Comparative Criticism* 14 (1992): 141–46.

Kon Satoshi. *Opus.* Manga. 1995–96. Translated by Zack Davisson as *Opus*. Milwaukie, Ore.: Dark Horse Manga, 2014.

Kotani Mari. Introduction to "Otaku Sexuality," by Saitō Tamaki. In Bolton, Csicsery-Ronay Jr., and Tatsumi, *Robot Ghosts and Wired Dreams*, 222–24.
———. "Otakuiin wa, otakuia no yume o mita wa" [The ota-queen dreams of an ota-queer]. In *Mōjō genron F kai* [Net-shaped discourse revision F], edited by Azuma Hiroki, 115–27. Tokyo: Seidosha, 2003.
———. "Techno-Gothic Japan: From Seishi Yokomizo's *The Death's-Head Stranger* to Mariko Ohara's *Ephemera the Vampire*." In *Blood Read: The Vampire as Metaphor in Contemporary Culture*, edited by Joan Gordon and Veronica Hollinger, 189–98. Philadelphia: University of Pennsylvania Press, 1997.
Koulikov, Mikhail. "The Origins of English-Language Anime Studies." *Anime and Manga Studies* (blog), March 17, 2015. https://animemanga studies.wordpress.com/2015/03/17/the-origins-of-english-language -anime-studies/.
Lacan, Jacques. "The Signification of the Phallus." In *Écrits: A Selection*, translated by Alan Sheridan, 281–91. New York: W. W. Norton, 1977.
Lamarre, Thomas. *The Anime Machine: A Media Theory of Animation*. Minneapolis: University of Minnesota Press, 2009.
———. "Born of Trauma: *Akira* and Capitalist Modes of Destruction." *positions: east asia cultures critique* 16, no. 1 (2008): 131–56.
———. "The First Time as Farce: Digital Animation and the Repetition of Cinema." In *Cinema Anime: Critical Engagements with Japanese Animation*, edited by Steven T. Brown, 161–88. New York: Palgrave, 2006.
Law, Jane Marie. *Puppets of Nostalgia: The Life, Death, and Rebirth of the Japanese Awaji Ningyō Tradition*. Princeton, N.J.: Princeton University Press, 1997.
Lunning, Frenchy, ed. *Mechademia*. 10 volumes. Minneapolis: University of Minnesota Press, 2006–16.
Lyotard, Jean-François. "Answering the Question: What Is Postmodernism?" Translated by Regis Durand. Appendix to Lyotard, *The Postmodern Condition*, 71–82.
———. *The Postmodern Condition: A Report on Knowledge*. Translated by Geoff Bennington and Brian Massumi. Minneapolis: University of Minnesota Press, 1984.
McCarthy, Helen. *Hayao Miyazaki, Master of Japanese Animation: Films, Themes, Artistry*. Berkeley, Calif.: Stone Bridge, 1999.
Miyazaki Hayao. "Biographical Chronology." In *Turning Point: 1997–2008*, translated by Beth Cary and Frederik L. Schodt, 431–47. San Francisco, Calif.: VIZ, 2014.
———. "Kenpō o kaeru nado motte no hoka" [Changing the constitution is out of the question]. In *Kenpō kaisei* [Constitutional revision]. Studio Ghibli *Neppū* special issue, July 2013. http://www.ghibli.jp/shuppan/np/009408/.
———. "Nihon no animeeshon ni tsuite." In *Nihon eiga no genzai* [Japanese film today], edited by Imamura Shōhei, 146–57. Tokyo, Iwanami, 1988;

translated by Beth Cary and Frederik L. Schodt as "Thoughts on Japanese Animation." In *Starting Point: 1979–1996*, 70–85. San Francisco, Calif.: VIZ, 2009.

———. "A 'Positive Pessimist': Japan's Animation Titan Hayao Miyazaki Returns with Another Marvel, *Howl's Moving Castle*. This Time He's Ready to Talk." Interview by Devin Gordon. *Newsweek*, June 20, 2005, 62. Expanded Academic ASAP.

Miyoshi, Masao, and Harry D. Harootunian. *Postmodernism and Japan*. Durham, N.C.: Duke University Press, 1989.

Monnet, Livia. "Invasion of the Women Snatchers: The Problem of A-Life and the Uncanny in *Final Fantasy: The Spirits Within*." In Bolton, Csicsery-Ronay Jr., and Tatsumi, *Robot Ghosts and Wired Dreams*, 193–221.

Murakami Takashi, ed. *Little Boy: The Arts of Japan's Exploding Subculture*. Translated by Linda Hoagland. New York: Japan Society; New Haven, Conn.: Yale University Press, 2005. Exhibition catalog.

Napier, Susan J. *Anime: From "Akira" to "Howl's Moving Castle."* Updated ed. New York: Palgrave, 2005.

———. *Anime: From "Akira" to "Princess Mononoke."* 1st ed. New York: Palgrave, 2001.

———. *From Impressionism to Anime: Japan as Fantasy and Fan Cult in the Mind of the West*. New York: Palgrave, 2007.

———. "Panic Sites: The Japanese Imagination of Disaster from *Godzilla* to *Akira*." *Journal of Japanese Studies* 19, no. 2 (1993): 327–51. Reprinted in *Contemporary Japan and Popular Culture*, edited by John Whittier Treat, 235–62. Honolulu: University of Hawai'i Press, 1996.

———. "Vampires, Psychic Girls, Flying Women, and Sailor Scouts: Four Faces of the Young Female in Japanese Popular Culture." In *The Worlds of Japanese Popular Culture: Gender, Shifting Boundaries, and Global Cultures*, edited by D. P. Martinez, 91–109. Cambridge: Cambridge University Press, 1998.

Natsume Fusanosuke, *Manga to sensō* [Manga and war]. Tokyo: Kōdansha, 1997.

Newitz, Annalee. "Magical Girls and Atomic Bomb Sperm: Japanese Animation in America." *Film Quarterly* 49, no. 1 (Fall 1995): 2–15.

Nichols, Peter M. "Home Video: Tokyo in 2019, Paris in 1880." Review of *Akira*. *New York Times*, July 20, 2001. ProQuest.

Noda Makoto, ed. *Zenryaku Oshii Mamoru-sama* [Dear Oshii Mamoru]. Tokyo: Futtowaaku, 1998.

Okada Toshio. *Otakugaku nyūmon* [Introduction to otakuology]. 1996. Tokyo: Shinchōsha OH! Bunko, 2000.

Orbaugh, Sharalyn. "Emotional Infectivity: Cyborg Affect and the Limits of the Human." *Mechademia* 3 (2008): 150–72.

———. "Sex and the Single Cyborg: Japanese Pop Culture Experiments in Subjectivity." In Bolton, Csicsery-Ronay Jr., and Tatsumi, *Robot Ghosts and Wired Dreams*, 172–92.

Ortabasi, Melek. "Indexing the Past: Visual Language and Translatability in Kon Satoshi's *Millennium Actress*," *Perspectives: Studies in Translatology* 14, no. 4 (2006): 278–91.

———. "National History as Otaku Fantasy: Satoshi Kon's *Millennium Actress*." In *Japanese Visual Culture: Explorations in the World of Manga and Anime*, edited by Mark MacWilliams, 274–94. Armonk, N.Y.: M. E. Sharpe, 2008.

Oshii Mamoru. *Blood the Last Vampire: Kemonotachi no yoru*. Tokyo: Kadokawa Horaa Bunko, 2000; translated by Camellia Nieh as *Blood The Last Vampire: Night of the Beasts*. Milwaukie, Ore.: DH Press, 2005.

———. Interview. *Internet Voice Magazine Alles* 6 (November 1995). Archived at https://web.archive.org/web/20001119140800/http://www.express.co.jp/ALLES/INDEX/6index_j.html.

———. Interview by Carl Gustav Horn. 1996. In *Anime Interviews: The First Five Years of Animerica, Anime and Manga Monthly (1992–97)*, edited by Trish Ledoux, 134–39. San Francisco, Calif.: Cadence, 1997.

———. "Last Commentary." In *The Analysis of "Ghost in the Shell,"* edited by Nozaki Tōru, Kubo Misuzu, Seki Junji, and Morita Hiroaki, n.p. Tokyo: Kōdansha, 1995.

———. "Profile." Gaburieru no yūutsu: Oshii Mamoru Official Site. Archived at https://web.archive.org/web/20140502013003/http://www.oshiimamoru.com/profile/profile.htm.

Oshii Mamoru and Miyazaki Hayao, "Jidai no keri o tsukeru tame ni." Dialogue. In *Oshii Mamoru zenshigoto: "Urusei yatsura" kara "Avaron" made* [Complete works of Mamoru Oshii: From *Urusei yatsura* to *Avalon*], edited by Uekusa Nobukazu, 82–89. Revised ed. Tokyo: Kinema Jumpō, 2001; translated by Ryoko Toyama as "Around the Movie *Patlabor 2*: To Put an End to the Era." Nausicaa.net. http://www.nausicaa.net/miyazaki/interviews/m_oshii_patlabor2.html.

Osmond, Andrew. *Satoshi Kon: The Illusionist*. Berkeley, Calif.: Stone Bridge, 2009.

Ōtomo Katsuhiro. *Akira*. Manga. 6 vols. Tokyo: Kōdansha, 1984–93; translated by Yoko Umezawa, Linda M. York, and Jo Duffy as *Akira*. 6 vols. New York: Kodansha Comics, 2009–11.

———. *Akira*. Manga. Translated by Yoko Umezawa as *Akira*. Color by Steve Oliff. English adaptation by Jo Duffy. 38 issues. New York: Epic Comics, 1988–95; Translated back into Japanese by Kuroma Hisashi as *Furu karaa Akira* [Full-color Akira]. 6 vols. Tokyo: Kōdansha, 2003–4.

———. *Akira Club*. Translated by Kumar Sivasubramanian. Milwaukie, Ore.: Dark Horse, 2007.

Ōtsuka Eiji. *Monogatari shōhiron kai* [A theory of narrative consumption revisited]. Tokyo: ASCII, 2012.

———. "World and Variation: The Reproduction and Consumption of Narrative." Translated with an introduction by Marc Steinberg. *Mechademia* 5 (2010): 99–116.

Patten, Fred. "Streamline Pictures—Part I." *Cartoon Research*. April 19, 2015. http://cartoonresearch.com/index.php/streamline-pictures-part-1/.

———. *Watching Anime, Reading Manga: 25 Years of Essays and Reviews*. Berkeley, Calif.: Stone Bridge, 2004.

Penney, Matthew. "Miyazaki Hayao and the Asia-Pacific War." *The Asia-Pacific Journal: Japan Focus*. http://apjjf.org/-Matthew-Penney/4766/article.html.

Pointon, Susan. "Transcultural Orgasm as Apocalypse: *Urotsukidoji: The Legend of the Overfiend*." *Wide Angle* 19, no. 3 (1997): 41–63.

"*R.O.D*" *Official Archive*. Translated by M. Kirie Hayashi. Richmond, ON: Udon Entertainment, 2013.

Richmond, Simon. *The Rough Guide to Anime: Japan's Finest from Ghibli to "Gankutsuō."* London: Rough Guides, 2009.

Rudd, David. "Building Castles in the Air: (De)Construction in *Howl's Moving Castle*." *Journal of the Fantastic in the Arts* 21, no. 2 (2010): 257–70. JStor.

Ruh, Brian. *Stray Dog of Anime: The Films of Mamoru Oshii*. 2nd ed. New York: Palgrave, 2013.

Ryan, Marie-Laure. *Narrative as Virtual Reality: Immersion and Interactivity in Literature and Electronic Media*. Baltimore, Md.: The Johns Hopkins University Press, 2001.

Saitō Chikashi and Naitō Keiji, eds. "*Patlabor The Movie*" *Archives*. Lead translator Dan Kanemitsu. N.p.: Bandai Visual USA, 2006. Included with *Patlabor: The Movie*. Limited collector's ed. DVD box set. Honneamise, 2006.

———, eds. "*Patlabor 2 The Movie*" *Archives*. Translated by Marc Schultz, Michael House, and Dan Kanemitsu N.p.: Bandai Visual USA, 2006. Included with *Patlabor 2: The Movie*. Limited collector's ed. DVD box set. Honneamise, 2006.

Saitō Tamaki. "Otaku no sekushuaritii." In *Hakase no kimyō na shishunki* [The doctor's strange adolescence], 17–56. Tokyo: Nihon Hyōronsha, 2003; adapted by the author and translated by Christopher Bolton as "Otaku Sexuality." In Bolton, Csicsery-Ronay Jr., and Tatsumi, *Robot Ghosts and Wired Dreams*, 224–49.

———. *Sentō bishōjo no seishin bunseki*. Tokyo: Ōta Shuppan, 2000; translated by J. Keith Vincent and Dawn Lawson as *Beautiful Fighting Girl*. Minneapolis: University of Minnesota Press, 2011.

Sakai, Naoki. *Voices of the Past: The Status of Language in Eighteenth-Century Japanese Discourse*. Ithaca, N.Y.: Cornell University Press, 1991.

Schodt, Frederik L. *Inside the Robot Kingdom: Japan, Mechatronics, and the Coming Robotopia*. Tokyo: Kodansha International, 1988.

Shirō Masamune. *Kōkaku kidōtai / The Ghost in the Shell*. Manga. Tokyo: Kōdansha, 1991; translated by Frederick Schodt and Toren Smith as *Ghost in the Shell*. 1st. ed. Milwaukie, Ore.: Dark Horse Comics, 1995.

Silvio, Carl. "Refiguring the Radical Cyborg in Mamoru Oshii's *Ghost in the Shell*." *Science Fiction Studies* 26, no. 1 (March 1999): 54–72.

Silvio, Teri. "Pop-Culture Icons: Religious Inflections of the Character Toy in Taiwan." *Mechademia* 3 (2008): 200–220.

Smith, Lindsay. "War, Wizards, and Words: Transformative Adaptation and Transformed Meanings in *Howl's Moving Castle.*" *The Projector: Film and Media Journal* 11, no. 1 (Fall/Spring 2011): n.p. http://www.theprojectorjournal.com.

Smith, Roberta. "From a Mushroom Cloud, a Burst of Art Reflecting Japan's Psyche." Review of "Little Boy: The Arts of Japan's Exploding Subculture." *New York Times*, April 8, 2005, East coast late edition. ProQuest.

Sobchack, Vivian. *The Address of the Eye: A Phenomenology of Film Experience.* Princeton, N.J.: Princeton University Press, 1992.

———. *Carnal Thoughts: Embodiment and Moving Image Culture.* Berkeley: University of California Press, 2004.

———. "Democratic Franchise and the Electronic Frontier." *Futures* 27, no. 7 (1995): 725–34.

———. *Screening Space: The American Science Fiction Film.* Rev. ed. New York: Ungar, 1987.

———. "Teenage Mutant Ninja Hackers: Reading *Mondo 2000.*" *South Atlantic Quarterly* 92, no. 4 (1993): 569–84.

Sontag, Susan. "A Note on Bunraku." *The Threepenny Review* 16 (Winter 1984): 16.

Standish, Isolde. "*Akira*, Postmodernism, and Resistance." In *The Worlds of Japanese Popular Culture: Gender, Shifting Boundaries, and Global Cultures*, edited by D. P. Martinez, 56–74. Cambridge: Cambridge University Press, 1998.

Steinberg, Marc. *Anime's Media Mix: Franchising Toys and Characters in Japan.* Minneapolis: University of Minnesota Press, 2012.

———. "The Trajectory of Apocalypse: Pleasure and Destruction in *Akira* and *Evangelion.*" *East Asia Forum* 8/9 (1999–2000): 1–31.

Stoker, Bram. *Dracula.* New York: Grosset & Dunlap, 1897. Project Gutenberg ebook. http://www.gutenberg.org/ebooks/345.

Studio Ghibli. *The Art of "Howl's Moving Castle."* Tokyo: Tokuma Shoten, 2005; translated by Yuji Oniki as *The Art of "Howl's Moving Castle."* San Francisco, Calif.: VIZ, 2005.

Suan, Stevie. *The Anime Paradox: Patterns and Practices through the Lens of Traditional Japanese Theater.* Leiden: Global Oriental, 2013.

Suematsu Ken'ichi, dir. *Butaiban Sennen joyū* [Millennium actress stage version]. Produced by Mizoguchi Mika. Performed by Shimizu Kaori, Nakamura Maria, Maebuchi Sanae, Yamane Chika, and Tachibana Ai. January 22, 2011. HEP Hall, Osaka.

———, dir. *Butaiban Sennen joyū* [Millennium actress stage version]. Produced by Mizoguchi Mika. Performed by Shimizu Kaori, Nakamura Maria, Maebuchi Sanae, Yamane Chika, and Matsumura Satomi. January 17–18, 2009. DVD. Lotus, n.d.

Talbot, Margaret. "The Auteur of Anime." *The New Yorker*, January 17, 2005, 64–75.

Tanaka Motoko. *Apocalypse in Contemporary Japanese Science Fiction*. New York: Palgrave, 2014.

Tanizaki Jun'ichirō. "Recollections of the Bunraku Puppets." Translated by Donald Keene. In *Bunraku: The Art of the Japanese Puppet Theater*, by Donald Keene, Hiroshi Kaneko, and Keizō Kaneko, 11–13. Tokyo: Kodansha International, 1965.

———. *Tade kuu mushi*. 1929. Tokyo, Shinchō Bunko, 1951; translated by Edward Seidensticker as *Some Prefer Nettles*. New York: Knopf, 1955.

Tatsumi Takayuki and Kotani Mari, eds. *Saibōgu feminizumu* [Cyborg feminism]. Tokyo: Treville, 1991.

Tom, Avery M. "Never Forget Your Protective Headgear!" *Animerica*, June 1994, 94.

Treat, John Whittier. "Yoshimoto Banana Writes Home: Shojo Culture and the Nostalgic Subject." *Journal of Japanese Studies* 19, no. 2 (Summer 1993): 353–87.

Ueno Toshiya, *Kurenai no metaru sūtsu: Anime to iu senjō* [Metalsuits the red: Wars in animation]. Tokyo: Kinokuniya Shoten, 1998.

Uji Kaganojō. *Takenokoshū (jo)*. In *Nihon shisō taikei*, vol. 61, *Kinsei geidōron* [Compendium of Japanese thought 61: Modern dramatic theory], 401–6. Tokyo: Iwanami Shoten, 1972; translated as "Preface to A Collection of Bamboo Shoots." In Gerstle, *Circles of Fantasy*, 183–88.

Vincent, J. Keith. "Making It Real: Fiction, Desire, and the Queerness of the Beautiful Fighting Girl." Introduction to Saitō, *Beautiful Fighting Girl*, ix–xxv.

Wells, Paul. "Playing the Kon Trick: Between Dates, Dimensions, and Daring in the Films of Satoshi Kon." *Cinephile* (University of British Columbia) 7, no. 1 (Spring 2011): 4–8.

Willemen, Paul. "The Fourth Look." In *Looks and Frictions: Essays in Cultural Studies and Film Theory*, 99–110. Bloomington: Indiana University Press / British Film Institute, 1994.

Wordsworth, William. Preface to *Lyrical Ballads*. 1802. In *Lyrical Ballads, 1798 and 1802*, by William Wordsworth and Samuel Taylor Coleridge, 95–115. Edited by Fiona Stafford. Oxford: Oxford University Press, 2013.

Yonezawa Yasuhiro. "Manga kara no ekusodasu: Ōtomo Katsuhiro ni tsuite no oboegaku 15 kō" [Exodus from manga: 15 memos on Ōtomo Katsuhiro]. In *Ōtomo Katsuhiro. Eureka* special issue (Aug. 1988): 149–50.

Yūda Yoshio. "The Formation of Early Modern Jōruri." *Acta Asiatica: Bulletin of the Institute of Eastern Culture* 28 (March 1975): 20–41.

———. *Jōrurishi ronkō* [Studies in the history of jōruri]. Tokyo: Chūō Kōronsha, 1975.

Index

Christopher Bolton is professor of comparative and Japanese literature at Williams College. He is the author of *Sublime Voices: The Fictional Science and Scientific Fiction of Abe Kōbō* and the coeditor of *Robot Ghosts and Wired Dreams: Japanese Science Fiction from Origins to Anime* (Minnesota, 2007).